ISBN 978-1-4400-7124-9
PIBN 10002260

THIRTY

INOR UPANISHAḌS

TRANSLATED BY

K. NĀRĀYAṆASVĀMI AIYAR

Translator of

Laghu Yoga Vāsishtha, Vāsuḍevamanana

&c. &c. &c.

MADRAS

1914

TO

THE ṚSHIS OF INDIA

WHO BY TREADING THE PATH

OF

THE UPANISHAḌS HAVE PERFECTED THEMSELVES

AND

REALISED THE GOAL

THIS HUMBLE EFFORṬ

TO SPREAD THEIR ANCIENT TEACHINGS IN A MODERN GARB

IS DEDICATED

BY ONE

WHO LOVES AND WORSHIPS THEM

AND TRIES TO WALK IN ṬHEIR FOOTSTEPS

AS THEIR HUMBLE AND DEVOTED DISCIPLE

ॐ

FOREWORD

For the first time it is, I believe, that the English translation of so many as 30 Upanishaḍs is being put forth before the public in a collected form. Ȧmong the Hinḍū Scriptures, the Veḍas hold the pre-eminent place. The Upanishaḍs which are culled from the Āraṇyaka-portions of the Veḍas—so-called because they were read in the Āraṇya (forest) after the learner had given up the life of the world—are regarded as the Veḍānṭa, or the end or final crown of the Veḍas. Veḍānṭa is also the end of all knowledge, since the word Veḍas means according to its derivation 'knowledge'. Rightly were the Upanishaḍs so considered, since their knowledge led a person to Āṭmā, the goal of life. The other portion of the Veḍas, *viz.*, Samhiṭas and Brāhmaṇas, conferred upon a man, if he should conform to the requisite conditions, the mastery of the Universe only which is certainly inferior to Āṭmā. It is these Upanishaḍs that to the western philosopher Schopenhauer were the "solace of life".

There are now extant, in all, 108 Upanishaḍs, of which the principal or major 12 Upanishaḍs commented upon by S'rī S'aṅkarāchārya and others were translated into English by Dr. Roer and Rāja Rājenḍra Lāl Miṭra and re-translated by Max Muller in his "Sacred Books of the East," together with one other Upanishaḍ called *Maiṭrāyaṇī*. Of the rest, 95 in number, two or three Upanishaḍs have appeared in English up to now, but never so many as are here presented to the public, so far as I am aware.

Many years ago, the late Sunḍara S'āsṭri, a good Sanscrit Scholar and myself worked together to put into English garb the Upanishaḍs that had not been attempted before, and succeeded in publishing most of those which are here gathered in the monthly issues of *The Theosophist*. The Kārmic agents willed that my late co-worker should abandon his physical garment at a premature age. Then I resolved upon throwing up my worldly business of pleading the cause of clients before the bench for that of pleading the cause of God before the public. The incessant travel in that cause since then for over 18 years from place to place in all parts of India left me no leisure until now to republish all the above translations in a book form. But when this year a little rest was afforded me, I was able to revise them as well as add a few more. I am conscious of the many faults from which this book suffers and have no other hope in it than that it will serve as a piece of pioneer work, which may induce real Yogins and scholars to come into the field and bring out a better translation.

There are many editions of the Upanishaḍs to be found in Calcutta, Bombay, Poona, South India and other places. But we found that the South Indian editions, which were nearly the same in Telugu or Granṭha characters, were in many cases fuller and more intelligible and significant. Hence we adopted for our translation South Indian editions. The edition of the 108 Upanishaḍs which the late Tukaram Tatya of Bombay has published in Ḍevanāgari characters approaches the South Indian edition. As the South Indian edition of the Upanishaḍs is not available for the study of all, I intend to have the recensions of that edition printed in Ḍevanāgari characters, so that even those that have a little knowledge of Sanscrit may be able to follow the original with the help of this translation.

Transliteration

In the transliteration of Sanscrit letters into the English alphabet certain difficulties present themselves. Let me take first the letter श. There are three letters in Sanscrit स, श, and ष. They are differently pronounced and one should not be confounded with another. For the first letter we have the English equivalent *S* and for the last *Sh*. But for the second one we have none whatsoever. The prominent writers in the field of Theosophy have been transliterating this letter into *Sh*. Hence in writing the word काशि they made it *Kāshi* in the English language. They utter it also in the same manner. To a South Indian ear, it is rather grating. The manṭras especially depend for their efficacy upon proper pronunciation. When we therefore utter the words wrongly, there is committed according to Sanscrit writers, Varṇa-Haṭyā-Ḍosha or the sin of the murder of letters or words. In my translation I have represented the letter श by S' and not by *Sh*, since I consider the latter to be a mistake. Other transliterations are :—

आ	ई	ऊ	ऋ	ङ	ञ	ट	ठ	ड	ढ	ण	त	थ	द	ध	ळ
ā	ī	ū	Ṛ	Ṅ	Ñ	T	Th	D	Dh	Ṇ	Ṭ	Ṭh	Ḍ	Ḍh	Ḷ

It would be well if our leaders of thought conferred together and came to some agreement upon the question of transliteration.

The Order of the Upanishaḍs

The Upanishaḍs translated have been classified under the headings of (1) Veḍānṭa, (2) Physiology, (3) Manṭra, (4) Sannyāsa and (5) Yoga. But these are not hard and fast divisions. For instance in the Sannyāsa and Yoga Upanishaḍs, manṭras also are given. But in the Mānṭric Upanishaḍs, Manṭras alone are given.

Veḍānṭa and Yoga Upanishaḍs

The Upanishaḍs that come under the headings of Veḍānṭa and Yoga are the most important. But it is the latter Upanishaḍs that are most occult in their character, since it is they that give clues to the mysterious forces located in nature and man, as well as to the ways by which they may be conquered. With reference to Veḍānṭa, the ancient teachers thereof have rightly ordained that none has the right to enter upon a study of it, unless he has mastered to a slight degree at least the Sāḍhana-Chaṭushtaya, or four means of salvation. He should not only be convinced in theory of the fact that Āṭmā is the only Reality, and all else are but the ephemeral things of the world, but he should also have outgrown in practice the craving for such transitory worldly things: besides he should have developed a fair mastery over the body and the mind. A non-compliance with these precedent conditions leads men into many anomalies. The orthodox and the clever without any practice are placed in a bad predicament through a study of these Upanishaḍs. In such Upanishaḍs as *Maiṭreya* and others, pilgrimages to holy places, the rituals of the Hinḍūs, ceremonial impurities at the time of birth and death, Manṭras, etc., are made light of. To the orthodox that are blind and strict observers of rites and ceremonies, statements like these give a rude shock. Hence Upanishaḍs are not meant for persons of this stamp. Nor are they intended for mere intellectual people who have no knowledge of practice about them, and are immersed in the things of the world. Some of us are aware of the manner in which men with brains alone have made a travesty of the doctrine of Māyā. Not a few clever but unprincipled persons actually endeavour to justify arguments of all kinds of dissipations and wrong conduct by the assertion that it is all Māyā. The old Ṛshis were fully aware of the fact that Veḍānṭa would be desecrated by those that had not complied with its precedent conditions. Only when the desires and the self are overcome and the heart is made pure, or as Upanishadic writers put it, the heart-knot is broken, only then the Āṭmā in the heart will be truly realised: and then it is that the Āṭmā in all universe is realised also, the universe being then seen as Māyā. But so long as the Āṭmā in the heart is not realised through living the life, the universe will not be realised as Māyā, and "God everywhere" will be but in words.

One special point worthy of notice in the Upanishaḍs is that all the knowledge bearing upon a subject is not put forward in one and the same place. We have to wade through a mass of materials and a number of Upanishaḍs, ere we can have a connected view of a subject. In modern days when a subject is taken up, all the available information is given in one place in a systematic manner. But not so in the Upanishaḍs.

Take the subject of Prāṇas which refer to life itself. In one Upanishaḍ, one piece of information is given, another in another and so on. And unless we read them all together and reconcile the seemingly discrepant statements, we cannot have a complete and clear knowledge of the subject. This process was adopted by the Ṛshis, probably because they wanted to draw out thereby the intellectual and spiritual faculties latent in the disciple, and not to make him a mere automaton. In these days when knowledge is presented in a well-assimilated form, it is no doubt taken up easily but it does not evoke the latent reasoning power so much. When therefore the disciple went in the ancient days to the teacher for the solution of a difficulty, having been unable to find it himself after hard thinking, it was understood easily and permanently because of the previous preparation of the mind, and was also reverently appreciated as a boon and godsend, because of the difficulty previously experienced. The function of the teacher was not only to explain the difficult points to the taught, but also to make him realise those things of which understanding was sought. As an illustration, we might take the case of the soul. The Guru not only explained the difficult passages or points relating to the soul, but also made the disciple leave the body or bodies and realise himself as the soul. As we cannot get such Gurus in the outer world nowadays, the only thing left to do instead is to secure the publication of simple treatises on matters of Veḍānṭa and Yoga for the benefit of the public. I hope, I shall before long be able to make a start in this direction.

In studying the Upanishaḍs on Veḍānṭa and Yoga, we find certain peculiarities which throw a light on their greatness. Both of them lay stress upon certain centres in the human body for development. The 12 major Upanishaḍs as well as the Veḍānṭa Upanishaḍs herein published deal with the heart and the heart alone; while the Yoga Upanishaḍs treat of many centres including the heart. For the purpose of simplification, all the centres may be divided under the main headings of head, heart and the portion of the body from the navel downwards.

But why? The key which will unlock these secrets seems to be this. All religions postulate that the real man is the soul, and that the soul has to reach God. Christianity states that God created the soul in His own image and that the soul has to rise to the full stature of God in order to reach Him. Hindūism says that Jīvāṭmā (the human soul) is an Āms'a or portion of Paramāṭmā, or God, which is to eventually unfold the powers of God, and compares it with a ray of the sun of God, or a spark out of the fire of God. In all religions, there is an unanimity of opinion that the soul is a likeness of God, having God's powers in latency to be unfolded hereafter. Let us therefore first understand the attributes of God. He is said to have omnipresence, omniscience and omnipotence. Hindūism translates these ideas into Saṭ, Chiṭ and Ānanḍa. They are eternal existence, infinite knowledge, and unlimited power. The soul identifying itself with the body thinks it lives for the life-term of the body only; cooped up by the brain, it imagines, it has only the knowledge circumscribed by the brain; carried away by the pleasures of the senses, it whirls about in the midst of them as if they constituted the Real Bliss. But when it wakes up from the dream of the lower things of the body and glances upwards to the higher world of Spirit, it discovers its delusions and finds itself to be of the same nature as the God above, who is eternal, all-knowing and all-powerful. And this discovery has to be made by each soul in the human body, in which it is functioning, through the three main centres of head, heart and navel. Through the heart, it cuts the heart-knot and realises its all-pervading character when it realises its eternity of existence; through the brain, it rises beyond it through its highest seat, *viz.*, Sahasrāra which corresponds to the pineal gland in the physical body, and obtains its omniscience; through the navel, according to the Upanishaḍs—it obtains a mastery over that mysterious force called Kuṇḍalinī which is located therein, and which confers upon it an unlimited power—that force being mastered only when a man arises above Kāma or passion. Psychologists tell us that desires when conquered lead to the development of will. When will is developed to a great degree, naturally great power, or omnipotence, ensues: our statement is that Kuṇḍalinī when conquered leads to unlimited powers and perfections, or Siḍḍhis like Aṇimā, etc., and that Kuṇḍalinī can only be conquered through rising above the desires of the senses.

From the foregoing it is clear that the Veḍānṭa Upanishaḍs are intended only for those devotees of God that want to have a development of the heart mainly, and not of the brain and the navel, and that the Yogic Upanishaḍs are intended for those that want to have an all-round development of the soul in its three aspects. Here I may remark that S'ri S'aṅkarāchārya and other commentators commented upon the 12 Upanishaḍs only, since other Upanishaḍs treating of Kuṇḍalinī, etc., are of an occult character and not meant for all, but only for the select few who are fit for private initiation. If they had proceeded to comment upon the minor Upanishaḍs also, they would have had to disclose certain secrets which confer powers and which are not meant, therefore, for all. It would be nothing but fatal to the community, were the secrets leading to the acquisition of such powers imparted indiscriminately to all. In the case of dynamite, the criminal using it may be traced, since it is of a physical nature, but in the case of the use of the higher powers, they are set in motion through the will, and can never be traced through ordinary means. Therefore in the Upanishaḍ called *Yoga-Kuṇḍalinī*, the final truths that lead to the realisation of the higher powers are said to be imparted by the Guru alone to the disciple who has proved himself worthy after a series of births and trials.

In order to expound the Upanishaḍs, especially those that bear upon Yoga, some one who is a specialist in Yoga—better still, if he is an Ādept—should undertake the task of editing and translating them. The passages in Yoga Upanishaḍs are very mystic sometimes; sometimes there is no nominative or verb, and we have to fill up the ellipses as best as we can.

One more remark may be made with reference to the Upanishaḍs. Each Upanishaḍ is said to belong to one of the Veḍas. Even if we take the 12 Upanishaḍs edited by Max Muller and others, we find some of them are to be found in the existing

Vedas and others not. Why is this? In my opinion this but corroborates the statement made by the *Vishṇu-Purāṇa* about the Vedas. It says that at the end of each Ḍwāpara Yuga, a Veda-Vyāsa, or compiler of the Vedas, incarnates as an Āvaṭāra of Vishṇu—a minor one—to compile the Vedas. In the Yugas preceding the Kali Yuga we are in, the Vedas were "one" alone though voluminous. Just before this Kali Yuga began, Kṛshṇa-Ḍwaipāyana Veda-Vyāsa incarnated, and, after withdrawing the Vedas that were not fit for this Yuga and the short-lived people therein, made with the aid of his disciples a division of the remaining portions into four. Hence perhaps we are unable to trace the Vedas of which some of the extant Upanishads form part.

ADYAR, *March* 1914. K. NARAYANASWAMI

MUKṬIKOPANISHAḌ

OF

S'UKLĀ-YĀJURVEḌA

AḌHYĀYA I

ADDRESSING with devotion and obedience S'ri-Rāma—the Lord Hari, at the end of His Samāḍhi, who being Himself changeless is the witness of the thousands of changes of Buḍḍhi, and who ever rests in Swarūpa-Ḍhyāna (the meditation on Reality) while seated under the bejewelled dome of the palace in the lovely city of Āyoḍhyā, in the midst of Sīṭā, Bharaṭa and Soumiṭri (Lakshmaṇa) S'aṭrughna and others, eulogised day and night by Sanaka and other hosts of Munis, as well as by Vasishtha, S'uka, and other devotees of Vishṇu—Hanūmān, after praising them, asked: "O Rāma, Thou art Paramāṭmā of the nature of Sachchiḍānanḍa. O foremost of the family of Raghu, I make prostrations to Thee again and again. O Rāma, I wish to know for the sake of emancipation, Thy nature as it really is. O Rāma, be Thou gracious enough to tell me that by which I shall be easily released from the bondage of mundane existence and by which I shall attain salvation."

(S'rī-Rāma replied:) "O mighty-armed one, well asked: hearken then to the truth uttered by Me. I am well established in Veḍānṭa (or the end of Veḍas or knowledge). Have thou recourse to Veḍānṭa well."

(Hanūmān again asked:) "O foremost of Raghus, what are Veḍānṭas? where do they abide? Pray enlighten me." (S'rī-Rāma replied:) "O Hanūmān, listen to Me. I shall truly describe to you the nature of Veḍānṭa. Through the expiratory breath of Myself—Vishṇu, the Veḍas were generated as many. Like the oil in the sesamum seeds, Veḍānṭa is well established (or latent) in the Veḍas."

(Hanūmān asked again:) "O Rāma, how many are the Veḍas and their branches? O Rāghava, what are the Upanishaḍs? Please, through Thy grace, tell me truly."

(S'rī-Rāma said:) "Through the divisions of Ṛgveḍa and others, the Veḍas are said to be four in number. Their branches are many. So also the Upanishaḍs. In Ṛgveḍa, there are branches, 21 in number. O son of Vāyu, there are 109 branches in Yajurveḍa. O conqueror of enemies, there are 1,000 branches in Sāmaveḍa. O best of Monkeys, there are 50 branches in Aṭharvaṇaveḍa. In each branch, there is one Upanishaḍ. Whoever with devotion to Me studies even one of the Ṛks (hymns) in these, attains the state of absorption, rare for the Munis to attain."

(Hanūmān asked:) "O Rāma, some excellent Munis have said there is one kind of salvation only, while others [stated that salvation is attained] through the uttering of Thy name or the initiation into Ṭāraka (Om) at Kās'ī (Benares); others through Sāṅkhya-Yoga, others through the Yoga of Devotion; other Mahārshis through the meditation upon the meaning of Mahāvākyas (the sacred sentences of the Veḍas). Salvation is stated to be of four kinds through the divisions of Sālokya and others."

(S'rī-Rāma replied:) "There is only one true emancipation. O Kapi (Monkey), even a person addicted to evil practices attains the salvation of Sālokya (My world) through the uttering of My name, but not of other worlds. Should one die in Brahma-nāḷa (the lotus-stalk—also street) in Kās'ī,[1] he attains My Ṭāraka (Manṭra). Such a person attains salvation without any rebirth; wherever he may die in Kās'ī, Mahes'wara initiates him by whispering My Ṭāraka (Manṭra) into his right ear. Such person, freed from all sins, attains My Swarūpa (Form). It is this that is termed Sālokya-Sārūpya salvation. The twice-born who is of virtuous conduct and who, without diverting his

[1] There is a street in Kāsi called Brahma-nāla.

intelligence on any other, meditates upon Me, the All-Ātmā, attains Sāmīpya (nearness) to Me.

"It is this that is termed Sālokya-Sārūpya-Sāmīpya salvation. The twice-born who according to the path opened by the teacher, meditates upon My immutable Reality attains Sāyujya (absorption) into Me, like the caterpillar into the wasp. This is the Sāyujya salvation which is productive of Brāhmic bliss and auspicious. Thus these kinds of salvation arise through the Upāsanā (worship) of Me.

" The only means by which the final emancipation is attained is through Māṇḍūkya-Upanishaḍ alone, which is enough for the salvation of all aspirants. If Jñāna is not attained thereby, study the 10 Upanishaḍs; thou shalt soon attain Jñāna, and then My Seat. O son of Āñjanā, if thy Jñāna is not made firm, practise (study) well the 32 Upanishaḍs. Thou shalt get release. If thou longest after Viḍehamukṭi (or disembodied salvation), study the 108 Upanishaḍs. I will truly state in order the (names of the) Upanishaḍs with their S'ānṭi (purificatory Manṭras). Hearken to them. (They are:) Īs'a, Kena, Katha, Pras'na, Muṇda, Māṇdūkya, Ṭiṭṭiri, Aiṭareya, Chhānḍogya, Bṛhaḍāraṇyaka, Brahma, Kaivalya, Jābāla, S'weṭās'waṭara, Hamsa, Āruṇi, Garbha, Nārāyaṇa, (Parama)-Hamsa, (Amṛṭa)-Binḍu, (Amṛṭa)-Nāḍa, (Aṭharva)-S'ira, (Aṭharva)-S'ikhā, Maiṭrāyaṇī, Kaushīṭaki, (Bṛhaṭ)-Jābāla, (Narasihma)-Ṭāpanī, Kālāgniruḍra, Maiṭreyī, Subāla, Kshurikā, Manṭrikā, Sarvasāra, Nirālamba, (S'uka)-Rahasya, Vajrasūchikā, Ṭejo-(Binḍu), Nāḍa-(Binḍu), Ḍhyāna-(Binḍu), (Brahma)-Viḍyā, Yoga-Ṭaṭṭwa, Āṭmaboḍhaka, Parivrāt (Nāraḍa-Parivrājaka), (Ṭri)-S'ikhī, Sīṭā, (Yoga)-Chūdā-(Maṇi) Nirvāṇa, Maṇdala-(Brāhmaṇa), Ḍakshiṇā-(Mūrṭi), S'arabha, Skanḍa, (Tripāḍvibhūṭi)-Mahā-Nārāyaṇa, Aḍwaya-(Ṭāraka), (Rāma)-Rahasya, (Rāma)-Ṭāpanī, Vāsuḍeva, Muḍgala, S'āṇdilya, Paiṅgala, Bhikshu, Mahaṭ-S'āriraka, (Yoga)-S'ikhā, Ṭurīyāṭīṭa, Sannyāsa, (Paramahamsa)-Parivrājaka, Akshamālikā, Avyakṭa, Ekākshara, (Anna)-Pūrṇā, Sūrya, Ākshi, Aḍhyāṭma, Kuṇdikā, Sāviṭr, īĀṭmā, Pās'upaṭa, Parabrahma, Avaḍhūṭa, Ṭripuraṭāpanī, Ḍevī, Ṭripurā, Kara, Bhāvanā, (Ruḍra)-Hṛḍaya, (Yoga)-Kuṇdalinī, Bhasma-(Jābāla) Ruḍrāksha, Gaṇapaṭi, Ḍars'ana, Tārasāra,

Mahāvākya, Pañchabrahma, (Prāṇa)-Agnihoṭra, Gopāla-Ṭāpanī, Kṛsbṇa, Yājñavalkya, Varāha, S'ātyāyanī, Hayagrīva, Ḍaṭṭāṭreya, Gāruda, Kali-(Sanṭāraṇa), Jābāla, Soubhāgya, Saraswaṭī-rahasya, Bahvricha, and Mukṭika. These 108 (Upanishaḍs) are able to do away with the three Bhāvanās [of doubt, vain thought, and false thought], conferring Jñāna and Vairāgya, and destroying the three Vāsanās [of book-lore, world and body].

"The twice-born—after learning the 108 Upanishaḍs, together with the S'ānṭi as prescribed both before and after from the mouth of a Guru well versed in the observances of Veḍic knowledge and study—become Jīvanmukṭas till the destruction of their Prārabḍha; in course of time as Prārabḍha is destroyed, they attain My disembodied salvation. There is no doubt of it. O son of Vāyu, these 108 Upanishaḍs, which are the essence of all the Upanishaḍs, and are capable of destroying all sins through their mere study, have been imparted by Me to you as a disciple. This science of the 108 Upanishaḍs taught by Me, is an occult one, and will free persons from bondage, whether they read them with or without knowledge. To gratify the desire of a supplicant, a kingdom may be given or wealth, but never shall the 108 Upanishaḍs be imparted to an atheist, an ungrateful person, one intent on vicious actions, one having no devotion towards Me, or one who loses his path in the cave of books. On no account shall they be given to one devoid of devotion. O Māruṭi, it is only after a thorough examination that they should be imparted to a disciple doing service (to a Guru), to a well-disposed son, or to one devoted to Me, following good observances, belonging to a good family, and being of good intelligence. Whoever studies or hears the 108 Upanishaḍs attains Me. There is no doubt of this. This is stated in the Ṛk (verse) thus—Viḍyā (Saraswaṭī) went to a Brāhmaṇa (and addressed him) thus: 'Protect me. I shall be thy treasure. Do not confide me to the envious, to one not treading the right path, or to the rogue. Then I shall be potent.' Impart this Āṭmanishtha-Viḍyā relating to Vishṇu to one after well examining him, who had studied much, is alert, intelligent, observant of the vow of celibacy, and serving [the Guru]."

Then Hanūmān asked S'rī-Rāmachanḍra to relate the S'ānṭi of each Upanishaḍ according to the divisions of Ṛgveḍa and others to which they belong. To which S'rī-Rāma replied: "Aiṭareya, Kaushīṭaki, Nāḍa-(Binḍu), Āṭma-Boḍha, Nirvāṇa, Muḍgala, Akshamālikā, Ṭripurā, Soubhāgya and Bahvricha—these 10 Upanishaḍs are of Ṛgveḍa and have the S'ānṭi beginning with 'Vāṅme-Manasi, etc'. Is'a, Bṛhaḍāraṇyaka, Jābāla, Hamsa, (Parama)-Hamsa, Subāla, Manṭrikā, Nirālamba, Ṭris'ikhī-Brāhmaṇa, Maṇḍala-Brāhmaṇa, Aḍwaya-Ṭāraka, Paiṅgala, Bhikshu, Ṭurīyāṭīṭa, Aḍhyāṭma, Tārasāra, Yājñavalkya, S'āṭyāyanī, and Mukṭika—these 19 Upanishaḍs are of S'ukla Yajurveḍa and have the S'ānti beginning with 'Pūrṇamaḍa, etc'.

"Katha, Ṭiṭṭiri, Brahma, Kaivalya, S'wetās'waṭara, Garbha, Nārāyaṇa, (Amṛṭa)-Binḍu, (Amṛṭa)-Nāḍa, Kālāgniruḍra, Kshurikā, Sarvasāra, S'ukarahasya, Ṭejo-(Binḍu), Ḍhyāna-(Binḍu), (Brahma)-Viḍyā, Yoga-Ṭaṭṭwa, Ḍakshiṇā-(Mūrṭi), Skanḍa, S'āriraka, (Yoga)-S'ikhā, Ekākshara, Akshi, Avaḍhūṭa, Kara, (Ruḍra)-Hṛḍaya, (Yoga)-Kuṇḍalinī, Pañchabrahma, (Prāṇa)-Agnihoṭra, Varāha, Kali-(Sanṭāraṇa), and Saraswaṭirahasya,—these 32 Upanishaḍs are of Kṛsbṇa Yajurveḍa and have the S'ānṭi beginning with 'Sahanāvavaṭu, etc'.

"Kena, Chhānḍogya, Āruṇi, Maiṭrāyaṇī, Maiṭreyī, Vajrasūchikā, (Yoga)-Chūḍā-(Maṇi), Vasuḍeva, Mahaṭ-Sannyāsa, Avyakṭa, Kuṇḍikā, Sāviṭrī, Ruḍrāksha, Jābāla, Dars'ana, and Jābāli,—these 16 Upanishaḍs are of Sāmaveḍa and have the S'ānti beginning with 'Āpyāyanṭu, etc'.

"Pras'na, Muṇḍaka, Māṇḍūkya, (Aṭharva)-S'ira, (Aṭharva)-S'ikhā, (Bṛhaṭ)-Jābāla, (Nṛsihma)-Ṭāpanī, (Nāraḍa-Parivrājaka), Sīṭā, S'arabha, Mahā-Nārāyaṇa, (Rāma)-Rahasya, (Rāma)-Tāpanī, S'ānḍilya, (Paramahamsa)-Parivrājaka, (Ānna)-Pūrṇā, Sūrya, Āṭma, Pās'upaṭa, Parabrahma, Ṭripuraṭāpanī, Ḍevī, Bhāvanā, Bhasma-(Jābāla), Gaṇapaṭi, Mahāvākya, Gopāla-Ṭāpanī, Kṛshṇa, Hayagrīva, Ḍaṭṭāṭreya, and Gāruda,—these 31 Upanishaḍs of Aṭharvaṇa-Veḍa have the S'ānṭi commencing with 'Bhaḍram-Karṇebhiḥ, etc'.

"Persons desirous of emancipation and having developed the four means of salvation should, with presents in their hands, approach a Guru full of faith, of good family, proficient in Veḍas, scripture-loving, of good qualities, straightforward, intent upon the welfare of all beings, and an ocean of compassion; and after studying under him, according to the rules, the 108 Upanishaḍs, he should ever be going through the process of studying, thinking and reflecting upon them. With the cessation of the three bodies through the destruction of Prārabḍha, they attain the state of Plenum without any Upāḍhis like the ether in the pot (after the pot is broken). This is the embodied salvation, this is the final emancipation. Therefore even those in Brahmaloka through the studying of Veḍānṭa from the mouth of Brahmā attain with Him the final emancipation. Hence to all these is stated the final emancipation through the Jñāna path, and not through Karma, Sāṅkhya-Yoga, and other Upāsanās. Thus is the Upanishaḍ."

Aḍhyāya II

Again Māruṭi (Hanūmān) addressed S'rī-Rāmachanḍra thus: "What is Jīvanmukṭi? what is Viḍehamukṭi? what is the authority therein? what about its perfection? what is the object of such a perfection?"

(S'rī-Rāma replied:) "The Ḍharma of a man's Chiṭṭa that has the characteristics of agency and enjoyment is fraught with pains and hence tends towards bondage. The control of it (the Chiṭṭa) is Jīvanmukṭi. Viḍehamukṭi follows when through the extinction of Prārabḍha, the removal of the vehicles [of the bodies] takes place like the ether in the pot [after the pot is broken]. The authority on the points of Jīvanmukṭi and Viḍehamukṭi is the 108 Upanishaḍs. Its object [of perfection] is the attaining of eternal bliss through the removal of the pains of agency, etc. This has to be achieved through human efforts. Like progeny obtained through the Puṭrakāmeshti sacrifice, wealth in trade, or heaven through the Jyoṭishtoma sacrifice, so Jīvanmukṭi is gained through Samāḍhi arising through Veḍānṭic study, and accomplished through human efforts. It has to be won through the extinction of all Vāsanās. Regarding it, there are verses thus: 'The efforts of man are stated to be of two kinds, those that transcend scriptures and those that are according to scriptures. Those that transcend scriptures tend to harm while those that are according to scriptures tend to Reality.' To men, true Jñāna does not arise through the Vāsanās of the world, scripture and body. Vāsanā is divided into two, the pure and the impure. If thou art led by the pure Vāsanās, thou shalt thereby soon reach by degrees My Seat. But should the old impure Vāsanās land thee in danger, they should be overcome through efforts. This river of Vāsanās towards objects, which flows in the pure and impure paths, should be diverted to the pure path through human efforts. The impure ones have to be transmuted into the pure. That which is diverted from the impure turns towards the pure. So also the reverse. This child, Chiṭṭa has to be fondled through human efforts. O killer of enemies, it is only when through means of practice both Vāsanās quite abandon thee, that thou wilt be able to realise the effects of [such] practice. Even in the case of doubt, the pure Vāsanās alone should be practised.

"O son of Vāyu, there is nothing wrong in the increase of the pure Vāsanās. The extinction of Vāsanās, Vijñāna and the destruction of Manas [as these three] when practised together for a long time are regarded, O great and intelligent one, as fruitful. So long as these are not equally practised again and again, so long the [Supreme] Seat is not attained, even after the lapse of hundreds of years. Even should one of these [three] be practised for a long time, it will not yield its fruit like a Manṭra imperfectly done. Through the practice of these for a long time, the firm knots of the heart are cut, without doubt, like the breaking of the threads in a lotus-stalk rent in twain. The illusory Samsāric Vāsanā that has arisen through the practice of [many] hundreds of lives never perishes except through the practice of Yoga for a long time. Therefore, O Somya [disciple], after having put away to a distance the desire of enjoyment through discriminative human effort, resort to these three alone. The wise know that a mind associated with Vāsanā tends to bondage, while a mind well freed from

Vāsanā is said to be an emancipated one. O Mahā-kapi [great Monkey] practise the state of a mind devoid of Vāsanā. Vāsanā perishes through well-conducted deliberation and truth. Through the absorption of Vāsanās, Manas attains quiescence like a lamp [without oil]. He whose mind, devoid of destruction, is [centred] on Me as of the nature of Chinmāṭra [consciousness alone], abandoning the Vāsanas, is no other than Myself of the nature of Sachchiḍānanḍa. Whether Sāmaḍhi and Karma are performed or not, one who has a supreme Chiṭṭa with a heart devoid of all desires is an emancipated person. He whose mind is freed from Vāsanās is not subject to the fruits arising from the performance or non-performance of actions, or Samāḍhi or Jñāna. Except through the entire giving up of Vāsanās and through Mouna [the observance of silence towards objects], the Supreme Seat is not attained. Though devoid of Vāsanās, the eye and other organs are involuntarily prompted to their (respective) external objects through habit. Just as the eye without any desire sees without any effort the objects that fall on it, so also the undaunted man of intelligence enters into the affairs [of the world] without any desire. O Māruṭi, the Munis know that as Vāsanā which is manifested through the consciousness of objects, which is of the nature of the object itself, and which is the cause of the origination and absorption of Chiṭṭa. This excessively fluctuating Chiṭṭa is the cause of birth, dotage and death, due to the identification of itself with objects practised firmly [for a long time]. Like the analogy of the seed and the tree, the vibration of Prāṇa arises through Vāsanā and (*vice versa*) the Vāsanā through the former—these forming the seed of Chiṭṭa. To the tree of Chiṭṭa, there are two seeds : the vibration of Prāṇa and Vāsanā. Should either of them perish, both perish soon. Through the actions of the world being done without attachment, through the abandoning of the [thought of the] reality of the universe and the conviction of the destructibility of the body, Vāsanā does not arise. Through the complete giving up of Vāsanā, Chiṭṭa becomes not-Chiṭṭa. When the mind does not think at all, being completely devoid of Vāsanā, then dawns the state of mindlessness which confers the great peace. So long as you are without a mind of [true] discrimination and are not a knower of the Supreme Seat, so long should you follow whatever has been decided by the teacher and the authorities of the sacred books. When your sins are burnt up and you are a knower of the Reality without any anxiety, then all the good Vāsanās even should be given up.

"The destruction of Chiṭṭa is of two kinds, that with form and that without form. [The destruction of] that with form is of the Jīvanmukṭa; (the destruction of), that without form being of the Viḍehamukṭa. O son of Vāyu, hearken to [the means of] the destruction of Chiṭṭa. That is said to be the destruction of Chiṭṭa when it, associated with all the attributes of Maiṭri (friendship) and others, becomes quiescent [without any resurrection]. There is no doubt of it. Then the Manas of a Jīvanmukṭa is free from fresh rebirth; to him, there is the destruction of Manas with form. But to the Viḍehamukṭa, there is the destruction of Manas without form. It is Manas that is the root of the tree of Samsāra with its thousands of shoots, branches, tender leaves and fruits. I think it to be Saṅkalpa alone. In order that the tree of Samsāra may wither soon, dry up its root through the quiescence of Saṅkalpa. There is only one means to control one's mind. That is to destroy the mind as soon as it rises. That is the (great) dawn. In the case of the wise, the mind is destroyed: but in the case of the ignorant, it is indeed a fetter. So long as the mind is not destroyed through the firm practice of the One Reality, so long as Vāsanās are prancing about in the heart like Veṭāla (goblin) in the night-time. The Vāsanās of enjoyment of one who has destroyed the egoism of Chiṭṭa and controlled the organs, the enemies, decay like lotuses in mid-winter. Pressing one hand against the other, setting teeth against teeth, and forcing one limb against the other, he should first conquer his mind.

"It is not possible on the part of the one-thoughted to control the mind by sitting up again and again except through the approved means. As a vicious rutting elephant is not subject to control except through the goad, so in the matter of the control of the mind, the effective means are the attainment of spiritual knowledge, association with the wise, the entire abdication of all Vāsanās and the control of prāṇas. While such are the [prescribed] means, should persons try to control the mind through violence, they are like those that search in darkness, having thrown aside the light (in their hands). Those who endeavour to control the mind through force are but trying to bind a mad elephant with the filaments of a lotus-stalk.

To the tree of the mind having the ever-growing branches of modifications, there are two seeds. One is the fluctuation of Prāṇa, and the other is the firmness of Vāsanā. The [One] All-pervading Consciousness is agitated by the fluctuation of Prāṇa. The means of Ḍhyāna by which [the one] Jñāna is attained through the one-pointedness of the mind is now imparted to you. After duly resolving back the things originated [in the universe] with all their changes, meditate upon that which remains—[*viz.*], Chinmāṭra (the consciousness alone), which is also Chiḍānanḍa (conscious-bliss). The wise say that the interval experienced by Yogins after the inspiration and before the (next) expiration is [the internal] Kumbhaka (cessation of breath); while the interval of complete equilibrium after expiration and before the next inspiration is the external Kumbhaka. Through the force of the practice of Ḍhyāna, the current of the modification of Manas devoid of Self that is of Brāhmic nature is said to be Samprajñāṭa Samāḍhi, while the mind with the utter quiescence of modifications that confers upon one supreme bliss is said to be Asamprajñāṭa-Samāḍhi that is dear unto Yogins. This [state] that is devoid of light, Manas and Buḍḍhi, and that is of the nature of Chiṭ (consciousness merely) is styled by the Munis Aṭaḍvyāvṛṭṭi Samāḍhi (a Samāḍhi that does not care or require the aid of another). It is Plenum above, below and in the middle, and is of the nature of S'iva (auspiciousness). This noumenal (or occult) Samāḍhi is itself Viḍhi-Mukha (sanctioned by books or Brahmā).

"The clinging to objects without previous or subsequent deliberation through intense thought [or longing] is stated to be Vāsanā. O chief of Monkeys, whatever is meditated upon by a person with ardent impetuosity without any other Vāsanā

—that he soon becomes. A person that is entirely subject to Vāsanā becomes of the nature of that. When he regards this [universe] as Saṭ [the Reality], then he is subject to delusion. Because of the many strong Vāsanās, he does not abandon the nature of the universe. This person of wrong vision sees everything under infatuation like one deluded. Vāsanās are of two kinds—the pure and the impure. The impure ones are the cause of rebirth, while the pure are the destroyers of it. The impure are said by the wise to be of the nature of intense Ajñāna, associated with the great Ahaṅkāra and generative of rebirth. Of what avail is the chewing again and again of the many S'āsṭric stories to one that has abandoned the seed of rebirth, having turned it into a burnt one? O Māruṭi, thou shouldst with effort seek the effulgence within. O tiger of Monkeys, whoever, after having abandoned the visible and the invisible, is as the One alone is not a mere knower of Brahman but is Brahman itself. One who having studied the four Veḍas and the various books does not cognize the reality of Brahman is like the ladle ignorant of the taste of the dainty. Therefore what other advice of indifference can be imparted to a person that has not attained the indifference to the impure Vāsanā of delusion [or body]? This body is very impure while the one [Āṭmā] that dwells in it is very pure. When the differences between the two are [thus] known, what then may be ordained as the purification? The bondage of Vāsanā is the [real] bondage, while the destruction of Vāsanā is salvation. After wholly abandoning the Vāsanās, give up even the desire for salvation. After first giving up the Vāsanā of objects dependent upon the Vāsanā of the mind, attract unto thyself the pure Vāsanās associated with Maiṭri [friendship] and others. Though engaged in the world with these pure Vāsanās, give up them too and retire within the quiescent desires and become of the form of the longing after Chiṭ alone. Then, O Māruṭi! giving up that also associated as it is with Manas and Buḍḍhi, mayst thou now left alone become firm in Me in Samāḍhi. O son of Vāyu! always worship My Reality that is destructive of pains, without sound, touch, form, decay, taste, destruction or smell, and without name and

Goṭra [clan]. I am that non-dual One (Brahman) that is of the nature of the visible (Jñāna), like unto the Ākās', supreme, always shining, without birth, non-dual, without destruction, without attachment and pervading all. I am the All, and of the nature of salvation. One should ever meditate upon Me thus: 'I am of the form of the visible [Jñāna], the pure, of changeless nature and have really no objects in Me. I am the ever-full Brahman, transverse and across, up and down.' Also meditate upon Me thus: 'I am birthless, deathless, ageless, immortal, self-shining, all-pervading, destructionless, causeless, pure beyond the effect (of the universe) and ever content.' When one's body becomes a prey to time, he gives up the state of Jīvanmukṭi, as the wind attains the motionless state.

"The following is said in the *Ṛg* [-Veḍa] also: Like the eye which is spread in the Ākās' (seeing all things without any obstacle), so the wise ever see the Supreme Seat of Vishṇu. The Brāhmaṇas that have ever the Divine vision praise in diverse ways and illumine the Supreme Seat of Vishṇu."

OM-ṬAṬ-SAṬ IS THE UPANISHAḌ.

SARVASĀRA-UPANISHAḌ[1]

OF

KṚSHṆA-YĀJURVEḌA

[In the text, all the questions are given first and then the answers follow. But the following arrangement is adopted to facilitate reference.]

1. What is Banḍha (bondage).

Āṭmā [the Self] falsely superimposing the body and others which are not-Self upon Himself, and identifying Himself with them—this iḍentification forms the bondage of the Self.

2. What is Moksha [emancipation]?

The freedom from that [identification] is Moksha.

3. What is Āviḍyā (Nescience)?

That which causes this identification—that indeed is Āviḍyā.

4. What is Viḍyā (knowledge)?

That which removes this identification is Viḍyā.

5. What are (meant by) the states of Jāgraṭ [the waking], Swapna [the dreaming], Sushupṭi [the dreamless sleeping] and Ṭurīya [the fourth]?

Jāgraṭ is that [state] during which Āṭmā enjoys the gross objects of senses as sound, etc., through the 14 organs[2] as Manas, etc., having the sun and the rest as their presiding deities.

Swapna is that [state] during which Āṭmā experiences, through the 14 organs associated with the Vāsanās [affinities],

[1] This Upanishaḍ and the next form a glossary of some of the terms of Veḍānṭa. 'Sarva-Sāra' is the all-essence or quintessence.

[2] They are the 5 organs of sense, the 5 organs of action and the 4 of Antaḥkaraṇa (the internal organ), *viz.*, Manas, Buḍḍhi, Chiṭṭa and Ahaṅkāra. Each is animated by a Ḍevaṭā or intelligential principle.

of the waking condition, sound and other objects which are of the form of the Vāsanās created for the time being, even in the absence of [the gross] sound and the others. Āṭmā experiences Sushupṭi when it does not experience sound and other objects of sense from the cessation of the functions of the 14 organs, there being no special enjoying consciousness on account of the absence of these organs.

Ṭurīya is that state during which Āṭmā is a witness to the existence of the above-mentioned three states, though it is in itself without (their) existence and non-existence and during which it is one uninterrupted Chaiṭanya (consciousness) alone. And that Chaiṭanya is that which is connected with the three states, which is without the three states, and which is pure.

6. What are the Annamaya, Prāṇamaya, Manomaya, Vijñānamaya and Ānanḍamaya Kos'as (sheaths)?

Annamaya sheath is the aggregate of the materials formed by food. When the ten Vāyus (Vital airs), Prāṇas and others, flow through the Annamaya sheath, then it is called the Prāṇamaya sheath. When Āṭmā connected with the above two sheaths performs the functions of hearing, etc., through the 14 organs of Manas and others, then it is called Manomaya sheath.

When in the (Ānṭaḥ-karaṇa) internal organs connected with the above three sheaths, there arise the modifications of contemplation, meditation, etc., about the peculiarities of the sheaths, then it is called Vijñānamaya sheath.

When the self-cause Jñāna is in its Self-bliss like the banyan tree in its seed, though associated with these four sheaths caused by Ajñāna, then it is called Ānanḍamaya sheath. Āṭmā which is associated with the Upāḍhi [vehicle] of these sheaths is figuratively called Kos'a.

7. What is meant by Karṭā (actor), Jīva, Pañchavarga [the five groups], Ksheṭrajña (the lord of the place), Sāksbi [the witness], Kūtasṭha and Anṭaryāmin (the latent guide)?

Karṭā (the actor) is the one who possesses the body and the internal organs through their respective desires proceeding from the idea of pleasure and pain. The idea of pleasure is that modification of the mind known as love. The idea of pain is that modification of the mind known as hate. The cause of pleasure and pain are sound, touch, form, taste and odour.

Jīva is that Aḍhyāsi [deluded one] that thinks that this body, which is obtained through the effects of good and bad Karmas, is one not so obtained.

Pañchavarga (the five groups) are (1) Manas, *viz.*, Manas, Buḍḍhi, Chiṭṭa and Ahaṅkāra (creating uncertainty, certitude, flitting thought and egoism), (2) Prāṇa, *i.e.*, Prāṇa, Āpāna, Vyāna Samāna and Uḍāna, (3) Saṭṭwa, *i. e.*, Saṭṭwa, Rajas, and Ṭamas. (4) the [five] elements: earth, water, fire, Vāyu and Ākās' and (5) Ḍharma and its opposite Āḍharma.

The original Āviḍyā which has the characteristics of the above 5 groups, which does not perish without Āṭma-Jñāna, which appears eternal through the presence of Āṭmā and which is the vehicle for [the manifestation of] Āṭmā, is the seed of the Liṅga [subtle] body. It is also called Hṛḍaya-granṭhi [the heart-knot].

The Chaiṭanya [consciousness] which is reflected and shines in it is Ksheṭrajña.

Sākshi [the witness] is that conscious one that is aware of the appearance and disappearance [of the three states] of the knower, the knowledge and the known, who is himself without [or not affected by] this appearance and disappearance, and who is self-radiant.

Kūtasṭha is he who is found without exception in the Buḍḍhi of all creatures from Brahmā down to ants, and who is shining as Āṭmā and dwells as witness to the Buḍḍhi of all creatures.

Anṭaryāmin is the Āṭmā that shines as the ordainer, being within all bodies like the thread [on which] beads [are strung] and serving to know the cause of the several differences of Kūtasṭha and others associated with him.

8. Who is Praṭyagāṭmā?

He is of the nature of truth, wisdom, eternity and bliss. He has no vehicles of body. He is abstract wisdom itself, like a mass of pure gold that is devoid of the changes of bracelet, crown, etc. He is of the nature of mere consciousness. He is that which shines as Chaiṭanya and Brahman. When He is subject to the vehicle of Âviḍyā and is the meaning of the word "Ṭwam" ('Thou' in "Ṭaṭṭwamasi"), then He is Praṭyagāṭmā.

9. Who is Paramāṭmā ?

It is He who is associated with truth, wisdom, eternity, bliss, omniscience, etc., who is subject to the vehicle of Māyā and who is the meaning of the word "Ṭaṭ" (or 'That' in "Ṭaṭṭwamasi").

10. What is Brahman ?

Brahman is that which is free from all vehicles, which is the Âbsolute Consciousness devoid of particularities, which is Saṭ (Be-ness), which is without a second, which is bliss and which is Māyā-less. It is different from characteristics of that expressed by the word "Ṭwam" (Thou) subject to Upāḍhis (vehicles), or the characteristics of 'That' expressed by the word "Ṭaṭ" subject to Upāḍhis. It is itself differenceless and is seen as the Seat of everything. It is the pure, the noumenal, the true and the indestructible.

Ând what is Saṭya (the true) ?

It is the Saṭ (Be-ness) which is the aim pointed out by the Veḍas. It is that which cannot be said to be Asaṭ (not-Be-ness). It is that which is not affected by the three periods of time. It is that which continues to exist during the three periods of time. It is that which is. It is one without a second. It has not the differences of similarity or dissimilarity ; or it is that which is the source of all ideas. It is that which does not perish even though space, time, matter, cause, etc., perish.

Ând what is Jñāna (wisdom) ?

It is self-light. It is that which illuminates all. It is that Âbsolute Consciousness which is without any obscuration. It is that Consciousness which has no beginning or end, which is perpetual and which is the witness to all modifications and their opposites.

Ând what is Ânanṭa (the eternal) ?

It is that which is without origin and destruction. It is that which is not subject to the six changes (*viz.*, birth, growth, manhood, decay, old age and death). It is free from all Upāḍhis. It is that Consciousness which, being all full and without destruction, permeates the created universe composed of Avyakṭa and others, like the earth in the modifications of clay, the gold in the modifications of gold, and thread in the modifications of thread.

And what is Ānanḍa (bliss) ?

It is the seat of all sentient beings, like the ocean of the water, is eternal, pure, partless and non-dual, and is the sole essence of Chiḍānanḍa (consciousness-bliss).

11. Of how many kinds are substances ?

There are three kinds, Saṭ (Be-ness), Āsaṭ (not-Be-ness) and Miṭhyā (Illusion).

Saṭ alone is Brahman. Āsaṭ is that which is not. Miṭhyā is the illusory ascription to Brahman of the universe that is not.

What is fit to be known is Brahman, the Āṭmā alone.

Brahma-Jñāna is the rooting out of all—bodies and such like—that are not Self, and the merging in Brahman, the Saṭ. The universe of Ākās' and others including Jīva is not-Āṭmā.

12. What is Māyā ?

The root of this not-Āṭmā is Māyā. She appears in Brahman like clouds, etc., in the sky. She has no beginning but has an end. She is subject to proof and not-proof. She neither is ; nor is not ; nor is she a combination of both (Saṭ and Āsaṭ). Her seat is indescribable. She has the varieties of differences as extolled by the wise. It is she that truly is not. Her nature is Ajñāna. She appears as Mūlaprakṛṭi, Guṇa-Sāmya (a state where the three Guṇas are found in equilibrium),[1] Aviḍyā (Nescience) and other forms, transforming herself into the form of the universe. Thus does a knower of Brahman cognize her.

---

[1] This refers to that slumbering or latent state of the universe—called also Mahā-Sushupṭi when the Guṇas are in equilibrium ; on re-awakening into activity when the Guṇas are disturbed, Mūlaprakṛṭi is called by the different names of Māyā, Aviḍyā, Ṭamas, etc.

NIRĀLAMBA[1]-UPANISHAḌ

OF

S'UKLĀ-YĀJURVEḌĀ

Hariḥ-Om. I shall relate in the form of a catechism whatever should be known for the removal of all miseries that befall these ignorant creatures [men].

What is Brahman? Who is Is'wara? Who is Jīva? What is Prakṛṭi? Who is Paramāṭmā? Who is Brahmā? Who is Vishṇu? Who is Ruḍra? Who is Inḍra? Who is Yama? Who is Sūrya? Who is Chanḍra? Who are Ḍevas? Who are Rākshasas? Who are Pis'āchas? Who are Manushyas? Who are Women? Who are Pas'us, etc.? What is Sṭhāvara? Who are Brāhmans and others? What is Jāṭi (caste)? What is Karma? What is Akarma? What is Jñāna? What is Ajñāna? What is Sukha? What is Ḍuḥkha? What is Swarga? What is Naraka? What is Banḍha? What is Moksha? Who is Upāsya? Who is Viḍwān? Who is Mūdha? What is Āsura? What is Ṭapas? What is Paramapaḍa? What is Grāhya? What is Agrāhya? Who is Sannyāsi? Thus are the questions.

1. What is Brahman?

It is the Chaiṭanya that appears, through the aspects of Karma and Jñāna, as this vast mundane egg composed of Mahaṭ, Āhaṅkāra and the five elements, earth, water, fire, Vāyu and Ākās'—that is secondless—that is devoid of all Upāḍhis [vehicles], that is full of all S'akṭis [potencies], that is without beginning and end, that is described as pure, beneficial, peaceful, and Guṇa-less and that is indescribable.

[1] Lit.—without support.

2. Who is Is'wara? and what are His characteristics? Bramhan itself, having through His S'akṭi called Prakṛṭi (matter) created the worlds and being latent in them, becomes the ruler of Buḍḍhi and Inḍriyas (organs of sense and action) as well as Brahmā (the creator) and others. Hence he is named Is'wara.

3. Who is Jīva?

Is'wara Himself, subject to the false superimposition upon Himself [of the idea] "I am the gross" through the [assumption of the] names and forms of Brahmā, Vishṇu, Ruḍra, Inḍra, and others is Jīva. Though one, he appears as many Jīvas, through the force of the different Karmas originating the bodies.

4. What is Prakṛṭi (matter)?

It is nothing else but the S'akṭi [potency] of Brahman which is of the nature of Buḍḍhi that is able to produce the many motley worlds by virtue of the mere presence of Brahman.

5. What is Paramāṭmā? The supreme Āṭmā or soul.

It is Brahman alone that is Paramāṭmā as it (the former) is far superior to bodies and others.

6. Who is Brahmā [the creator]?
7. Who is Vishṇu [the preserver]?
8. Who is Ruḍra [the destroyer]?
9. Who is Inḍra?
10. Who is Yama [the angel of death]?
11. Who is Sūrya [the Sun]?
12. Who is Chanḍra [the Moon]?
13. Who are Ḍevas [the Angels]?
14. Who are Āsuras [the Demons]?
15. Who are Pis'āchas [the evil spirits]?
16. Who are Manushyas [the men]?
17. Who are Women?
18. What are beasts, etc.?
19. What are the Sṭhāvaras [fixed ones]?
20. Who are Brāhmans and others?

That Brahman is Brahmā, Vishṇu, Ruḍra and Inḍra, Yama, Sun and Moon, Ḍevas, Āsuras, Pis'āchas, men, women, beasts, etc., the fixed ones, Brāhmans and others. Here there is no manyness in the least degree: all this is verily Brahman.

21. What is Jāṭi (caste)

It cannot refer to the skin, the blood, the flesh or the bone. There is no caste for Āṭmā; caste is only conventional.

22. What is Karma?

Karma is that action alone which is performed by the organs and ascribed to Āṭmā as "I do" (*viz.*, agency being attributed to Āṭmā).

23. What is Akarma [or non-Karma]?

Akarma is the performance, without any desire for the fruits, of the daily and occasional rites, sacrifices, vows, austerities, gifts and other actions that are associated with the egoism of the actor and the enjoyer, and that are productive of bondage, rebirth, etc.

24. What is Jñāna?

It is the realisation by direct cognition of the fact that in this changing universe there is nothing but Chaiṭanya [the one life] that is Consciousness, that is of the form of the seer and the seen, pervading all things, that is the same in all, and that is not subject to changes like pot, cloth, etc. This realisation is brought about by means of the subjugation of the body and the senses, the serving of a good Guru (teacher), the hearing of the exposition of Veḍānṭic doctrines and constant meditation thereon.

25. What is Ajñāna?

It is the illusory attribution, like the snake in the rope, of many Āṭmās (souls) through the diverse Upāḍhis [or vehicles] of the angels, beasts, men, the fixed ones, females, males, castes and orders of life, bondage and emancipation, etc., to Brahman that is secondless, all-permeating and of the nature of all.

26. What is Sukha (happiness)?

It is a state of being of the nature of bliss, having cognized through experience the Reality of Sachchiḍānanḍa [or that which is be-ness, consciousness and bliss].

27. What is Ḍuḥkha (pains)?

It is the mere Saṅkalpa [or the thinking] of the objects of mundane existence [or of not-Self according to the Bombay Edition].

28. What is Swarga (heaven)?

It is the association with Saṭ [either good men or Brahman which is Saṭ, the true].

29. What is Naraka (hell)?

It is the association with that which brings about this mundane existence which is Āsaṭ [the false].

30. What is Banḍha [bondage]?

Such Saṅkalpas [thoughts] as "I was born," etc., arising from the affinities of beginningless Ajñāna form bondage.

The thought obscuration [or mental ignorance] of the mundane existence of "mine" in such as father, mother, brother, wife, child, house, gardens, lands, etc., forms bondage.

The thoughts of I-ness as actor, etc., are bondage.

The thought of the development in oneself of the eight Siḍḍhis (higher psychical powers) as Āṇimā and others[1] is bondage.

The thought of propitiating the angels, men, etc., is bondage.

The thought of going through the eight means of Yoga[2] practice, Yama, etc., is bondage.

The thought of performing the duties of one's own caste and order of life is bondage.

The thought that command, fear and doubt are the attributes of [or pertain to] Āṭmā is bondage.

The thought of knowing the rules of performing sacrifices, vows, austerity and gift is bondage. Even the mere thought of desire for Moksha (emancipation) is bondage. By the very act of thought, bondage is caused.

31. What is Moksha [emancipation]?

Moksha is the (state of) the annihilation, through the discrimination of the eternal from the non-eternal, of all thoughts of bondage, like those of "mine" in objects of pleasure and pain, lands, etc., in this transitory mundane existence.

32. Who is Upāsya [or fit to be worshipped]?

That Guru (or spiritual instructor) who enables (the disciple) to attain to Brahman, the Consciousness that is in all bodies.

[1] There are 18 Siḍḍhis, 8 higher and 10 lower.

[2] They are Yama, Niyama, etc.

33. Who is S'ishya (the disciple)?

The disciple is that Brahman alone that remains after the consciousness of the universe has been lost (in him) through Brāhmic wisdom.

34. Who is Viḍwān (the learned)?

It is he who has cognized the true form (or reality) of his own consciousness that is latent in all.

35. Who is Mūdha [the ignorant]?

He who has the egoistic conception of the body, caste, orders of life, actor, enjoyer and others.

36. What is Āsura [the demoniacal]?

It is the Ṭapas [austerity] practised by one inflicting trouble on the Āṭmā within through Japa [or inaudible muttering of Manṭras], abstinence from food, Agnihoṭra [the performance of the worship of fire], etc., attended with cruel desire, hatred, pain, hypocrisy and the rest for the purpose of acquiring the powers of Vishṇu, Brahmā, Ruḍra, Inḍra and others.

37. What is Ṭapas?

Ṭapas is the act of burning—through the fire of direct cognition of the knowledge that Brahman is the truth and the universe, a myth—the seed of the deep-rooted desire to attain the powers of Brahmā, etc.

38. What is Paramapaḍa [the supreme abode]?

It is the seat of the eternal and emancipated Brahman which is far superior to Prāṇas (the vital airs), the organs of sense and actions, the internal organs (of thought), the Guṇas and others, which is of the nature of Sachchiḍānanḍa and which is the witness to all.

39. What is Grāhya [or fit to be taken in]?

Only that Reality of Absolute Consciousness which is not conditioned by space, time or substance.

40. What is Agrāhya?

The thought that this universe is truth—this universe which is different from one's Self and which being subject to Māyā (or illusion) forms the object of (cognition of) Buḍḍhi and the organs.

41. Who is the Sannyāsi [ascetic]?

Ā Sannyāsi is an ascetic who having given up all the duties of caste and orders of life, good and bad actions, etc., being freed from [the conceptions of] "I" and "mine" and having taken his refuge in Brahman alone, roams at large practising Nirvikalpa Samāḍhi and being firmly convinced of "I am Brahman" through the realisation of the meaning of such sacred (Veḍic) sentences as "Thou art That" "Āll this is verily Brahman" and "Here there is no manyness in the least". He only is an emancipated person. He only is fit to be adored. He only is a Yogin. He only is a Paramahamsa. He only is an Avaḍhūṭa. He only is a Brahman. Whoever studies the *Nirālamba-Upanishaḍ* becomes, through the grace of Guru, pure like fire. He becomes pure like Vāyu (air). He does not return. He is not born again: nay he is not born again.

Such is the Upanishaḍ.

MAIṬREYA-UPANISHAḌ

OF

SĀMAVEḌA

Ā KING named Bṛhaḍraṭha, thinking this body to be impermanent and having acquired indifference (to objects), retired to the forest, leaving his eldest son to rule over (his) kingdom. With hands uplifted and eyes fixed on the sun, he performed a severe Ṭapas (or religious austerity). Āt the end of a thousand days, the Lord S'ākāyanya Muni, a knower of Ātmā, who was like fire without smoke, and who was as a scorching fire with his Ṭejas (spiritual lustre) approached (him) and addressed the King thus: "Rise, rise and choose a boon." The King prostrated before him and said: "O Lord, I am not an Āṭmaviṭ (or knower of Āṭmā). Thou art a *Ṭaṭṭwaviṭ*, we hear. Please enlighten me about Saṭṭva (the state of Saṭ or Brahman)." (To which) the Muni replied thus: "O thou that art born of the race of Ikshwāku: To begin with, your question is difficult (of explanation): do not question me. Āsk for any other thing you desire." Thereupon the King touched the feet of S'ākāyanya and recited the (following) verse:

"What is the use of these to me or any other? Oceans dry up. Mountains sink down. The positions of Ḍhruva (the Polar Star) and of trees change. Earth is drowned. The Suras (angels) run away, leaving their (respective) places. (While such is the case), I am He in reality. Therefore of what avail to me is the gratification of desires, since one who clings to the gratification of desires is found to return again and again to this Samsāra (mundane existence)? Thou art able to extricate me (out of this Samsāra). I am drowned like a frog in a dry well. Thou art my refuge.

"O Lord! this body was the result of sexual intercourse. It is without wisdom; it is hell (itself). It came out through the urinary orifice. It is linked together by bones. It is coated over with flesh. It is bound by skin. It is replete with fæces, urine, Vāyu (air), bile, phlegm, marrow, fat, serum and many other impurities. O Lord! to me in such a foul body (as this), thou art my refuge."

Thereupon Lord S'ākāyanya was pleased and addressed the King thus: "O Mahārāja, Bṛhaḍraṭha, the flag of the Ikshwāku race, thou art an Āṭmajñānī. Thou art one that has done his duty. Thou art famous by the name of Maruṭ." At which the King asked: "O Lord! in what way, can you describe Āṭmā?" To which he replied thus: "Sound, touch, and others which seem to be Arṭha (wealth) are in fact Anarṭha (evil). The Bhūṭāṭmā (the lower Self) clinging to these, never remembers the Supreme Seat. Through Ṭapas, Saṭṭwa (quality) is acquired; through Saṭṭwa, a (pure) mind is acquired; and through mind, (Parama-) Āṭmā, (the higher Self) is reached. Through attaining Āṭmā, one gets liberation. Just as fire without fuel is absorbed into its own womb, so Chiṭṭa (thought) through the destruction of its modifications is absorbed into its own womb (source). To a mind that has attained quiescence and truth, and which is not affected by sense-objects, the events that occur to it through the bondage of Karma are merely unreal. It is Chiṭṭa alone that is Samsāra. It should be cleansed with effort. Whatever his Chiṭṭa (thinks), of that nature he becomes. This is an archaic mystery. With the purifying of Chiṭṭa, one makes both good and bad Karmas to perish. One whose mind is thus cleansed attains the indestructible Bliss (through his own Self). Just as Chiṭṭa becomes united with an object that comes across it, so why should not one (be released) from bondage, when one is united with Brahman. One should meditate in the middle of the lotus of the heart, Parames'wara (the highest Lord) who is the witness to the play of Buḍḍhi, who is the object of supreme love, who is beyond the reach of mind and speech, who has no beginning or end, who is Saṭ alone being of the nature of light only, who is beyond meditation, who can neither be given up nor grasped (by the mind), who is without equal or superior, who is the permanent, who is of unshaken depth, who is without light or darkness, who is all-pervading, changeless and vehicleless, and who is wisdom of the nature of Moksha (salvation). I am He—that Paramāṭmā who is the eternal, the pure, the liberated, of the nature of wisdom, the true, the subtle, the all-pervading, the secondless, the ocean of bliss, and one that is superior to Praṭyagāṭmā (the lower Self). There is no doubt about it. How will calamity (or bondage) approach me who am depending upon my own bliss in my heart, who have put to shame the ghost of desires, who look upon this universe as (but) a jugglery and who am not associated with anything. The ignorant with their observance of the castes and orders of life obtain their fruits according to their Karmas. Men who have given up all duties of castes, etc., rest content in the bliss of their own Self. The distinctions of caste and orders of life have divisions among them, have beginning and end, and are very painful. Therefore having given up all identification with sons and as well as body, one should dwell in that endless and most supreme Bliss."

Aḍhyāya II

Then Lord Maiṭreya went to Kailās and having reached it asked Him thus: "O Lord! please initiate me into the mysteries of the highest Ṭaṭṭwa." To which Mahāḍeva replied: "The body is said to be a temple. The Jīva in it is S'iva alone. Having given up all the cast-off offerings of Ajñāna, one should worship Him with So'ham (I am He). The cognition of everything as non-different from oneself is Jñāna (wisdom). Abstracting the mind from sensual objects is Ḍhyāna (meditation). Purifying the mind of its impurities is Snāna (bathing). The subjugation of the Inḍriyas (sensual organs) is S'aucha (purification). One should drink the nectar of Brahman and beg food for maintaining the body. Having one (thought) alone, he should live in a solitary place without a second. The wise man should observe thus: then he obtains Absolution.

"This body is subject to birth and death. It is of the nature of the secretion of the father and mother. It is impure, being the seat of happiness and misery. (Therefore) bathing is prescribed for touching it. It is bound by the Ḍhāṭus (skin, blood, etc.), is liable to severe diseases, is a house of sins, is impermanent and is of changing appearance and size. (Therefore) bathing is prescribed for touching it. Foul matter is naturally oozing out always from the nine holes. It (body) contains bad odour and foul excrement. (Therefore) bathing is prescribed for touching it. It is connected (or tainted) with the child-birth impurity of the mother and is born with it. It is also tainted with death impurity. (Therefore) bathing is prescribed for touching it. (The conception of) "I and mine" is the odour arising from the besmeared dung and urine. The release from it is spoken of as the perfect purification. The (external) purification by means of water and earth is on account of the worldly. The destruction of the threefold affinities (of S'āsṭras, world and body) generates the purity for cleansing Chiṭṭa. That is called the (real) purification which is done by means of the earth and water of Jñāna (wisdom) and Vairāgya (indifference to objects).

"The conception of Aḍwaiṭa (non-dualism) should be taken in as the Bhiksha (alms-food); (but) the conception of Ḍwaiṭa (dualism) should not be taken in. To a Sannyāsī (ascetic), Bhiksha is ordained as dictated by the S'āsṭra and the Guru. After becoming a Sannyāsī, a learned man should himself abandon his native place and live at a distance, like a thief released from prison. When a person gives up Ahaṅkāra (I-am-ness) the son, wealth the brother, delusion the house, and desire the wife, there is no doubt that he is an emancipated person. Delusion, the mother is dead. Wisdom, the son is born. In this manner while two kinds of pollution have occurred, how shall we (the ascetics) observe the Sanḍhyās (conjunction periods)? The Chiṭ (consciousness) of the sun is ever shining in the resplendent Ākās' of the heart. He neither sets nor rises; while so, how shall we perform the Sanḍhyās? Ekānṭa (solitude) is that state of one without second as determined by the words of a Guru. Monasteries or forests are not solitudes. Emancipation is only for those who do not doubt. To those who doubt, there is no salvation even after many births. Therefore one should attain faith. (Mere) abandoning of the Karmas or of the Manṭras uttered at the initiation of a Sannyāsī (ascetic) will not constitute Sannyāsa. The union of Jīva (-Āṭmā) (the lower Self) and Parama (-Āṭmā) (the higher Self) at the two Sanḍhis (morning and evening) is termed Sannyāsa. Whoever has a nausea for all Ishaṇa (desires) and the rest as for vomited food, and is devoid of all affection for the body, is qualified for Sannyāsa. At the moment when indifference towards all objects arises in the mind, a learned person may take up Sannyāsa. Otherwise, he is a fallen person. Whoever becomes a Sannyāsī on account of wealth, food, clothes and fame, becomes fallen in both (as a Sannyāsī and as houesholder); (then) he is not worthy of salvation.

"The thought of (contemplation upon) Ṭaṭṭwas is the transcendental one; that of the S'āsṭras, the middling, and that of Manṭras, the lowest. The delusion of pilgrimages is the lowest of the lowest. Like one, who, having seen in water the reflection of fruits in the branches of trees, tastes and enjoys them, the ignorant without self-cognition are in vain overjoyed with (as if they reached) Brahman. That ascetic is an emancipated person who does not abandon the internal alms-taking (*viz.*, the meditation upon the non-dual), generating Vairāgya as well as faith the wife, and wisdom the son. Those men (termed) great through wealth, age, and knowledge, are only servants to those that are great through their wisdom as also to their disciples. Those whose minds are deluded by My Māyā, however learned they may be, do not attain Me, the all-full Āṭmā, and roam about like crows, simply for the purpose of filling up their belly, well burnt up (by hunger, etc.). For one that longs after salvation, the worship of images made of stone, metals, gem, or earth, is productive of rebirth and enjoyment. Therefore the ascetic should perform his own heart-worship alone, and relinquish external worship in order that he may not be born again. Then like a vessel full to its brim in an ocean, he is full within and full without. Like a vessel void in the ether, he is void within and void without. Do not become (or differentiate between) the Āṭmā that knows or the Āṭmā that is known. Do become of the form of that which remains, after having given up all thoughts. Relinquishing with their Vāsanās the seer, the seen and the visual, worship Āṭmā alone, the resplendent supreme presence. That is the real supreme State wherein all Saṅkalpas (thoughts) are at rest, which resembles the state of a stone, and which is neither waking nor sleeping."

Aḍhyāya III

"I am "I" (the Self). I am also another (the not-Self). I am Brahman. I am the Source (of all things). I am also the Guru of all worlds. I am of all the worlds. I am He. I am Myself alone. I am Siḍḍha. I am the Pure. I am the Supreme. I am. I am always He. I am the Eternal. I am stainless. I am Vijñāna. I am the Excellent. I am Soma. I am the All. I am without honour or dishonour. I am without Guṇas (qualities). I am S'iva (the auspicious). I am neither dual or non-dual. I am without the dualities (of heat or cold, etc.) I am He. I am neither existence nor non-existence. I am without language. I am the Shining. I am the Glory of void and non-void. I am the good and the bad. I am Happiness. I am without grief. I am Chaiṭanya. I am equal (in all). I am the like and the non-like. I am the eternal, the pure, and the ever felicitous. I am without all and without not all. I am Sāṭṭwika. I am always existing. I am without the number one. I am without the number two. I am without the difference of Saṭ and Āsaṭ. I am without Saṅkalpa. I am without the difference of manyness. I am the form of immeasurable Bliss. I am one that exists not. I am the one that is not another. I am without body, etc. I am with asylum. I am without asylum. I am without support. I am without bondage or emancipation. I am the pure Brahman. I am He. I am without Chiṭṭa, etc. I am the supreme and the Supreme of the supreme. I am ever of the form of deliberation and yet am without deliberation. I am He. I am of the nature of the Ākāra and Ukāra as also of Makāra. I am the earliest. The contemplator and contemplation I am without. I am One that cannot be contemplated upon. I am He. I have full form in all. I have the characteristics of Sachchiḍānanḍa. I am of the form of places of pilgrimages. I am the higher Self and S'iva. I am neither the thing defined nor non-defined. I am the non-absorbed Essence. I am not the measurer, the measure or the measured. I am S'iva. I am not the universe. I am the Seer of all. I am without the eyes, etc. I am the full grown. I am the Wise. I am the Quiescent. I am the Destroyer. I am without any sensual organs. I am the doer of all actions. I am One that is content with all Veḍānṭas (either books or Âṭmic Wisdom). I am the easily attainable. I have the name of one that is pleased as well as one that is not. I am the fruits of all silence. I am always of the form of Chinmāṭra (Âbsolute Consciousness). I am always Saṭ (Be-ness) and Chiṭ (Consciousness). I am one that has not anything in the least. I am not one that has not anything in the least. I am without the heart-Granṭhi (knot). I am the Being in the middle of the lotus. I am without the six changes. I am without the six sheaths and without the six enemies. I am within the within. I am without place and time. I am of the form of happiness having the quarters as My garment. I am the emancipated One, without bondage. I am without the "no". I am of the form of the partless. I am the partless. I have Chiṭṭa, though released from the universe. I am without the universe. I am of the form of all light. I am the Light (Jyoṭis) in Chinmāṭra (Âbsolute Consciousness). I am free from the three periods (of time past, present, and future). I am without desires. I am without body. I am One that has no body. I am Guṇaless. I am alone. I am without emancipation. I am the emancipated One. I am ever without emancipation. I am without truth or untruth. I am always One that is not different from Saṭ (Be-ness). I have no place to travel. I have no going, etc. I am always of the same form. I am the Quiescent. I am Purushoṭṭama (the Lord of Souls). There is no doubt that he who has realised himself thus, is Myself. Whoever hears (this) once becomes himself Brahman, yea, he becomes himself Brahman. Thus is the Upanishaḍ."

KAIVALYA[1]-UPANISHAḌ

OF

KṚSHṆA-YĀJURVEḌA

HARIH-OM. Then[2] Ās'walāyana went to Lord Parameshtī (Brahmā) and addressed Him thus: "Please initiate me into Brahmavidyā (Divine Wisdom), which is the most excellent, which is ever enjoyed by the wise, which is mystic, and by which the learned, after having soon freed themselves from all sins, reach Purusha, the Supreme of the supreme."

To him the Grandfather (thus) replied: "Know (It) through S'raḍḍhā (faith), Bhakṭi (devotion), Ḍhyāna (meditation), and Yoga. Persons attain salvation not through Karma, progeny or wealth but through Sannyāsa (renunciation) alone. Ascetics of pure mind through (the realisation of) the meaning well-ascertained by Veḍānṭa-Vijñāna and through Sannyāsa-Yoga enter into That which is above Swarga (heaven) and is in the cave (of the heart). They all attain Paramāṭmā[3] in the Brahma-world and are (finally) emancipated.

"Being seated in a pleasant posture in an unfrequented place with a pure mind, and with his neck, head, and body erect, having given up the duties of the (four) orders of life, having subjugated all the organs, having saluted his Guru with devotion, having looked upon the heart (-lotus) as being free from Rajoguṇa and as pure, and having contemplated in its (heart's) centre Parames'wara who is always with His consort Umā, who is pure and free from sorrow, who is unthinkable and invisible, who is of endless forms, who is of the nature of happiness,

[1] Lit., isolation- or emancipation-Upanishaḍ.

[2] After attaining Sāḍhana-Chaṭushtaya or the four means of salvation.

[3] Hiraṇyagarbha or the higher Self.

who is very quiescent, who is of the form of emancipation, who is the source of Māyā, who has no beginning, middle or end, who is One, who is All-Pervading, who is Chiḍānanḍa (Consciousness-Bliss), who is formless, who is wonderful, who is the Lord (of all), who has three eyes, who has a blue neck, (Nīlakaṇtha), and who is serenity (itself)—the Muni attains Paramāṭmā, the womb of all elements, the Āll-Witness, and above Ṭamas. He only is Brahmā. He only is S'iva. He only is Inḍra. He only is the indestructible. He only is the Supreme. He only is the Self-Shining. He only is Vishṇū. He only is Prāṇa. He only is Time. He only is Agni (fire). He only is the moon. He only is all things that exist or will hereafter exist. He only is eternal. Having known Him, one crosses death. There is no other path to salvation. He only attains Parabrahman who sees in himself all elements and himself in all elements. There is no other means. Having constituted his body an Āraṇi (the lower attritional piece of wood) and Praṇava (Om), the upper Āraṇi, a wise man burns Ajñāna by the churning of meditation.

"It is only He (Paramāṭmā) who, deluded by Māyā, assumes a body with the internal organs and does everything. It is only He who in the waking state is gratified with women, food, drink, and other diverse enjoyments. In the dreaming state, the Jīva enjoys pleasures and pains in the several worlds which are created by His Māyā. In the dreamless sleeping state when all are absorbed, He, replete with Ṭamas, attains the state of happiness. Then through the force of the Karmas of previous births, that Jīva again wakes up and goes to sleep. Āll the diversified objects (of the universe) emanate from the Jīva, who sports in the three bodies (gross, subtle and causal). The three bodies are finally absorbed in Him who is the source of all, who is Bliss, and who is Ābsolute Wisdom. From Him, arise Prāṇa, Manas, all the organs of sense and action, Ākās', Vāyu, Āgni, water and the earth supporting all. Parabrahman, which is of all forms, which is the Supreme Ābode of this universe, which is the most subtle of the subtle and which is eternal, is only yourself. You are only That. One who knows himself to be that Parabrahman that shines as the universe in the waking, dreaming, dreamless and other states, will be relieved from all bondage. I am that Saḍās'iva, (or the eternal happiness) who is other than the enjoyer, the enjoyed, and the enjoyment in the three seats (or bodies), and who is witness and Chinmāṭra. Āll emanate from Me alone. Āll exist in Me alone. Āll merge into Me alone. I am that non-dual Brahman. I am the atom of atoms; so am I the biggest (of all). I am this diversified universe. I am the oldest of all. I am Purusha. I am Īs'a (the Lord). I am of the form of Jyoṭis (light) and of the form of happiness. I have neither hands nor feet. I have power unthinkable. I see without eyes. I hear without ears. I am omniscient. I have one kind of form only. None is able to know Me fully. I am always of the form of Chiṭ. I am the One that should be known through all the Veḍas. I am the Guru who revealed the Veḍānṭā. I am only He who knows the true meaning of Veḍānṭa. I have no sins or virtues. I have no destruction. I have no birth, body, organs of sense or action, or Buḍḍhi. To Me there is no earth, water or fire. There is no Vāyu; there is no Ākās'. He who thinks Paramāṭmā as being in the cave (of the heart), as having no form, as being secondless, as being the witness of all and as being neither Saṭ nor Āsaṭ, attains the pure form of Paramāṭmā.

"Whoever recites this Upanishaḍ belonging to Yajurveḍa, he becomes as pure as Agni (fire). He becomes purified from the sins of theft of gold. He becomes purified from the sins of drinking alcohol. He becomes purified from the sins of murder of a Brāhman. He becomes purified from the sins of commission (of those that ought not to be done) and the sins of omission (of those that ought to be done). Therefore he becomes a follower of Brahman. Were one who has stepped beyond the duties of the four orders of life to recite (this Upanishaḍ) always or even once, he acquires the wisdom that destroys the ocean of Samsāra. Therefore having known Him, he attains the Kaivalya State (or state of isolation or emancipation)—yea, he attains the Kaivalya State."

OM-ṬAṬ-SAṬ.

AMṚṬABINḌU[1]-UPANISHAḌ

OF

KṚSHṆA-YĀJURVEḌĀ

Om. Manas (mind) is said to be of two kinds, the pure and the impure. That which is associated with the thought of desire is the impure, while that which is without desire is the pure. To men, their mind alone is the cause of bondage or emancipation. That mind which is attracted by objects of sense tends to bondage, while that which is not so attracted tends to emancipation. Now inasmuch as to a mind without a desire for sensual objects there is stated to be salvation, therefore an aspirant after emancipation should render his mind ever free from all longing after material objects. When a mind freed from the desires for objects and controlled in the heart attains the reality of Āṭmā, then is it in the Supreme Seat. Till that which arises in the heart perishes, till then it (Manas) should be controlled. This only is (true) wisdom. This only is true Ḍhyāna (meditation). Other ways are but long or tedious. It (Brahman) is not at all one that can be contemplated upon. It is not one that cannot be contemplated upon. It is not capable of contemplation, (and yet) it should be contemplated upon. Then one attains Brahman that is devoid of partiality. Yoga should be associated with Swara (sound, accent). (Brahman) should be meditated upon without Swara. By meditating without Swara upon Brahman, that which *is* cannot become non-existent. Such a Brahman is partless, devoid of fancy and quiescent (or free from the action of mind). Whoever cognizes "I" to be that Brahman

[1] Lit., the immortal germ.

attains certainly Brahman. A wise man having known that Brahman, that is without fancy, without end, without cause, or example, beyond inference and without beginning, is emancipated. There is (for him then) no destruction, no creation, no person in bondage, no devotee, no aspirant for salvation, no emancipated person. This is the truth. Āṭmā that should be contemplated upon is One in (the three states), the waking, the dreaming, and the dreamless sleep. There is no rebirth to him who goes beyond the three states. The one Bhūṭāṭmā of all beings is in all beings. Like the moon (reflected) in water, he appears as one and as many. While a pot is being carried (from one place to another), the Ākās' (ether) that is within it is not carried (along with it). As the pot alone is carried, Jīva (within the body) may be likened to the Ākās'. Like the pot, the body has various kinds of forms. The body which perishes again and again is not conscious of its own destruction. But he (the Jīva) knows (it) always. He who is enveloped by the Māyā of sound, is never able to come to (or see) the sun (of Parabrahman) from the darkness (of ignorance). Should such darkness be cleared, then he alone sees the non-dual state. Parabrahman is S'abḍākshara.[1] What remains after the cessation of S'abḍa-Veḍas, that is Akshara (indestructible), should be meditated upon by a learned man who wishes to secure quiescence to his Āṭmā.

Two Viḍyās (sciences) are fit to be known, *viz.*, S'abḍabrahman and Parabrahman. One who has completely mastered S'abḍabrahman attains Parabrahman. Having studied well the books, the learned man should persevere studiously in Jñāna (the acquisition of knowledge) and Vijñāna (Self-realisation according to such knowledge). Then he should discard the whole of the books, as a person in quest of grain gives up the straw. Though there are cows of different colours, yet their milk is of the same colour. Like milk is seen Jñāna, and like cows are seen the different kinds of forms (in the universe). As ghee is latent in milk, so is Vijñāna (Self-realisation) latent in every being. Through churning always the Manas with the

[1] It is the indestructible known through the sound or the Veḍas.

churning-stick of Manas and the string of Jñāna, **Parabrahman** that is partless, calm and quiescent should be brought out like fire from the wood. I am that Brahman. That Vāsuḍeva who is support of all beings, who lives in all and who protects all creatures is Myself. That Vāsuḍeva is Myself.

Such is the Upanishaḍ.

OM-ṬAṬ-SAṬ.

ĀṬMABOḌHA[1]-UPANISHAḌ

OF

ṚGVEḌA

Om. Prostrations to Nārāyaṇa wearing conch, discus, and mace,[2] by whom the Yogī is released from the bondage of the cycle of rebirth through the utterance of Him who is of the form of Praṇava, the Om, composed of the three letters Ā, U, and M, who is the uniform bliss and who is the Brahmapurusha (all-pervading Purusha). Om. Therefore the reciter of the Manṭra "Om-namo-Nārāyaṇāya" reaches the Vaikuṇtha world. It is the heart-Kamala (lotus), *viz.*, the city of Brahman. It is effulgent like lightning, shining like a lamp. It is Brahmaṇya (the presider over the city of Brahman) that is the son of Ḍevakī. It is Brahmaṇya that is Maḍhusūḍana (the killer of Maḍhu). It is Brahmaṇya that is Puṇdarīkāksha (lotus-eyed). It is Brahmaṇya, Vishṇu that is Achyuṭa (the indestructible). He who meditates upon that sole Nārāyaṇa who is latent in all beings, who is the causal Purusha, who is causeless, who is Parabrahman, the Om, who is without pains and delusion and who is all-pervading—that person is never subject to pains. From the dual, he becomes the fearless non-dual. Whoever sees this (world) as manifold (with the differences of I, you, he, etc.), passes from death to death. In the centre of the heart-lotus is Brahman, which is the All, which has Prājñā as Its eye and which is established in Prajñāna[3] alone. To creatures,

1 This Upanishaḍ treats of Āṭmic instruction.

2 The three symbols stand for Ākāsa, Manas, and Buḍḍhi.

3 In the Māṇdūkya Upanishaḍ, Prajñā is said to be the Jīva in the third state and Prajñāna is its attribute. Prajñāna is Prakarsha Jñāna or special wisdom, *viz.*, of looking over the past and the future.

Prajñāna is the eye and Prājñā is the seat. It is Prajñāna alone that is Brahman. A person who meditates (thus), leaves this world through Prajñāna, the Āṭmā and ascending attains all his desires in the Supreme Swarga deathless. Oh! I pray Thee, place me in that nectar-everflowing unfailing world where Jyoṭis (the light) always shines and where one is revered. (There is no doubt) he attains nectar also. Om-namaḥ.

I am without Māyā. I am without compare. I am solely the thing that is of the nature of wisdom. I am without Āhaṅkāra (I-am-ness). I am without the difference of the universe, Jīva and Is'wara. I am the Supreme that is not different from Praṭyagāṭmā (individual Āṭmā). I am with ordinances and prohibitions destroyed without remainder. I am with Ās'ramas (observances of life) well given up. I am of the nature of the vast and all-full wisdom. I am one that is witness and without desire. I reside in My glory alone. I am without motion. I am without old age—without destruction—without the differences of My party or another. I have wisdom as chief essence. I am the mere ocean of bliss called salvation. I am the subtle. I am without change. I am Āṭmā merely, without the illusion of qualities. I am the Seat devoid of the three Guṇas. I am the cause of the many worlds in (My) stomach. I am the Kūtasṭha-Chaiṭanya (supreme Cosmic-mind). I am of the form of the Jyoṭis (light) free from motion. I am not one that can be known by inference. I alone am full. I am of the form of the stainless salvation. I am without limbs or birth. I am the essence which is Saṭ itself. I am of the nature of the true wisdom without limit. I am the state of excellent happiness. I am One that cannot be differentiated. I am the all-pervading and without stain. I am the limitless and endless Saṭṭwa alone. I am fit to be known through Veḍānṭa. I am the one fit to be worshipped. I am the heart of all the worlds. I am replete with Supreme Bliss. I am of the nature of happiness, which is Supreme Bliss. I am pure, secondless, and eternal. I am devoid of beginning. I am free from the three bodies (gross, subtle, and causal). I am of the nature of wisdom. I am the emancipated One. I have a wondrous form. I am free from impurity.

I am the One latent (in all). I am the equal Āṭmā of eternal Vijñāna. I am the refined Supreme Truth. I am of the nature of Wisdom-Bliss alone.

Though I cognize as the secondless Āṭmā by means of discriminative wisdom and reason, yet is found the relation between bondage and salvation. Though to Me the universe is gone, yet it shines as true always. Like the truth in the (illusory conception of a) snake, etc., in the rope, so the truth of Brahman alone is, and is the substratum on which this universe is playing. Therefore the universe is not. Just as sugar is found permeating all the sugar-juice (from which the sugar is extracted), so I am full in the three worlds in the form of the non-dual Brahman. Like the bubbles, waves, etc., in the ocean, so all beings, from Brahmā down to worm, are fashioned in Me; just as the ocean does not long after the motion of the waves, so to Me, there is no longing after sensual happiness, being Myself of the form of (spiritual) Bliss. Just as in a wealthy person the desire for poverty does not arise, so in Me who am immersed in Brāhmic Bliss, the desire for sensual happiness cannot arise. An intelligent person who sees both nectar and poison rejects poison; so having cognized Āṭmā, I reject those that are not-Āṭmā. The sun that illuminates the pot (both within and without) is not destroyed with the destruction of the pot; so the Sākshī (witness) that illuminates the body is not destroyed with the destruction of the body. To Me there is no bondage; there is no salvation, there are no books, there is no Guru; for these shine through Māyā and I have crossed them and am secondless. Let Prāṇas (vital airs) according to their laws be fluctuating. Let Manas (mind) be blown about by desire. How can pains affect Me who am by nature full of Bliss? I have truly known Āṭmā. My Ajñāna has fled away. The egoism of actorship has left Me. There is nothing I should yet do. Brāhman's duties, family, Goṭra (clan), name, beauty, and class—all these belong to the gross body and not to Me who am without any mark (of body). Inertness, love, and joy—these attributes appertain to the causal body and not to Me, who am eternal and of changeless nature. Just as an owl sees darkness only in the sun, so a fool sees only darkness in the self-shining Supreme Bliss. Should the clouds screen the eyesight, a fool thinks there is no sun; so an embodied person full of Ajñāna thinks there is no Brahman. Just as nectar which is other than poison does not commingle with it, so I, who am different from inert matter, do not mix with its stains. As the light of a lamp, however small, dispels immense darkness, so wisdom, however slight, makes Ajñāna, however immense, to perish. Just as (the delusion) of the serpent does not exist in the rope in all the three periods of time (past, present, and future), so the universe from Ahaṅkāra (down) to body does not exist in Me who am the non-dual One. Being of the nature of Consciousness alone, there is not inertness in Me. Being of the nature of Truth, there is not non-truth to Me. Being of the nature of Bliss, there is not sorrow in Me. It is through Ajñāna that the universe shines as truth.

Whoever recites this Āṭmaboḍha-Upanishaḍ for a Muhūrṭa (48 minutes) is not born again—yea, is not born again.

SKAṆḌA[1]-UPANISHAḌ

OF

KṚSHṆA-YĀJURVEḌĀ

Oм. O Mahāḍeva (Lord of Ḍevas), I am indestructible through a small portion of Thy grace. I am replete with Vijñāna. I am S'iva (Bliss). What is higher than It? Truth does not shine as such on account of the display of the anṭaḥkaraṇa (internal organs). Through the destruction of the anṭaḥkaraṇa, Hari abides as Samviṭ (Consciousness) alone. As I also am of the form of Samviṭ, I am without birth. What is higher than It? All inert things being other (than Āṭmā) perish like dream. That Achyuṭa (the indestructible or Vishṇu), who is the seer of the conscious and the inert, is of the form of Jñāna. He only is Mahāḍeva. He only is Mahā-Hari (Mahāvishṇu). He only is the Jyoṭis of all Jyoṭis (or Light of all lights). He only is Parames'vara. He only is Parabrahman. That Brahman I am. There is no doubt (about it). Jīva is S'iva. S'iva is Jīva. That Jīva is S'iva alone. Bound by husk, it is paddy; freed from husk, it is rice. In like manner Jīva is bound (by karma). If karma perishes, he (Jīva) is Saḍās'iva. So long as he is bound by the bonds of karma, he is Jīva. If freed from its bonds, then he is Saḍās'iva. Prostrations on account of S'iva who is of the form of Vishṇu, and on account of Vishṇu who is of the form of S'iva. The heart of Vishṇu is S'iva. The heart of S'iva is Vishṇu. As I see no difference[2] (between these two), therefore to me are prosperity and life. There is no difference—between S'iva and

[1] Skanḍa is the son of Siva and is represented on earth by Sanaṭkumāra.

[2] This will give a rude shock to the followers of Siva and Vishṇu in India, who wage useless war as to the supremacy of Vishṇu and Siva.

Kes'ava (Vishṇu). The body is said to be the divine temple. The S'iva (in the body) is the God Saḍās'iva[1] (in the temple).

Having given up the cast-off offerings of ajñāna, one should worship Him with the thought "I am He". To see (oneself) as not different (from Him) is (jñāna) wisdom. To make the mind free from sensual objects is ḍhyāna (meditation). The giving up of the stains of the mind is snāna (bathing). The subjugation of the senses is s'oucha (cleansing). The nectar of Brahman should be drunk. For the upkeep of the body, one should go about for alms and eat. He should dwell alone in a solitary place without a second. He should be with the sole thought of the non-dual One. The wise person who conducts himself thus, attains salvation. Prostrations on account of S'rīmaṭ Param-Jyoṭis (Supreme Light) abode! May prosperity and long life attend (me). O Narasimha![2] O Lord of Ḍevas! through Thy grace, persons cognize the true nature of Brahman that is unthinkable, undifferentiated, endless, and immutable, through the forms of the Gods, Brahmā, Nārāyaṇa, and S'aṅkara.

Like the eye (which sees without any obstacle the things) spread in the ākās', so the wise always see the supreme abode of Vishṇu. Brāhmans with divine eyes who are always spiriṭually awake, praise in diverse ways and illuminate the supreme abode of Vishṇu. Thus is the teaching of the Veḍas for salvation.

Thus is the Upanishaḍ.

---

[1] Saḍāsiva, lit., eternal bliss. This is one of the names applied to Siva as also Mahāḍeva.

[2] Narasimha, lit., Man-lion. This refers to one of the incarnations of Vishṇu when he killed the evil power Hiraṇyakasipu.

PAIṄGALA-UPANISHAḌ[1]

OF

S'UKLA-YĀJURVEḌA

Aḍhyāya I

Om. Paiṅgala, having served under Yājñavalkya for twelve years, asked him to initiate him into the supreme mysteries of Kaivalya. To which Yājñavalkya replied thus: "O gentle one, at first, this (universe) was Saṭ (Be-ness) only. It (Saṭ) is spoken of as Brahman which is ever free (from the trammels of matter), which is changeless, which is Truth, Wisdom, and Bliss, and which is full, permanent, and one only without a second. In It, was like a mirage in the desert, silver in mother-of-pearl, a person in the pillar, or colour, etc., in the crystals, mūlaprakṛṭi, having in equal proportions the guṇas, red,[2] white, and black, and being beyond the power of speech. That which is reflected in it is Sākshi-Chaiṭanya (lit., the witness-consciousness). It (mūlaprakṛṭi) undergoing again change becomes with the preponderance of Saṭṭva (in it), Āvaraṇa[3] S'akṭi named avyakṭa. That which is reflected in it (Avyakṭa) is Īs'vara-Chaiṭanya. He (Īs'vara) has Māyā under his control, is omniscient, the original cause of creation, preservation, and dissolution, and the seed of this universe. He causes the universe which was latent in Him, to manifest itself through the bonds of karma of all creatures like a painted canvas unfurled. Again through the extinction

[1] This Upanishaḍ is so called after the questioner.

[2] Rajas, Saṭṭva and Ṭamas colours.

[3] Āvaraṇa Ṣakṭi literally means the veiling or contracting power. This is it that produces egoism. It may be called the centripetal force.

of their karmas, he makes it disappear. In Him alone is latent all the universe, wrapped up like a painted cloth. Then from the supreme (Āvaraṇa) S'akṭi, dependent on (or appertaining to Īs'vara, arose, through the preponderance of Rajas, Vikshepa[1] S'akṭi called Mahaṭ. That which is reflected in it is Hiraṇyagarbha-Chaiṭanya. Presiding (as He does) over Mahaṭ, He (Hiraṇyagarbha) has a body, both manifested and unmanifested.[2] From Vikshepa S'akṭi of Hiranyagarbha arose, through the preponderance of Ṭamas, the gross S'akṭi called ahaṅkāra. That which is reflected in it is Virāt-Chaiṭanya. He (Virāt) presiding over it (ahaṅkāra) and possessing a manifested body becomes Vishṇu, the chief Purusha and protector of all gross bodies. From that Āṭmā arose ākās'; from ākās' arose vāyu, from vāyu agni, from agni apas, and from apas pṛṭhivī. The five ṭanmāṭras[3] (rudimentary properties) alone are the guṇas (of the above five). That generating cause of the universe (Īs'vara) wishing to create and having assumed ṭamo-guṇa, wanted to convert the elements which were subtle ṭanmāṭras into gross ones. In order to create the universe, he divided into two parts each of those divisible elements; and having divided each moiety into four parts, made a fivefold mixture, each element having moiety of its own original element and one-fourth of a moiety of each of the other elements, and thus evolved out of the fivefold classified gross elements, the many myriads of Brahmāṇdas (Brahmā's egg or macrocosm), the fourteen worlds pertaining to each sphere, and the spherical gross bodies (microcosm) fit for the (respective) worlds. Having divided the Rajas-essence of the five elements into four parts, He out of three such parts created (the five) prāṇas having fivefold function. Again out of the (remaining) fourth part, He created karmendriyas (the organs of action). Having divided their Saṭṭva-essence into four parts, He out of three such parts created the anṭaḥkaraṇa (internal organ) having fivefold

[1] Vikshepa Ṣakti (lit.,) is the expanding power. It may be called the centrifugal force.

[2] The account given here though differing from that in other books may be justified.

[3] They are sound, touch, form, taste, and odour.

function. Out of the (remaining) fourth part of S'aṭṭva-essence, he created the jñānenḍriyas (organs of sense). Out of the collective totality of Saṭṭva-essence, He created the ḍevaṭās (deities) ruling over the organs of sense and actions. Those (ḍevaṭās) He created, He located in the spheres (pertaining to them). They through His orders, began to pervade the macrocosm. Through His orders, Virat associated with ahaṅkāra created all the gross things. Through His orders, Hiraṇyagarbha protected the subtle things. Without Him, they that were located in their spheres were unable to move or to do anything. Then He wished to infuse cheṭana (life) into them. Having pierced the Brahmāṇda (Brahmā's egg or macrocosm) and Brahmaranḍhras (head-fontanelle) in all the microcosmic heads, He entered within. Though they were (at first) inert, they were then able to perform karmas like beings of intelligence. The omniscient Īs'vara entered the microcosmic bodies with a particle of Māyā and being deluded by that Māyā, acquired the state of Jīva. Identifying the three bodies with Himself, He acquired the state of the actor and enjoyer. Associated with the attributes of the states of jāgraṭ, svapna, sushupṭi, trance, and death and being immersed in sorrow, he is (whirled about and) deluded like water-lift or potter's wheel, as if subject to birth and death."

Aḍhyāya II

Paiṅgala again addressed Yājñavalkya thus: "How did Īs'vara, who is the creator, preserver, and destroyer and the Lord of all the worlds, acquire the state of Jīva?" To which Yājñavalkya replied: "I shall tell in detail the nature of Jīva and Īs'vara, together with a description of the origin of the gross, subtle, and kāraṇa (causal) bodies. Hear attentively with one-pointed mind.

"Īs'vara having taken a small portion of the quintuplicated mahā-bhūṭas, (the great elements), made in regular order the gross bodies, both collective and segregate. The skull, the skin, the intestines, bone, flesh, and nails are of the essence of pṛṭhivī. Blood, urine, saliva, sweat and others are of the essence of āpas. Hunger, thirst, heat, delusion, and copulation are of the essence of agni. Walking, lifting, breathing and others are of the essence of vāyu. Passion, anger, etc., are of the essence of ākās'. The collection of these having touch and the rest is this gross body that is brought about by karma, that is the seat of egoism in youth and other states and that is the abode of many sins. Then He created prāṇas out of the collective three parts of Rajas-essence of the fivefold divided elements. The modifications of prāṇa are prāṇa, apāna, vyāna, udāna, and samāna; nāga, kūrma, kṛkara, ḍevaḍaṭṭa and dhanañjaya are the auxiliary prāṇas. (Of the first five), the heart, anus, navel, throat and the whole body are respectively the seats. Then He created the karmenḍriyas out of the fourth part of the Rajas-guṇa. Of ākās' and the rest the mouth, legs, hands, and the organs of secretion and excretion are the modifications. Talking, walking, lifting, excreting, and enjoying are their functions. Likewise out of the collective three parts of Saṭṭva-essence, He created the anṭaḥkaraṇa (internal organ). Anṭaḥkaraṇa,[1] manas, buḍḍhi, chiṭṭa, and ahaṅkāra are the modifications. Saṅkalpa (thought), certitude, memory, egoism, and anusanḍhāna (inquiry) are their functions. Throat, face, navel,[2] heart, and the middle of the brow are their seats. Out of the (remaining) fourth part of Saṭṭva-essence, He created the jñānenḍriyas (organs of sense). Ear, skin, eyes, tongue, and nose are the modifications. Sound, touch, form, taste, and odour are their functions. Ḍik (the quarters), Vāyu, Ārka (the sun), Varuṇa, As'vini Ḍevas, Inḍra, Upenḍra, Mṛṭyu (the God of death), Prajāpaṭi, the Moon, Vishṇu the four-faced Brahmā and S'ambhu (S'iva) are the presiding deities of the organs. There are the five kos'as (sheaths), *viz.*, annamaya, prāṇamaya, manomaya, vijñānamaya, and ānanḍamaya. Annamaya sheath is that which is created and developed out of the essence of food, and is absorbed into the earth which is of the form of food. It alone is the gross body. The prāṇas with the karmenḍriyas (organs of action) is the prāṇamaya

[1] The fifth aspect of anṭaḥkaraṇa is made to be itself, having the function of anusanḍhāna or inquiry, though others call it otherwise.

[2] Navel is the seat of chiṭṭa.

sheath. Manas with the jñānenḍriyas (organs of sense) is the manomaya sheath. Buḍḍhi with the jñānenḍriyas is the vijñānamaya sheath. These three sheaths constitute the liṅgas'arīra (or the subtle body). (That which tends to) the ajñāna (ignorance) of the Reality (of Āṭmā) is the ānanḍamaya sheath. This is the kāraṇa body. Moreover the five organs of sense, the five organs of action, the five prāṇas and others, the five ākās' and other elements, the four internal organs, aviḍyā, passion, karma, and ṭamas—all these constitute this town (of body).

" Virāt, under the orders of Īs'vara having entered this microcosmic body, and having buḍḍhi as his vehicle, reaches the state of Vis'va. Then he goes by the several names of Vijñānāṭma, Chiḍābhāsa, Vis'va, Vyāvahārika, the one presiding over the waking gross body and the one generated by karma. Sūṭrāṭmā, under the orders of Īs'vara, having entered the microcosmic subtle body, and having manas as his vehicle, reaches the Ṭaijasa state. Then he goes by the names of ṭaijasa, prāṭibhāsika and svapnakalpiṭa (the one bred out of dream). Then under the orders of Īs'vara, he who is coupled with avyakṭa, the vehicle of Māyā having entered the microcosmic kāraṇa body, reaches the state of prajñā. He goes then by the names of prājña, avichchinna, and pāramārṭhika and sushupṭhi-abhimānī (the presider over sushupṭi). Such sacred sentences, as Ṭaṭṭvamasi (That art thou) and others, speak of the identity with the Brahman of the Pāramārṭhika-Jīva enveloped by ajñāna, which is but a small particle of avyakṭa ; but not vyāvahārika and prāṭibhāsika (Jīvas). It is only that chaiṭanya which is reflected in anṭaḥkaraṇa that attains the three states. When it assumes the three states of jāgraṭ, swapna, and sushupṭi, it is like a water-lift as if grieved, born and dead. There are five avasṭhās—jāgraṭ, swapna, sushupṭi, mūrchchhā (trance), and death. Jāgraṭ avasṭhā is that in which there is the perception of objects, of sound, etc., through the grace of the ḍevaṭā presiding over each of them. In it, the Jīva, being in the middle of the eyebrows and pervading the body from head to foot, becomes the agent of actions, such as doing, hearing and others. He becomes also the enjoyer of the fruits thereof; and such a person doing karma for the fruits thereof goes to other worlds and enjoys the same there. Like an emperor tired of worldly acts (in the waking state), he strives to find the path to retire into his abode within. The svapna avasṭhā is that in which, when the senses are at rest, there is the manifestation of the knower and the known, along with the affinities of (things enjoyed in) the waking state. In this state Vis'va alone, its actions in the waking state having ceased, reaches the state of Ṭaijasa (of ṭejas or effulgence), who moves in the middle of the nādīs (nerves), illuminates by his lustre the heterogeneity of this universe which is of the form of affinities, and himself enjoys according to his wish. The sushupṭi avasṭhā is that in which the chiṭṭa is sole organ (at play). Just as a bird, tired of roaming, flies to its nest with its stomach filled, so the Jīva being tired of the actions of the world in the waking and dreaming states, enters ajñāna and enjoys bliss. Then trance is attained which resembles death, and in which one with his collection of organs quails, as it were, through fear and ajñāna, like one beaten unexpectedly by a hammer, club or any other weapon. Then death avasṭhā is that which is other than the avasṭhās of jāgraṭ, svapna, sushupṭi, and trance, which produces fear in all Jīvas from Brahmā down to small insects and which dissolves the gross body. The Jīva, that is surrounded by aviḍyā and the subtle elements, takes with it the organs of sense and action, their objects, and prāṇas along with the kāmio karmas and goes to another world, assuming another body. Through the ripening of the fruits of previous karmas, the Jīva has no rest like an insect in a whirlpool. It is only after many births that the desire of emancipation arises in man through the ripening of good karma. Then having resorted to a good Guru and served under him for a long time, one out of many attains moksha, free from bondage. Bondage is through non-inquiry and moksha through inquiry. Therefore there should always be inquiry (into Āṭmā). The Reality should be ascertained through aḍhyāropa (illusory attribution) and apavād (withdrawal or recession of that idea). Therefore there should be always inquiring into the universe, Jīva and Paramāṭmā. Were the true nature of Jīva and the universe known, then there remains Brahman which is non-different from Praṭyagāṭmā."

AḌHYĀYA III

Then Paiṅgala asked Yājñavalkya to offer an exposition on the mahāvākyas (sacred sentences of the Veḍas). To which Yājñavalkya replied: "One should scrutinise (the sacred sentences), Ṭaṭṭvamasi (That art thou), Ṭvamṭaḍasi (Thou art That), Ṭwambrahmāsi (Thou art Brahman) and Ahambrahmāsmi (I am Brahman). The word 'Ṭaṭ' denotes the cause of the universe that is variegated beyond perception, has the characteristics of omniscience, has Māyā as His vehicle and has the attributes of Sachchiḍānanḍa. It is He that is the basis of the notion 'I' which has the differentiated knowledge produced by anṭaḥkaraṇa; and it is He that is denoted by the word 'Ṭwam' (Thou). That is the undifferentiated Brahman which remains as the aim (or meaning) of the words Ṭaṭ and Ṭvam after freeing itself from Māyā and Aviḍyā which are respectively the vehicles of Paramāṭmā and Jīvāṭmā. The inquiry into the real significance of the sentences Ṭaṭṭvamasi and Ahambrahmāsmi forms (what is called) s'ravaṇa (hearing—the first stage of inquiry). To inquire in solitude into the significance of s'ravaṇa is manana. The concentration of the mind with one-pointedness upon that which should be sought after by s'ravaṇa and manana is niḍiḍhyāsana. Samāḍhi is that state in which chiṭṭa having given up (the conception of the difference of) the meditator and the meditation, becomes of the form of the meditated like a lamp in a place without wind. Then arise the modifications pertaining to Āṭmā. Such (modifications) cannot be known; but they can only be inferred through memory (of the samāḍhi state). The myriads of karmas committed in this beginningless cycle of rebirths are annihilated only through them. Through proficiency in practice, the current of nectar[1]

[1] It is said that in samāḍhi astral nectar flows from the head down which the Yogins are said to drink and which gives them infinite bliss.

always rains down in diverse ways. Therefore those who know Yoga call this samāḍhi, ḍharma-megha (cloud). Through these (modifications of Āṭmā), the collection of affinities is absorbed without any remainder whatever. When the accumulated good and bad karmas are wholly destroyed, these sentences (Ṭaṭṭvamasi and Ahambrahmāsmi), like the myrobalan in the palm of the hand, bring him face to face with the ultimate Reality, though It was before invisible. Then he becomes a Jīvanmukṭa.

"Īs'vara wished to produce non-quintuplication (or involution) in the fivefold differentiated elements. Having drawn into their cause Brahmā's egg and its effects of worlds, and mixed together the subtle organs of sense and action and the four internal organs and dissolved all things composed of the elements into their cause, the five elements, He then caused pṛṭhivī to merge into water, water into agni, agni into vāyu, and vāyu into ākās', ākās' into ahaṅkāra, akaṅkāra into mahaṭ, mahaṭ into avyakṭa, and avyakṭa into Purusha in regular order. Virāt, Hiraṇyagarbha and Īs'vara being freed from the vehicle of Māyā, are absorbed into Paramāṭmā. This gross body composed of the five differentiated elements and obtained through accumulated karma, is merged into its subtle state of non-quintuplicated elements, through the extinction of (bad) karṃa and increase of good ḳarma, then attains its kāraṇa (causal) state and (finally) is absorbed into its cause, (*viz.,*) Kūtasṭha-Praṭyagāṭma. Vis'va and Ṭaijasa and Prājña, their upāḍhi (of aviḍyā) having become extinct, are absorbed in Praṭyagāṭmā. This sphere (of universe) being burnt up by the fire of jñāna is absorbed along with its cause into Paramāṭmā. Therefore a Brāhmaṇa should be careful and always meditate upon the identity of Ṭaṭ and Ṭvam. Then Āṭmā shines, like the sun freed from the (obscuration of the) clouds. One should meditate upon Āṭmā in the midst (of the body) like a lamp within a jar.

"Āṭmā, the Kūtasṭha, should be meditated upon as being of the size of a thumb, as being of the nature of the jyoṭis (light) without smoke, as being within, illuminating all and as being indestructible. That Muni (sage) who meditates (upon Āṭmā always) until sleep or death comes upon him passes into the state of (Jīvanmukṭi) emancipation like the immovable state of the wind. Then there remains that One (Brahman) without sound, touch, free from destruction, without taste or odour, which is eternal, which is without beginning or end, which is beyond the Ṭaṭṭva of Mahaṭ, and which is permanent and without stain or disease."

Aḍhyāya IV

Then Paiṅgala addressed Yājñavalkya thus: "To the wise, what is their karma? And what is their state?" To which Yājñavalkya replied: "A lover of moksha, having humility[1] and other possessions (or virtues), enables twenty-one generations to cross (to Āṭmā). One through his being a Brahmaviṭ[2] alone enables 101 generations to cross. Know Āṭmā to be the rider and the body as the chariot. Know also buḍḍhi as the charioteer and manas as the reins. The wise say the organs are the horses, the objects are the roads (through which the horses travel) and the hearts are the moving balloons. Mahārshis say that Āṭmā, when associated with the sense organs and manas, is the enjoyer. Therefore it is the actual Nārāyaṇa alone that is established in the heart. Till his prārabḍha karma[3] is worn out, he exists (in his body) as in the (cast-off) slough of a serpent (without any desire for the body). An emancipated person having such a body roves about like a moon gladdening all with no settled place of abode. He gives up his body whether in a sacred place, or in a chaṇḍāla's (outcaste's) house (without any distinction whatever), and attains salvation. Such a body (when seen by a person) should be offered as a sacrifice to ḍik (the quarters) or should be buried (underground). It is only to Purusha (the wise) that sannyāsa (renunciation) is ordained and not to others. In case of the

[1] Humility and other virtues twenty in number are described in *Bhagavaḍ-Giṭā*, Chapter XIII.

[2] There are four classes of Brahma Jñānīs or initiates of whom this is one.

[3] That portion of past karma which is being enjoyed in this life.

death of an ascetic who is of the form (or has attained the nature) of Brahman, there is no pollution (to be observed); neither the ceremonies of fire (as burning the body, homa, etc.); nor the piṇda (balls of rice), nor ceremonies of water, nor the periodical ceremonies (monthly and yearly). Just as a food once cooked is not again cooked, so a body once burnt (by the fire of wisdom) should not be burnt (or exposed to fire) again. To one whose body was burnt by the fire of wisdom there is neither s'rāḍḍha[1] (required to be performed), nor (funeral) ceremony. So long as there is the upāḍhi (of non-wisdom) in one, so long should he serve the Guru. He should conduct himself towards his Guru's wife and children as he does to his Guru. If being of a pure mind, of the nature of immaculate Chiṭ and resigned, and having the discrimination arising from the attainment of wisdom "I am He," he should concentrate his heart on Paramāṭmā and obtain firm peace in his body, then he becomes of the nature of Jyoṭis, void of manas and buḍḍhi. Of what avail is milk to one content with nectar? Of what avail are the Veḍas to him who has known his Āṭmā thus? For a Yogin content with the nectar of wisdom, there is nothing more to be done. If he has to do anything, then he is not a knower of Ṭaṭṭva. Praṭyagāṭmā though far (or difficult of attainment), is not far; though in the body, he is devoid of it (since) he is all-pervading. After having purified the heart and contemplated on the One without disease (*viz.*, Brahman), the cognizing of 'I' as the supreme and the all is the highest bliss. Like water mixed with water, milk with milk, and ghee with ghee, so Jīvāṭmā and Paramāṭmā are without difference. When the body is rendered bright through wisdom and the buḍḍhi becomes of the partless One, then the wise man burns the bondage of karma through the fire of Brahma-jñāna. Then he becomes purified, of the nature of the non-dual named Parmes'vara and the light like the stainless ākās'. Like water mixed with water, so Jīva (-Āṭmā) becomes upāḍhiless (or freed from the bonds of matter). Āṭmā is, like ākās', of an invisible form. (Therefore) the inner Āṭmā is invisible like vāyu. Though he is within and without, he is the immovable

[1] The yearly ceremonies in honour of the dead.

Āṭmā. Through the torch of wisdom, the internal Āṭmā sees (or knows).

"A wise man, in whatever place or manner he dies, is absorbed in that place like the all-pervading ākās'. It should be known that Āṭmā is absorbed as truly as the ākās' in the pot (when broken). Then he attains the all-pervading wisdom-light that is without support. Though men should perform ṭapas standing on one leg for a period of 1,000 years, it will not, in the least, be equal to one-sixteenth part of ḍhyānayoga. One desirous of knowing what jñāna (wisdom) and jñeya (the object to be known) are, will not be able to attain his desired end, even though he may study the S'āsṭras for 1,000 years. That which is alone should be known as the indestructible. That which exists (in this world) is only impermanent. (Therefore) after having given up (the study of) the many S'āsṭras, one should worship that which is saṭya (truth). The many karmas, purity (of mind and heart), japa (the muttering of manṭras), sacrifice and pilgrimages—all these should be observed till Ṭaṭṭva is known. For Mahāṭmās (noble souls) to be always in (the conception of) 'I am Brahman' conduces to their salvation. There are two causes (that lead) to bondage and emancipation. They are 'mine' and 'not mine'. Through 'mine' creatures are bound, whereas through 'not mine' they are released from bondage. When the mind attains the state of Uumani (above manas, *viz.*, when it is destroyed), then there is never the conception of duality. When the Uumani state occurs, then is the supreme Seat (attained). (After which) wherever the mind goes, there is the supreme Seat (to it, *viz.*, the mind enjoys salvation wherever it is). That which is equal in all is Brahman alone. One may attain the power to strike the ākās' with his fist; he may appease his hunger by eating husks (of grain), but never shall he attain emancipation who has not the self-cognition, 'I am Brahman'.

"Whoever recites this Upanishaḍ becomes as immaculate as Agni. He becomes as pure as Brahmā. He becomes as pure as Vāyu. He becomes like one who has bathed in all the holy waters. He becomes like one who has studied all the Veḍas. He becomes like one that has undergone all veḍic observances. He obtains the fruit of the recitation of Iṭihāsas[1], Purāṇas and Ruḍramanṭras a lakh of times. He becomes like one that has pronounced Praṇava (Om) ten thousand times. He purifies his ancestors ten degrees removed and his descendants ten degrees removed. He becomes purified of all those that sit with him for dinner. He becomes a great personage. He becomes purified from the sins of the murder of a Brāhman, the drinking of alcohol, theft of gold, and sexual cohabitation with Guru's wife, and from the sins of associating with those that commit such sins.

"Like the eye pervading the ākas' (seeing without effort everything above), a wise man sees (always) the supreme Seat of Vishṇu. The Brāhmaṇas who have always their spiritual eyes wide open praise and illuminate in diverse ways the supreme Seat of Vishṇu. Om: This Upanishaḍ is truth."

---

[1] Iṭihāsas are the *Rāmāyaṇa* and the *Mahābhāraṭa*.

AḌHYĀṬMA-UPANISHAḌ[1]

OF

S'UKLA-YAJURVEḌA

The One Āja (unborn) is ever located in the cave (of the heart) within the body. (Pṛṭhivī) the earth is His body; though He pervades the earth, it does not know Him. The waters are His body; though He pervades the waters, they do not know Him. Āgni is His body; though He pervades agni, it does not know Him. Vāyu is His body; though He pervades vāyu, it does not know Him. Ākās' is His body; though He pervades ākās', it does not know Him. Manas is His body; though He pervades manas, it does not know Him. Buḍḍhi is His body; though He pervades buḍḍhi, it does not know Him. Ahaṅkāra is His body; though He pervades ahaṅkāra, it does not know Him. Chiṭṭa is His body; though He pervades chiṭṭa, it does not know Him. Avyakṭa is His body; though He pervades avyakṭa, it does not know Him. Akshara is His body; though He pervades akshara, it does not know Him. Mṛṭyu is His body; though He pervades mṛṭyu, it does not know Him. He who is the inner soul of all creatures and the purifier of sins, is the one divine Lord Nārāyaṇa.

The wise should through the practice of deep meditation of Brahman leave off the (recurrent) conception of "I" and "mine" in the body and the senses which are other than Āṭmā. Having known himself as Praṭyagāṭmā, the witness of buḍḍhi and its actions, one should ever think "So'ham" ("I am That") and leave off the idea of Āṭmā in all others. Shunning the pursuits of the world, the body and the S'āsṭras, set about removing the false attribution of self. In the case of a Yogin staying always in his own Āṭmā, his mind perishes having known his Āṭmā as the Āṭmā of all, through inference, Veḍas

[1] This Upanishaḍ is also called Ṭurīyāṭīṭa Avaḍhūṭa Upanishaḍ.

and self-experience. Never giving the slightest scope to sleep, worldly talk, sounds, etc., think of Āṭmā, (in yourself) to be the (supreme) Āṭmā. Shun at a distance like a chaṇḍāla (the thought of) the body, which is generated out of the impurities of parents and is composed of excreta and flesh. Then you will become Brahman and be (in a) blessed (state). O Sage, having dissolved (Jīva-) Āṭmā into Paramāṭmā with the thought of its being partless, like the ether of a jar in the universal ether, be ever in a state of taciturnity. Having become that which is the seat of all Āṭmās and the self-resplendent, give up the macrocosm and microcosm like an impure vessel. Having merged into Chiḍāṭmā, which is ever blissful, the conception of "I" which is rooted in the body, and having removed the (conception of) Liṅga (here the sign of separateness), become ever the Kevala (alone). Having known "I am that Brahman" in which alone the universe appears like a town in a mirror, become one that has performed (all) his duty, O sinless one. The ever-blissful and the self-effulgent One being freed from the grip of ahaṅkāra attains its own state, like the spotless moon becoming full (after eclipse).

With the extinction of actions, there arises the extinction of chinṭā. From it arises the decay of vāsanās; and from the latter, arises moksha; and this is called Jīvanmukṭi. Looking upon everything in all places and times as Brahman brings about the destruction of vāsanās through the force of vāsanās of sāṭṭvic nature. Carelessness in Brahmanishthā by (or meditation of Brahman) should not in the least be allowed (to creep in). Knowers of Brahman style (this) carelessness, in Brāhmic science, as death (itself). Just as the moss (momentarily) displaced (in a tank) again resumes its original position, in a minute, so Māyā envelops even the wise, should they be careless (even for a moment). He who attains the Kaivalya state during life becomes a Kevala even after death of his body. Ever devoted to samāḍhi, become a nirvikalpa (or the changeless one), O sinless one. The granṭhi (or knot) of the heart, full of ajñāna, is broken completely only when one sees his Āṭmā as secondless through nirvikalpa samāḍhi.

Now, having strengthened the conception of Āṭmā and well given up that of "I" in the body, one should be indifferent as he would be towards jars, cloth, etc. From Brahmā down to a pillar, all the upāḍhis are only unreal. Hence one should see (or cognize) his Āṭmā as all-full and existing by itself (alone). Brahmā is Swayam (Āṭmā); Vishṇu is Āṭmā; Ruḍra is Āṭmā; Inḍra is Āṭmā; all this universe is Āṭmā and there is nothing but Āṭmā. By expelling (from the mind) without any remainder all objects which are superimposed on one's Āṭmā, one becomes himself Parabrahman the full, the secondless and the actionless. How can there be the heterogeneity of the universe of saṅkalpa and vikalpa in that One Principle which is immutable, formless and homogeneous? When there is no difference between the seer, the seen, and sight, there being the decayless and Chiḍāṭmā, full like the ocean at the end of a Kalpa and effulgent, all darkness, the cause of false perception, merges in it. How can there be heterogeneity in that one supreme Principle which is alike? How can there be heterogeneity in the highest Ṭaṭṭva which is One? Who has observed any heterogeneity in sushupṭi (the dreamless sleep), where there is happiness only? This vikalpa has its root in chiṭṭa only. When chiṭṭa is not, there is nothing. Therefore unite the chiṭṭa with Paramāṭman in its Praṭyāgāṭmic state. If one knows Āṭmā as unbroken bliss in itself, then he drinks always the juice (or essence) of bliss in his Āṭmā, whether internally or externally.

The fruit of vairāgya is boḍha (spiritual wisdom); the fruit of boḍha is uparaṭi (renunciation); s'ānṭi (sweet patience) is attained out of the enjoyment of the bliss of one's Āṭmā, and this s'ānṭi is the fruit of uparaṭi. If the latter in each of these is absent, the former is useless. Nivṛṭṭi (or the return path) leads to the highest contentment and (spiritual) bliss is said to be beyond all analogy. That which has Māyā as its upāḍhi is the womb of the world; that true one which has the attribute of omniscience, etc., and has the variegated mystery is denoted by the word "Ṭaṭ" (that). That is called Āpara (the other or inferior) which shines through meditation upon the idea and the world asmaṭ[1] and the consciousness of which is developed by anṭaḥkaraṇa. By separating the upāḍhis Māyā and aviḍyā from Parā and Jīva (cosmic and human Āṭmās respectively), one realises Parabrahman which is partless and Sachchiḍānanḍa. Making the mind dwell upon such sentences (or ideas) as the above constitutes s'ravaṇa (hearing). It becomes manana (contemplation) when such ideas are quieted (in one) through logical reasoning. When (their) meaning is confirmed through these (two processes), the concentration of the mind on it alone constitutes niḍiḍhyāsana. That is called samāḍhi in which the chiṭṭa, rising above the conception of the contemplator and contemplation, merges gradually into the contemplated, like a light undisturbed by the wind. Even the mental states are not known (at the time when one is within the scope of Āṭmā). But they are only inferred from the recollection which takes place after samāḍhi. Through this samāḍhi are destroyed crores of karmas which have accumulated during cycles of births without beginning and pure ḍharma is developed. Knowers of Yoga call this samāḍhi, ḍharma-megha (cloud), inasmuch as it showers nectarine drops of karma in great quantities, when all the hosts of vāsanās are destroyed entirely through this, and when the accumulated karmas, virtuous and sinful, are rooted out. Then that in which speech was hidden till now, appears no longer so, and shines as Saṭ; and direct cognition reveals itself, like the myrobalan in the palm of the hand. Vairāgya begins from where the vāsanās cease to arise towards objects of enjoyment. The cessation of the rising of the idea of "I" is the highest limit of buḍḍhi; uparaṭi begins from where the mental states once destroyed do not again arise. That ascetic is said to possess Sṭhiṭaprajñā who enjoys bliss always and whose mind is absorbed in Brahman that is formless and actionless. That state of mind is termed prajñā that realises the oneness of Brahman and Āṭmā after deep inquiry, and that has the vṛṭṭi of nirvikalpa and chinmāṭra. He who possesses this always is a Jīvanmukṭa. He is a Jīvanmukṭa who has neither the conception of "I" in the body and the senses, nor

[1] I and its inflexions.

the conception of another (different from himself) in everything else. He is a Jīvanmukṭa who sees through his prajñā no difference between his own Āṭmā and Brahman as well as between Brahman and the universe. He is a Jīvanmukṭa who preserves equanimity of mind, either when revered by the good or reviled by the vicious. One who has cognized the true nature of Brahman is not subject to rebirth as before. But were he so subjected, then he is not a true knower, the knowing of Brahman being external only. A man is subject to prārabḍha[1] so long as he is affected by pleasure, etc. The attainment of a result is always preceded by action; and nowhere is it without karma. Through the cognition "I am Brahman" are destroyed the karmas accumulated during hundreds of crores of previous births, like the actions in the dreaming state (that are destroyed) during the waking state.

An ascetic having known himself as associateless and indifferent like ether, is not at all affected by any of his karmas at any time. Just as the ether is not affected by the alcoholic smell through its contact with a pot, so Ātmā is not affected by the guṇas produced by its upāḍhi. The prārabḍha karma that has begun to act before the dawn of jñāna is not checked by it; and one should reap its fruit, as in the case of an arrow discharged at a target. An arrow that is discharged towards an object with the idea that it is a tiger, does not stop when it (the tiger) is found to be a cow; but it (even) pierces the mark through its speed, without stopping. When one realises his Āṭmā as free from old age and death, then how will prārabḍha affect him? Prārabḍha accomplishes (its work) only when one considers his body as Āṭmā. This conception of Āṭmā as body is not at all a desirable one; so it should be given up along with prārabḍha, since it is simply a delusion to attribute prārabḍha to this body. How can there be reality to that which is superimposed upon another? How can there be birth to that which is not real? How can there be death to that which is not born? How can there be prārabḍha to that which is unreal? The Veḍa speaks of prārabḍha in an external sense only, to satisfy those

[1] The result of past karma now enjoyed.

foolish persons that doubt, saying: "If jñāna can destroy all the results of ajñāna (such as body, etc.), then whence is the existence of this body to such a one?" but not to inculcate to the wise the existence of the body.

Āṭmā is all-full, beginningless, endless, immeasurable, unchangeable, replete with Saṭ, Chiṭ, and Ānanḍa, decayless, the one essence, the eternal, the differentiated, the plenum, the endless, having its face everywhere, the one that can neither be given up nor taken up, the one that can neither be supported nor be made to support, the guṇaless, the actionless, the subtle, the changeless, the stainless, the indescribable, the true nature of one's Āṭmā, above the reach of speech and mind, the one full of Saṭ, the self-existent, the immaculate, the enlightened, and the incomparable; such is Brahman, one only without a second. There are not in the least many. He who knows his Āṭmā himself through his own cognition, as the one who is not restricted by any, is a Siḍḍha (one that has accomplished his object), who has identified his Āṭmā with the one changeless Āṭmā. Whither is this world gone, then? How did it appear? Where is it absorbed? It was seen by me just now, but now it is gone. What a great miracle! What is fit to be taken in? and what to be rejected? What is other (than Āṭmā)? And what is different (from It)? In this mighty ocean of Brahman full of the nectar of undivided bliss, I do not see, hear, or know anything. I remain in my Āṭmā only and in my own nature of Saṭ, Ānanḍarūpa. I am an asaṅga (or the associateless). I am an asaṅga. I am without any attributes. I am Hari (the Lord taking away sin). I am the quiescent, the endless, the all-full and the ancient. I am neither the agent nor the enjoyer. I am the changeless and the decayless. I am of the nature of pure enlightenment. I am the one and the perpetual bliss.

This science was imparted to Apānṭaraṭama who gave it to Brahmā. Brahmā gave it to Ghora-Aṅgiras. Ghora-Aṅgiras gave it to Raikva, who gave it to Rāma. And Rāma gave it to all beings. This is the teaching of Nirvāṇa; and this is the teaching of the Veḍas; yea, this is the teaching of the Veḍas. Thus ends the Upanishaḍ.

SUBĀLA-UPANISHAḌ

OF

S'UKLĀ-YĀJURVEḌĀ

KHAṆDA I

THEN he (Raikva[1]) asked: "What was at first?" To which (He the Lord) replied:

"There was neither Saṭ [2] nor asaṭ nor Saṭ-asaṭ. From it, ṭamas (darkness) was evolved. From ṭamas came bhūṭāḍi;[3] from bhūṭāḍi came ākās', from ākās', vāyu; from vāyu, agni (fire); from agni, āpas (water); and from āpas, pṛṭhivī (earth). Then it became an egg. After remaining so for one (divine) year, it split into two and became earth below,[4] the ākās' above and in the midst, the infinite Purusha of a divine form of myriads of heads, eyes, feet and hands. Prior to the bhūṭas (elements), he had evolved Mṛṭyu (time or death) of three letters [5], three heads, and three feet, and having a khaṇda-paras'u [6] (broken

[1] In the Chhānḍogya Upanishaḍ, Raikva is said to be the imparter of Samvargavidyā.

[2] The absolute (Parabrahman) is neither Saṭ (Be-ness) nor asaṭ (not-Be-ness) nor a commingling of both. It is neither spirit nor matter nor a commingling of both.

[3] Bhūṭāḍi is tāmasa ahaṅkāra according to Vishṇu Purāṇa.

[4] "Above and below" refers not to the position but only to the state, of matter, gross or subtle. "In the midst" implies that ākās and earth are soaked in and with spirit.

[5] This refers to the first triune manifestation of Purusha or spirit through time when only there is activity. Mṛṭyu or Kāla is the first manifestation whereas Yama (or the God of death) is the secondary one dealing with the death of creatures lower down.

[6] Khaṇda means divided or with parts. Parasu literally injuring another. Hence Mṛṭyu with his khaṇda-parasu divided eternal time into its parts and conditions the absolute through primordial matter. In the Purāṇas and other books, Mṛṭyu and Yama are represented as having an axe broken in a conflict.

axe). To him, Brahmā (the Purusha) spoke. He entered Brahmā himself and evolved mentally the seven sons [1] and these Havirāts (or sons) as well as the seven prajāpaṭis (progenitors). Brāhmaṇas [2] were born from His mouth, Kshaṭṭriyas from His hands, Vais'yas from His thighs, and from the feet were born the S'uḍras. The moon was born from His manas (mind), the sun from His eyes, vāyu from (His) ears and prāṇas from (His) heart. Thus all things were born."

Khaṇḍa II

" From apāna came Nishāḍas, Yakshas, Rākshasas, and Ganḍharvas. From (His) bones, arose the mountains. From His hairs arose the herbs and the trees. From His forehead, Ruḍra was born through His anger. The breath of this great Being became the Ṛgveḍa, Yajurveḍa, Sāmaveḍa, Aṭharvaveḍa, S'īkshā (the science of the proper pronunciation and articulation of sounds), Kalpa (the science of methodology), Vyākaraṇa (grammar), Nirukṭa (glossarial explanation of obsolete and other terms in Veḍas), Chhanḍas (prosody or veḍic metre), Jyoṭisha (astronomy), Nyāya (logic), Mīmāmsā (including rituals and veḍānṭa), Ḍharmas'āsṭras, commentaries, glosses and all beings. This Āṭmā (or the Self of Purusha) is Hiraṇyajyoṭis (or golden or effulgent Light) into which all the universe is absorbed. He divided Āṭmā (his Self) into two moieties; out of one moiety, the woman was created; and out of the other, man. Having become a Ḍeva, He created the Ḍevas. Having become a Ṛshi, He created the Ṛshis; also He created Yakṣhas, Rākshasas, Ganḍharvas, wild and domestic beasts and others such as cows, bulls, mares and horses, she-asses and asses and Vis'vambhara (the Supporter) and Vis'vambharā (the earth). Becoming Vais'vānara (fire) at the end (of creation), He burnt up all objects. Then (in dissolution), pṛṭhivī was absorbed in āpas, āpas in agni, agni in vāyu, vāyu in ākas', ākas' in inḍriyas (organs),

[1] This refers to the septenary manifestation from the triune one; also to the sub-septenary ones.

[2] In other words beings of Saṭṭva, Rajas and Ṭamas and an admixture of these were born.

indriyas into ṭanmāṭras (rudimentary properties), ṭanmāṭras into bhūṭāḍi, bhūṭāḍi into mahaṭ, mahaṭ into avyakṭa, avyakṭa into akshara (the indestructible), akshara into ṭamas (darkness). Ānd ṭamas becomes one with the supreme Lord. Ānd then there is neither Saṭ nor asaṭ, nor Saṭ-asaṭ. This is the teaching of Nirvāṇa and this is the teaching of the Veḍas. Yea, This is the teaching of the Veḍas."

KHAṆḌA III

" Āt first, there was Āsaṭ, unborn, non-existent, unsupported, soundless, touchless, formless, tasteless, odourless, and decayless. The undaunted man never grieves, as he knows Āṭmā to be great, all-pervading and unborn. It (Āṭmā) is prāṇaless, mouthless, earless, tongueless, manas-less, ṭejas-less, eyeless, nameless, goṭraless (or clanless), headless, handless, feetless, non-unctuous, bloodless, non-measurable, neither long nor short, neither gross nor atomic, neither great nor small, endless, indescribable, non-returnable, non-luminous, not hidden, having neither inside nor outside, neither eating anything nor being eaten by others. Some one (out of many) attains to this (Āṭmā) by the six means of saṭya (truth), ḍāna (charity), ṭapas (religious austerities), non-injury to any creature, celibacy and complete indifference to worldy objects ;[1] and there are no other means. Whoever feels happy with the thought 'I know That', that learned person's prāṇa will never get out of his body at the moment of death, but will become absorbed in Brahman ; and being absorbed in Brahman, he attains the state of Brahman Itself as he who knows this."

KHAṆḌA IV

" In the middle of the heart is a red fleshy mass in which is the ḍahara-lotus. Like the lotus, it opens into many (petals). There are ten openings in the heart. The (different kinds of) prāṇas are located there. Whenever he (Āṭmā) is united with

---

[1] The word anāsakena (non-injury) is repeated in the text which is wrong.

prāṇa, he sees cities with rivers and other variegated things; when united with vyāna, he sees Ḍevas and Ṛshis; when united with apāna, he sees Yakshas, Rākshasas and Ganḍharvas; when united with uḍāna, he perceives the celestial world, Ḍevas, Skanḍa (Kārṭikeya or the six-faced Mars), and Jayanṭa (Inḍra's son); when united with samāna, he sees the celestial world and the treasures (of Kubera); when united with rambhā (a nādi hereafter given out), he sees whatever is seen or not seen, heard or not heard, eaten or not eaten, asaṭ or Saṭ and all else.

"There are ten nādis; in each of these are seventy-one. And these become 72,000 branch nādis. When Āṭmā sleeps therein, it produces sound; but when Āṭmā sleeps in the second kos'a (or sheath) then it sees this world and the higher as also knows all the sounds. This is spoken of as samprasāḍa (deep sleep rest). Then prāṇa protects the body. The nādis are full of blood, of the colours green, blue, yellow, red, and white. Now this ḍahara-lotus has many petals like a lily. Like a hair divided into 1,000 parts, the nādis called hiṭa are. The divine Āṭmā sleeps in the ākās' of the heart, in the supreme kos'a (or ānanḍamaya sheath); sleeping there, it has no desires, no dreams, no ḍeva-worlds, no yajñas or sacrificer, no mother or father, no relative, no kinsman, no thief, or no Brāhman-slayer. Its body is ṭejas (resplendent effulgence) and of the nature of nectar (or the immortal). It is as if in sport, a water-lotus. When he returns again to the waking state by the same way (he quitted or went in before to the heart), he is Samrāt[1]. Thus says he."

Khaṇḍa V[2]

"That which joins one place (or centre) with another is the nādis which bind them. The eye is aḍhyāṭmā (pertaining to the body); the visible objects are āḍhibhūṭa (pertaining to the

[1] Lit., one producing sound.

[2] In this chapter are given out the several correspondences of the ḍevas (or the presiding spiritual deities) and of the objects to the five organs of sense, the five organs of action, and the anṭahkaraṇa (or lower mind) composed of manas, buḍḍhi, ahaṅkāra, and chiṭṭa.

elements) and the sun is aḍhiḍaivaṭa (spiritual). The nādis form their bond (or connect them). He who moves in the eye, in the visible, in the sun, in the nādis, in prāna, in vijñāna,[1] in ānanḍa, in the ākās' of the heart, and within all else—That is Āṭmā. It is that which should be worshipped. It is without old age, death, fear, sorrow, or end.

" The ear is adhyāṭma, the audible aḍhibhūṭa, and ḍik (the quarters) is aḍhiḍaivaṭa. The nādis bind them. He who moves in the ear, in the audible, in the quarters, in the nādis, in prāṇa, in vijñāna, in ānanḍa, in the ākās' of the heart, and within all else—That is Āṭmā. It is that which should be worshipped. It is without old age, death, fear, sorrow, or end.

" The nose is aḍhyāṭma, the odoriferous aḍhibhūṭa, and the earth is aḍhiḍaivaṭa. The nādis bind them. He who moves in the nose, the odoriferous, the earth, the nādis, prāṇa, vijñāna, ānanḍa, the ākās' of the heart, and within all else—That is Āṭmā. It is that which should be worshipped. It is without old age, death, fear, sorrow, or end.

"The tongue is aḍhyāṭma: the tastable aḍhibhūṭa, and Varuṇa is aḍhiḍaivaṭā. The nādis bind them. He who moves in the tongue, the tastable, Varuṇa, the nādis, prāṇa, vijñāna, ānanḍa, the ākas' of the heart, and within all else—That is Āṭmā. It is that which should be worshipped. It is without old age, death, fear, sorrow, or end.

" The skin is aḍhyāṭma, the tangiferous aḍhibhūṭa, and the vāyu is aḍhiḍaivaṭa. The nādis bind them. He who moves in the skin, the tangiferous, the vāyu, the nādis, prāṇa, vijñāna, ānanḍa, the ākās' of the heart, and within all else—That is Āṭmā. It is that which should be worshipped. It is without old age, death, fear, sorrow, or end.

" Vāk (speech) is aḍhyāṭma, that which is acted upon by vāk is aḍhibhūṭa, and Āgni is Aḍhiḍaivaṭa. The nādis bind them. He who moves in vāk, that which is acted upon by vāk, Āgni, the nādis, prāṇa, vijñāna, the ākas' of the heart, and within all else—That is Āṭmā. It is that which should be worshipped. It is without old age, death, fear, sorrow, or end.

[1] Probably prāṇa, vijñāna, and ānanḍa refer to the sheaths formed by them.

"The hand is aḍhyāṭma, that which can be handled is aḍhibhūṭa, and Inḍra is aḍhiḍaivaṭa. The nādis bind them. He who moves in the hand, that which can be handled by it, Inḍra, the nādis, prāṇa vijñāna, ānanḍa, the ākās' of the heart, and within all else—That is Āṭmā. It is that which should be worshipped. It is without old age, death, fear, sorrow, or end.

"The feet is aḍhyāṭma, that which is walked upon is aḍhibhūṭa, and Vishṇu (or Upenḍra) is aḍhiḍaivaṭa. The nādis bind them. He who moves in the feet, that which is walked upon, Vishṇu, the nādis, prāṇa, vijñāna, ānanḍa, the ākās' of the heart, and within all else—That is Āṭmā. It is that which should be worshipped. It is without old age, death, fear, sorrow, or end.

"The anus is aḍhyāṭma, the excreta is aḍhibhūṭa, and Mṛṭyu is aḍhiḍaivaṭa. The nādis bind them. He who moves the anus, the excreta, Mṛṭyu, the nādis, prāṇa, vijñāna, ānanḍa, the ākās' of the heart, and within all else—That is Āṭmā. It is that which should be worshipped. It is without old age, death, fear, sorrow, or end.

"The genitals is aḍhyāṭma, the secretion is aḍhibhūṭa, and Prajāpaṭi is aḍhiḍaivaṭa. The nādis bind them. He who moves in the genitals, secretion, Prajāpaṭi, the nādis, prāṇa, vijñāna, ānanḍa, the ākās' of the heart, and within all else—That is Āṭmā. It is that which should be worshipped. It is without old age, death, fear, sorrow, or end.

[1] "Manas is aḍhyāṭma, the thinkable is aḍhibūṭa, and the moon is Aḍhiḍaivaṭa. The nādis bind them. He who moves in the manas, the thinkable, the moon, the nādis, prāṇa, vijñāna, ānanḍa, the ākās' of the heart, and within all else—That is Āṭmā. It is that which should be worshipped. It is without old age, death, fear, sorrow, or end.

"Buḍḍhi is aḍhyāṭma, the certainly knowable is aḍhibhūṭa, and Brahmā is aḍhiḍaivaṭa. The nādis bind them. He who moves in buḍḍhi, the certainly knowable, Brahmā, the nādis, prāṇa, vijñāna, ānanḍa, the ākās' of the heart, and within all else—That

[1] Although in the original manas, buḍḍhi, etc., are in the middle, yet they are inserted here after the karmenḍriyas.

is Āṭmā. It is that which should be worshipped. It is without old age, death, fear, sorrow, or end.

"Āhaṅkāra is aḍhyāṭma, that which is acted upon by ahaṅkāra is aḍhibhūṭa, and Ruḍra is aḍhiḍaivaṭa. The nādis bind them. He who moves in ahaṅkāra, that which is acted upon by ahaṅkāra, Ruḍra, the nādis, prāṇa, vijñāna, ānanḍa, the ākās' of the heart, and within all else—That is Āṭmā. It is that which should be worshipped. It is without old age, death, fear, sorrow, or end.

"Chiṭṭa is aḍhyāṭma, that which is acted upon by chiṭṭa (producing fluctuation of thought) is aḍhibhūṭa, and Ksheṭrajña is aḍhiḍaivaṭa. The nādis bind them. He who moves in chiṭṭa, that which is acted upon by chiṭṭa, Ksheṭrajña, the nādis, prāṇa, vijñāna, ānanḍa, the ākas' of the heart, and within all else—That is Āṭmā. It is that which should be worshipped. It is without old age, death, fear, sorrow, or end.

"He is the knower of all, the Lord of all, the ruler of all, the one latent in all, the one worshipped for the happiness of all, but Himself not worshipping (or seeking) any happiness, the one worshipped by all, the Veḍas and other books and to which all this is food, but who does not become the food of another; moreover, the one who, as the eye, is the ordainer of all, the one who as annamaya is Bhūṭāṭmā; the one who as prāṇamaya is Inḍriyāṭmā, the one as manomaya is Saṅkalpāṭmā, the one who as vijñānamaya is Kālāṭmā, the one who as ānanḍamaya is Layāṭmā, is one and not dual. How can it be said to be mortal? How can it be said that there is not immortality in It? It is neither internal prajñā nor external prajñā nor both, nor Prajñānaghana; it is neither prajñā nor not-prajñā; it is neither known nor is it to know anything. Thus is the exposition of Nirvāṇa; and thus is the exposition of the Veḍas; yea, thus is the exposition of the Veḍas."

KHAṆḌA VI

"At first there was not anything in the least. These creatures were born through no root, no support but the Divine Ḍeva, the one Nārāyaṇa.[1] The eye and the visible are Nārāyaṇa;

[1] Nārāyaṇa is the Universal Self. This chapter gives out the pantheistic theory that the whole universe is nothing but God Nārāyaṇa.

the ear and the audible are Nārāyaṇa; the tongue and the 'tastable' are Nārāyaṇa; the nose and the 'smellable' are Nārāyaṇa; the skin and the tangible are Nārāyaṇa; manas and that which is acted upon by it are Nārāyaṇa; buḍḍhi and that which is acted upon by it are Nārāyaṇa; ahaṅkāra and that which is acted upon by it are Nārāyaṇa; chiṭṭa and that which is acted upon by it are Nārāyaṇa; vāk and that which is spoken are Nārāyaṇa; the hand and that which is lifted are Nārāyaṇa; the leg and that which is walked upon are Nārāyaṇa; the anus and the excreted are Nārāyaṇa; the genitals and the enjoyment of pleasure are Nārāyaṇa. The originator and the ordainer as also the agent and the causer of changes, are the Divine Ḍeva Nārāyaṇa only. Āḍiṭyas, Ruḍras, Maruṭs, Vasus, Ās'vins, the Ṛk, Yajus, and Sāma, Manṭras, Āgni, clarified butter and oblation—all these are Nārāyaṇa. The origin and the combination are the Divine Ḍeva Nārāyaṇa only. Mother, father, brother, residence, asylum, friends and dependents are Nārāyaṇa only. The divine nādis known as virājā, suḍars'anā, jiṭā, saumyā, moghā, kumārā, amṛṭā, saṭyā, sumaḍhyamā, nāsīrā, s'is'irā, surā, sūryā, and bhāsvaṭī (fourteen nādis in all), that which thunders, sings and rains, *viz.*, Varuṇa, Aryamā (sun), Chanḍramas (moon), Kalā (part), Kavi (S'ukra), the creator Brahmā and Prajāpaṭi, Inḍra, Kāla (or time) of days, half-days, Kalpa, the upper, and the directions—all these are Nārāyaṇa. That which was and will be is this Purusha only. Like the eye (which sees without any obstacle) the thing spread in the ākās', the wise ever see this supreme seat of Vishṇu. Brāhmaṇas who are ever spiritually awake, praise in diverse ways and illuminate the supreme abode of Vishṇu. Thus is the exposition to the attaining of Nirvaṇa; thus is the teaching of the Veḍas; yea, thus is the teaching of the Veḍas."

KHAṆḌA VII

"Within the body, is the one eternal Āja (unborn), located in the cave (of the heart). Earth is His body. Though He moves in the earth, earth does not know Him. Waters are His body. Though He moves in the waters, waters do not know Him. Ṭejas is His body. Though He moves in ṭejas, ṭejas does not know Him. Vāyu is His body. Though He moves in vāyu, vāyu does not know Him. Ākās' is His body. Though He moves in ākās', ākās' does not know Him. Manas is His body. Though He moves in manas, manas does not know Him. Buḍḍhi is His body. Though He moves in buḍḍhi, buḍḍhi does not know Him. Āhaṅkāra is His body. Though He moves in ahaṅkāra, ahaṅkāra does not know Him. Chiṭṭa is His body. Though He moves in chiṭṭa, chiṭṭa does not know Him. Avyakṭa is His body. Though He moves in avyakṭa, avyakṭa does not know Him. Akshara is His body. Though He moves in akshara, akshara does not know Him. Mṛṭyu (death) is His body. Though He moves in Mṛṭyu, Mṛtyu does not know Him. Such an one is the Āṭmā within all creatures, the remover of all sins and the Divine Ḍeva, the one Nārāyaṇa.

"This knowledge was imparted (by Nārāyaṇa) to Apānṭaraṭama who in turn imparted it to Brahmā. Brahmā imparted it to Ghora-Aṅgiras. He imparted it to Raikva, who in turn imparted it to Rāma. Rāma imparted it to all creatures. This is the teaching of Nirvāṇa; this is the teaching of the Veḍas; yea, this is the teaching of the Veḍas."

Khaṇḍa VIII

"The Āṭmā of all which is immaculate, is located within the cave in the body. Āṭmā which lives in the midst of the body filled with fat, flesh and phlegm in a seat very closely shut up with shining many-coloured walls resembling a Ganḍharva city and with the (subtle) essence going out of it (to other parts of the body), which seat may be likened to a plantain flower and is ever agitated like a water-bubble—this Āṭmā is of an unthinkable form, the Divine Ḍeva, associateless and pure, has ṭejas as its body, is of all forms, the Lord of all, the unthinkable and the bodiless, placed within the cave, immortal, shining, and bliss itself. He is a wise person who cognizes Āṭmā thus, and not one who does not do so."

Khaṇḍa IX

Once Raikva questioned Him (Lord) thus: "O Lord, in whom does everything disappear (or merge)?" He replied thus: "That which (or he who) disappears in the eye becomes the eye only; that which disappears in the visible becomes the visible only; that which disappears in the sun becomes sun only; that which disappears in Virāt becomes Virāt only; that which disappears in prāṇa becomes prāṇa only; that which disappears in vijñāna becomes vijñāna only; that which disappears in ānanḍa becomes ānanḍa only; that which disappears in ṭurya becomes ṭurya only—(all these) attain that which is deathless, fearless, sorrowless, endless, and seedless."

Then He continued "That which disappears in the ear becomes ear itself; that which disappears in the audible becomes the audible only; that which disappears in ḍik (space) becomes ḍik only; that which disappears in suḍaras'ana (discus) becomes suḍars'ana only: that which disappears in apāna becomes apāna only; that which disappears in vijñāna becomes vijñāna only; that which disappears in ānanḍa become ānanḍa only; that which disappears in ṭurya becomes ṭurya only—(all these) attain that which is deathless, fearless, sorrowless, endless, and seedless."

Then He continued: "That which disappears in the nose becomes nose only; that which disappears in the odoriferous becomes odoriferous only; that which disappears in pṛṭhivī becomes pṛṭhivī only; that which disappears in jiṭam (victory) becomes victory only; that which disappears in vyāna becomes vyāna only; that which disappears in vijñāna becomes vijñāna only; that which disappears in bliss becomes bliss only; that which disappears in ṭurya becomes ṭurya only—(all these) attain that which is deathless, fearless, sorrowless, endless, and seedless."

Then He continued: "That which disappears in the mouth becomes the mouth only; that which disappears in the tasted becomes the tasted only; that which disappears in Varuṇa becomes Varuṇa only; that which disappears in soumya (moon or Mercury) becomes soumya only; that which disappears in uḍāna becomes uḍāna only; that which disappears in vijñāna becomes vijñāna only; that which disappears in bliss becomes bliss only; that which disappears in ṭurya becomes ṭurya only—(all these) attain that which is deathless, fearless, sorrowless, endless, and seedless."

Then He continued: "That which disappears in the skin becomes the skin only; that which disappears in touch becomes touch only; that which disappears in vāyu becomes vāyu only; that which disappears in cloud becomes cloud only; that which disappears in samāna becomes samāna only; that which disappears in vijñāna becomes vijñāna only; that which disappears in bliss becomes bliss only; that which disappears in ṭurya becomes ṭurya only—(all these) attain that which is deathless, fearless, sorrowless, endless, and seedless."

Then He continued: "That which disappears in vāk becomes vāk only; that which disappears in speech becomes speech only; that which disappears in Agni becomes Agni only; that which disappears in kumārā becomes kumārā only; that which disappears in hostility becomes hostility itself; that which disappears in vijñāna become vijñāna only; that which disappears in bliss becomes bliss only; that which disappears in ṭurya becomes ṭurya only—(all these) attain that which is deathless, fearless, sorrowless, endless, and seedless."

Then He continued: "That which disappears in the hand becomes the hand only; that which disappears in that which is lifted by the hand becomes that which is lifted by the hand; that which disappears in Inḍra becomes Inḍra only; that which disappears in the nectar becomes the nectar only; that which disappears in mukhya becomes mukhya only; that which disappears in vijñāna becomes vijñāna only; that which disappears in blisss becomes bliss only; that which disappears in ṭurya becomes ṭurya only—(all these) attain, that which is deathless, fearless, sorrowless, endless, and seedless."

Then He continued: "That which disappears in the leg becomes the leg only; that which disappears in that which is walked upon becomes that which is walked upon; that which disappears in Vishṇu becomes Vishṇu only; that which disappears in saṭya becomes saṭya only; that which disappears in the suppression of the breath and voice becomes the suppression of the breath and voice; that which disappears in vijñāna becomes vijñāna only; that which disappears in bliss becomes bliss only; that which disappears in ṭurya becomes ṭurya only—(all these) attain that which is deathless, fearless, sorrowless, endless, and seedless."

Then He continued: "That which disappears in the anus becomes the anus only; that which disappears in that which is excreted becomes that which is excreted; that which disappears in Mṛṭyu becomes Mṛṭyu only; that which disappears in spirituons liquor becomes spirituous liquor only; that which disappears in hurricane becomes hurricane only; that which disappears in vijñāna becomes vijñāna only; that which disappears in bliss becomes bliss only; that which disappears in ṭurya becomes ṭurya only—(all these) attain that which is deathless, fearless, sorrowless, endless, and seedless."

Then He continued: "That which disappears in the genitals becomes the genitals only; that which disappears in that which is enjoyed becomes that which is enjoyed; that which disappears in that which is Prajāpaṭi becomes Prajāpaṭi only; that which disappears in nāsīnām becomes nāsīnām only; that which disappears in kurmira becomes kurmira only; that which disappears in vijñāna becomes vijñāna only; that which disappears in bliss becomes bliss only; that which disappears in ṭurya becomes ṭurya only—(all these) attain that which is deathless, fearless, sorrowless, endless, and seedless."

Then He continued: "That which disappears in manas becomes manas itself; that which disappears in the thinkable becomes the thinkable itself; that which disappears in the moon becomes the moon itself; that which disappears in s'is'u becomes s'is'u itself; that which disappears in s'yena becomes s'yena itself; that which disappears in vijñāna becomes vijñāna itself; that which disappears in ānanḍa becomes ānanḍa itself; that which disappears in ṭurya becomes ṭurya itself—(all these) attain that which is deathless, fearless, sorrowless, endless, and seedless."

Then He continued: "That which disappears in buḍḍhi becomes buḍḍhi itself; that which disappears in the certainly knowable becomes the certainly knowable itself; that which disappears in Brahmā becomes Brahmā himself; that which disappears in Kṛshṇa becomes Kṛshṇa himself; that which disappears in Sūrya becomes Sūrya itself; that which disappears in vijñāna becomes vijñāna itself; that which disappears in ānanḍa becomes ānanḍa itself; that which disappears in ṭurya becomes ṭurya itself—(all these) attain that which is deathless, fearless, sorrowless, endless, and seedless."

Then He continued: "That which disappears in ahaṅkāra becomes ahaṅkāra itself; that which disappears in that which is acted upon by ahaṅkāra becomes that itself; that which disappears in Ruḍra becomes Ruḍra himself; that which disappears in asura becomes asura itself; that which disappears in s'veṭa becomes s'veṭa itself; that which disappears in vijñāna becomes vijñāna itself; that which disappears in ānanḍa becomes ānanḍa itself; that which disappears in ṭurya becomes ṭurya itself—(all these) attain that which is deathless, fearless, sorrowless, endless, and seedless."

Then He continued: "That which disappears in chiṭṭa becomes chiṭṭa itself; that which disappears in that which is acted upon by chiṭṭa becomes that itself; that which disappears in Ksheṭrajña becomes Ksheṭrajña itself; that which disappears in bhāsvaṭī becomes bhāsvaṭī itself; that whch disappears in nāga becomes nāga itself; that which disappears in vijñāna becomes vijñāna itself; that which disappears in ānanḍa becomes ānanḍa itself; that which disappears in ṭurya becoms ṭurya itself—(all these) attain that which is deathless, fearless, sorrowless, endless, and seedless."

"He who knows this as seedless in this manner becomes himself seedless. He is neither born, nor dies, nor is deluded, nor split, nor burnt, nor cut—yea, he does not feel angry, and hence he is said to be Āṭmā, capable of burning all. Such an Āṭmā is neither attained by a hundred sayings, nor by (the reading of) many scriptures, nor by mere intelligence, nor by hearing from others, nor by understanding, nor by Veḍas, nor by scriptures, nor by severe ṭapas, nor sāṅkhya, nor yoga, nor observances of the orders of the life, nor by any other means (than the following). Devoted Brāhmaṇas who repeat the Veḍas according to rules and who worship Him with praise attain Him. He who is quiescent, self-controlled, indifferent to worldly objects and resigned, having centred his mind on Āṭmā sees Āṭmā and becomes one with the Āṭmā of all, as also he who knows this."

KHAṆDA X

Then Raikva asked Him: "O Lord, where do all things rest? He replied: "In the worlds of Rasāṭala (or nether worlds)."

"In what are these (Rasāṭala worlds) woven warp and woof?" He replied: "In the worlds of Bhūḥ."

"In what are these (worlds of Bhūḥ) woven warp and woof?" He replied: "In the worlds of Bhuvaḥ."

"In what are these (Bhuvaḥ worlds) woven warp and woof?" "In the worlds of Suvaḥ."

"In what are these (Suvaḥ worlds) woven warp and woof?" "In the worlds of Mahaḥ."

"In what are these (Mahaḥ worlds) woven warp and woof?" "In the Janaloka."

"In what are these (Jana worlds) woven warp and woof?" "In the Ṭapoloka."

"In what are these (Ṭapolokas) woven warp and woof?" "In the Saṭya loka."

"In what are these (Saṭya worlds) woven warp and woof?" "In the Prajāpaṭi loka."

"In what are these (Prajāpaṭi worlds) woven warp and woof?" "In the Brahmaloka."

"In what are these (Brahma worlds) woven warp and woof?" "In the Sarvaloka."

"In what are these (Sarva lokas) woven warp and woof?" "In Āṭmā—which is Brahman, like beads (in a rosary) warp-wise and woof-wise."

Then he said: "All these rest in Āṭmā, and he who knows this, becomes Āṭmā itself. Thus is the exposition of Nirvāṇa.

Thus is the exposition of the Veḍas ; yea, thus is the exposition of the Veḍas."

KHAṆḌA XI

Again Raikva asked Him : "O Lord ! what is the seat of Āṭmā which is replete with vijñāna ? and how does it leave the body and pervade the universe ?" To this He replied : "There is a mass of red flesh in the middle of the heart. In it, there is a lotus called ḍahara. It buds forth in many petals like a water-lily. In the middle of it is an ocean (samuḍra).[1] In its midst is a koka[2] (bird). In it there are four nādis. They are ramā, aramā, Ichchhā, and punarbhava. Of these, ramā leads a man of virtue to a happy world. Āramā leads one of sins into the world of sins. (Passing) through Ichchhā (nādi), one gets whatever he remembers. Through punarbhava, he splits open the sheaths; after splitting open the sheaths, he splits open the skull of the head ; then he splits open pṛṭhivī ; then āpas ; then ṭejas ; then vāyu ; then ākās'. Then he splits open manas ; then bhūṭāḍi ; then mahaṭ ; then avyakṭa ; then akshara ; then he splits open mṛṭyu and mṛṭyu becomes one with the supreme God. Beyond this, there is neither Saṭ nor asaṭ, nor Saṭ-asaṭ. Thus is the exposition of Nirvāṇa ; and thus is the exposition of the Veḍas ; yea, thus is the exposition of the Veḍas."

KHAṆḌA XII[3]

"Anna (food) came from Nārāyaṇa. It was first cooked in Brahmaloka in the Mahā-samvarṭaka fire. Again it was cooked in the sun ; again it was cooked in kravyāḍi (lit., the fire that burns raw flesh, etc.) ; again it was cooked in jwālakīla (the flaming kīla) ; then it became pure and not stale (or fresh). One should eat whatever has fallen to his lot and without begging ; one should never beg any (food)."

[1] The ocean probably refers to ākāsic space.
[2] Koka probably refers to Hamsa.
[3] In this chapter are related the different fires, the first or primordial anna or food-substance has to pass through in order to become the gross food.

KHAṆDA XIII

"The wise man should conduct himself like a lad, with the nature of a child, without company, blameless, silent and wise and without exercising any authority. This description of Kaivalya is stated by Prajāpaṭi. Having found with certitude the supreme seat, one should dwell under a tree with torn cloths, unaccompanied, single and engaged in samāḍhi. He should be longing after the attaining of Āṭmā and having attained this object, he is desireless, his desires have decayed. He fears none, though he finds the cause of death in such as elephants, lions, gadflies, musquitoes, ichneuma, serpents, Yakshas, Rākshasas, and Ganḍharvas. He will stand like a tree. Though cut down, he will neither get angry nor tremble. He will stand (or remain) like a lotus. Though pierced, he will neither get angry nor tremble. He will stand like ākās'; though struck, he will neither get angry nor tremble. He will stand by Saṭya (truth), since Āṭmā is Saṭya.

"Pṛṭhivī is the heart (or centre) of all odours; āpas is the heart of all tastes; ṭejas is the heart of all forms; vāyu is the heart of all touch; ākās' is the heart of all sounds; avyakṭa is the heart of gīṭās (or sounds); mṛṭyu is the heart of all Saṭṭvas; and mṛṭyu becomes one with the Supreme. And beyond Him, there is neither Saṭ nor asaṭ, nor Saṭ-asaṭ. Thus is the exposition of Nirvāṇa; thus is the exposition of the Vedas; yea, thus is the exposition of the Veḍas."

KHAṆDA XIV[1]

"Pṛṭhivi is the food, and āpas is the eater; āpas is the food, and jyoṭis (or fire) is the eater; jyoṭis is the food, and vāyu is the eater; vāyu is the food, and ākās' is the eater; and akās' is the food and the inḍriyas (organs) are the eaters; inḍriyas are the food and manas is the eater; manas is the food, and buḍḍhi is the eater; buḍḍhi is the food, and avyakṭa is the eater; avyakṭa is the food, and akshara is the eater; akshara is the food, and

[1] The causes and effects are herein given out, the cause of an effect becoming itself the effect of a higher cause.

mṛṭyu is the eater; and mṛṭyu becomes one with the Supreme. Beyond Him, there is neither Saṭ nor asaṭ, nor Saṭ-asaṭ. Thus is the exposition of Nirvāṇa, and thus is the exposition of the Veḍas; yea, thus is the exposition of the Veḍas."

Khaṇḍa XV

Ågain Raikva asked: "O Lord, when this Vijñāna-ghana goes out (of the body or the universe), what does it burn and how?" To which He replied: "When it goes away, it burns prāṇa, apāna, vyāna, uḍāna, samāna, vairambha, mukhya, anṭar-yāma, prabhañjana, kumāra, s'yena, kṛshṇa, s'veṭa, and nāga. Then it burns pṛṭhivī, āpas, ṭejas, vāyu, and ākās'; then it burns the waking, the dreaming, the dreamless sleeping and the fourth states as well as the maharlokas and worlds higher; then it burns the lokāloka (the highest world forming a limit to the other worlds). Then it burns ḍharma and aḍharma. Then it burns that which is beyond, is sunless, limitless, and worldless. Then it burns mahaṭ; it burns avyakṭa; it burns akshara; it burns mṛṭyu; and mṛṭyu becomes one with the great Lord. Beyond Him, there is neither Saṭ nor asaṭ, nor Saṭ-asaṭ. Thus is the exposition of Nirvāṇa, and thus is the exposition of the Veḍas; yea, thus is the exposition of the Veḍas."

Khaṇḍa XVI

"This Subāla-Bīja-Brahma-Upanishaḍ should neither be given out nor taught to one who has not controlled his passions, who has no sons, who has not gone to a Guru, and having become his disciple has not resided with him for a year, and whose family and conduct are not known. These doctrines should be taught to him who has supreme devotion to the Lord and as much to his Guru. Then these truths shine in his great soul. Thus is the exposition of Nirvāṇa; thus is the exposition of the Veḍas; yea, thus is the exposition of the Veḍas."

ṬEJOBINḌU[1]-UPANISHAḌ

OF

KṚSHṆA-YĀJURVEḌĀ

CHAPTER I

PARAM-ḌHYĀNA (the supreme meditation) should be upon ṭejobinḍu, which is the Āṭmā of the universe, which is seated in the heart, which is of the size of an atom, which pertains to S'iva, which is quiescent and which is gross and subtle, as also above these qualities. That alone should be the ḍhyāna of the Munis as well as of men, which is full of pains, which is difficult to meditate on, which is difficult to perceive, which is the emancipated one, which is decayless and which is difficult to attain. One whose food is moderate, whose anger has been controlled, who has given up all love for society, who has subdued his passions, who has overcome all pairs (heat and cold etc.), who has given up his egoism, who does not bless anyone nor take anything from others, and also who goes where they naturally ought not to go, and naturally would not go where they like to go—such persons also obtain three[2] in the face. Hamsa is said to have three seats. Therefore know it is the greatest of mysteries, without sleep and without support. It is very subtle, of the form of Soma, and is the supreme seat of Vishṇu. That seat has three faces, three guṇas and three ḍhāṭus, and is formless, motionless, changeless, sizeless, and supportless. That seat is without upāḍhi, and is above the reach of speech and

[1] Ṭejas is spiritual light and binḍu is seed; hence the seed or source of spiritual light.

[2] This probably refers to the triangle appearing in the disciples.

mind. It is Svabhāva (Self or nature) reachable only by bhāva (being). The indestructible seat is associateless, without bliss, beyond mind, difficult to perceive, emancipated and changeless. It should be meditated upon as the liberated, the eternal, the permanent and the indestructible. It is Brahman, is aḍhyāṭma (or the deity presiding as Āṭmā) and is the highest seat of Vishṇu. It is inconceivable, of the nature of Chiḍāṭmā and above the ākās', is void and non-void, and beyond the void, and is abiding in the heart. There is (in It) neither meditation nor meditator, nor the meditated, nor the non-meditated. It is not the universe. It is the highest space; it is neither supreme nor above the supreme. It is inconceivable, unknowable, non-truth, and not the highest. It is realised by the Munis, but the Ḍevas do not know the supreme One. Āvarice, delusion, fear, pride, passion,, anger, sin, heat, cold, hunger, thirst, thought and fancy—(all these do not exist in It). (In It) there is no pride of (belonging to) the Brāhmaṇa caste, nor is there the collection of the knot of salvation. (In It) there is no fear, no happiness, no pains, neither fame nor disgrace. That which is without these states is the supreme Brahman.

Yama[1] (forbearance), niyama (religious observance), ṭyāga (renunciation), mouna (silence) according to time and place, āsana (posture), mūlabanḍha, seeing all bodies as equal, the position of the eye, prāṇa-samyamana (control of breath), praṭyāhāra (subjugation of the senses), ḍhāraṇa, āṭma-ḍhyāna and samāḍhi—these are spoken of as the parts (of yoga) in order. That is called yama in which one controls all his organs (of sense and actions) through the vijñāna that all is Brahman; this should be practised often and often. Niyama, in which there is the supreme bliss enjoyed through the flowing (or inclination) of the mind towards things of the same (spiritual) kind, (*viz.*, Brahman) and the abandoning of things differing from one another is practised by the sages as a rule. In ṭyāga (renunciation), one abandons the manifestations (or objects) of the universe through the cognition of Āṭmā that is Saṭ and Chiṭ. This is practised by the great and is the giver of immediate salva-

[1] All these parts of yoga are explained here from the standpoint of veḍānṭa.

tion. Mouna (the silence), in which, without reaching That, speech returns along with mind, is fit to be attained by the Yogins and should be ever worshipped by the ignorant (even). How is it possible to speak of "That", from which speech returns? How should it be described as the universe as there is no word to describe it? It is "That" which is (really) called silence, and which is naturally understood (as such). There is silence in children, but with words (latent); whereas the knowers of Brahman have it (silence) but without words. That should be known as "the lonely seat" in which there is no man in the beginning, middle, or end, and through which all this (universe) is fully pervaded. The illusion of Brahmā and all other beings takes place within one twinkling (of His eye). That should be known as āsana (posture), in which one has with ease and without fatigue(uninterrupted) meditation of Brahman; that is described by the word kāla (time), that is endless bliss and that is secondless. Everything else is the destroyer of happiness. That is called siḍḍhāsana (siḍḍha-posture) in which the siḍḍhas (psychical personages) have succeeded in realising the endless One as the support of the universe containing all the elements, etc. That is called the mūlabanḍha, which is the Mūla (root) of all worlds, and through which the root Chiṭṭa is (banḍha) bound. It should be always practised by the Rājayogins.

One after having known the equality of the aṅgas (or parts of yoga) point to one and the same Brahman, should be absorbed in that equal (or uniform) Brahman; if not, there is not that equality (attained). Then like a dry tree, there is straightness (or uniformity throughout). Making one's vision full of spiritual wisdom, one should look upon the world as full of Brahman. That vision is very noble. It is (generally) aimed at the tip of the nose; but it should be directed towards that seat (of Brahman) wherein the cessation of seer, the seen, and sight will take place, and not towards the tip of the nose. That is called prāṇāyāma (the control of breath), in which there is the control of the modifications (of mind) through the cognition of Brahman in all the states of chiṭṭa, and others. The checking of (the conception of the reality of) the universe, is said to be expiration. The conception of "I am Brahman" is inspiration. The holding on (long) to this conception without agitation is cessation of breath. Such is the practice of the enlightened. The ignorant close their nose. That should be known as praṭyāhāra, through which one sees Āṭmā (even) in the objects of sense, and pleases chiṭṭa through manas. It should be practised often and often. Through seeing Brahman wherever the mind goes, the ḍhāraṇa of the mind is obtained. Ḍhāraṇā is thought of highly by the wise. By ḍhāraṇā is meant that state where one indulges in the good thought, "I am Brahman alone," and is without any support. This ḍhyāna is the giver of supreme bliss. Being first in a state of changelessness, and then thoroughly forgetting (even) that state owing to the cognition of the (true) nature of Brahman—this is called samāḍhi. This kind of bliss should be practised (or enjoyed) by a wise person till his cognition itself united in a moment with the state of praṭyag (Āṭmā). Then this King of Yogins becomes a Siḍḍha, and is without any aid (outside himself). Then he will attain a state, inexpressible and unthinkable.

When samāḍhi is practised, the following obstacles arise with great force—absence of right inquiry, laziness, inclination to enjoyment, absorption (in material object), ṭamas, distraction, impatience, sweat, and absent-mindedness. All these obstacles should be overcome by inquirers into Brahman. Through bhāva-vṛṭṭis (worldly thoughts), one gets into them. Through s'ūnya-vṛṭṭis (void or empty thoughts), one gets into them. But through the vṛṭṭis of Brahman, one gets fullness. Therefore one should develop fullness through this means (of Brahman). He who abandons this vṛṭṭi of Brahman, which is very purifying and supreme—that man lives in vain like a beast. But he who understands this vṛṭṭi (of Brahman), and having understood it makes advances in it, becomes a good and blessed person, deserving to be worshipped by the three worlds. Those who are greatly developed through the ripening (of their past karmas) attain the state of Brahman; others are simply reciters of words.

Those who are clever in arguments about Brahman, but are without the action pertaining to Brahman, and who are greatly attached to the world—those certainly are born again and again (in this world) through their ajñāna; (the former) never remain, even for half a moment—without the vṛṭṭi of Brahman, like Brahmā and others, Sanaka,[1] etc., S'uka and others. When a cause is subject to changes, it (as an effect) must also have its cause. When the cause ceases to exist in truth, the effect perishes through right discrimination. Then that substance (or principle) which is beyond the scope of words, remains pure. Ȧfter that, vṛṭṭi jñāna arises in their purified mind; through meditation with transcendental energy, there arises a firm certitude. Ȧfter reducing the visible into the invisible state, one should see everything as Brahman. The wise should ever stay in bliss with their understanding full of the essence of Chiṭ. Thus ends the first chapter of Ṭejobinḍu.

CHAPTER II

Then the Kumāra[2] asked S'iva: "Please explain to me the nature of Chinmāṭra, that is the partless non-dual essence." The great S'iva replied: "The partless non-dual essence is the visible. It is the world, it is the existence, it is the Self, it is manṭra, it is action, it is spiritual wisdom, it is water. It is the earth, it is ākās', it is the books, it is the three Veḍas, it is the Brahman, it is the religious vow, it is Jīva, it is Ȧja (the unborn), it is Brahmā, it is Vishṇu, it is Ruḍra; it is I, it is Ȧṭmā, it is the Guru. It is the aim, it is sacrifice, it is the body, it is manas, it is chiṭṭa, it is happiness, it is viḍyā; it is the undifferenṭiated, it is the eternal, it is the supreme, it is everything. O six-faced one, different from It there is nothing. None, none but It; It is I. It is gross, it is subtle, it is knowable, it is thou; it is the mysterious; it is the knower; it is existence, it is mother, it is father, it is brother, it is husband, it is Sūṭra (Ȧṭmā), it is Virāt.

[1] Sanaka is one of the four Kumāras in the Purāṇas who refused to create; Suka is the son of Veḍa-Vyās.

[2] The Kumāra is the son of Siva called Kārṭikēya the six-faced, symbolising the six-faced Mars in one sense.

It is the body, it is the head, it is the internal, it is the external, it is full, it is nectar, it is goṭra (clan), it is gṛha (the house), it is the preservable, it is the moon, it is the stars, it is the sun, it is the holy seat. It is forgiveness, it is patience, it is the guṇas, it is the witness. It is a friend, it is a relative, it is an ally, it is the king, town, kingdom and subjects. It is Om, japa, meditation, the seat, the one worthy to be taken (in), the heart, the Jyoṭis, Swarga (heaven) and Self."

" All the partless and non-dual essence should be regarded as Chinmāṭra. Chinmāṭra alone is the Absolute Consciousness; and this partless non-dual essence alone is the (real) essence. All having consciousness alone except those having changes, are Chinmāṭra. All this is Chinmāṭra. He is Chinmaya; the state of Āṭmā is known as Chinmāṭra and the partless non-dual essence. The whole world is Chinmāṭra. Your state and my state are Chinmāṭra. Ākās', earth, water, vāyu, agni, Brahmā, Vishṇu, S'iva and all else that exist or do not, are Chinmāṭra. That which is the partless non-dual essence is Chinmāṭra. All the past, present, and future are Chinmāṭra. Substance and time are Chinmāṭra. Knowledge and the knowable are Chinmāṭra. The knower is Chinmāṭra. Everything is Chinmāṭra. Every speech is Chinmāṭra. Whatever else is Chinmāṭra. Asaṭ and Saṭ are Chinmāṭra. The beginning and end are Chinmāṭra; that which is in the beginning and end is Chinmāṭra ever. The Guru and the disciple are Chinmāṭra. If the seer and the seen are Chinmāṭra, then they are always Chinmaya. All things wondrous are Chinmāṭra. The (gross) body is Chinmāṭra, as also the subtle and causal bodies. There is nothing beyond Chinmāṭra. I and thou are Chinmāṭra. Form and non-form are Chinmāṭra. Virtue and vice are Chinmāṭra. The body is a symbol of Chinmāṭra. Saṅkalpa, knowing, manṭra, and others, the gods invoked in manṭras, the gods presiding over the eight quarters, the phenomenal and the supreme Brahman are nothing but Chinmāṭra. There is nothing without Chinmāṭra. Māyā is nothing without Chinmāṭra. Pūjā (worship) is nothing without Chinmāṭra. Meditation, truth, sheaths and others, the (eight) vasus, silence, non-silence, and indifference to objects

—are nothing without Chinmāṭra. Everything is from Chinmāṭra. Whatever is seen and however seen—it is Chinmāṭra so far. Whatever exists and however distant, is Chinmāṭra. Whatever elements exist, whatever is perceived, and whatever is veḍānṭa—all these are Chinmāṭra. Without Chinmāṭra, there is no motion, no Moksha and no goal aimed at. Everything is Chinmāṭra. Brahman that is the partless non-dual essence is known to be nothing but Chinmāṭra. Thou, O Lord, art the partless non-dual essence (stated) in the books, in me, in Thee, and in the ruler. He who thus perceives 'I' as of one homogeneity (pervading everywhere) will at once be emancipated through this spiritual wisdom. He is his own Guru with this profound spiritual wisdom. Thus ends the second chapter of Ṭejobinḍu."

Chapter III

The Kumāra addressed his father (again): "Please explain to me the realisation of Āṭmā." To which the great S'iva said: "I am of the nature of the Parabrahman. I am the supreme bliss. I am solely of the nature of divine wisdom. I am the sole supreme, the sole quiescence, the sole Chinmaya, the sole unconditioned, the sole permanent and the sole Saṭṭva. I am the 'I' that has given up 'I'. I am one that is without anything. I am full of Chiḍākās'. I am the sole fourth one. I am the sole one above the fourth (state of ṭurya). I am of the nature of (pure) consciousness. I am ever of the nature of the bliss-consciousness. I am of the nature of the non-dual. I am ever of a pure nature, solely of the nature of divine wisdom, of the nature of happiness, without fancies, desires or diseases, of the nature of bliss, without changes or differentiations, and of the nature of the eternal one essence and Chinmāṭra. My real nature is indescribable, of endless bliss, the bliss above Saṭ and Chiṭ and the interior of the interior. I am beyond reach of manas and speech. I am of the nature of Āṭmic bliss, true bliss and one who plays with (my) Āṭmā. I am Āṭmā and Saḍās'iva. My nature is Āṭmic spiritual effulgence. I am the essence of the jyoṭis of Āṭmā. I am without beginning, middle, or end. I am like the sky. I am solely Saṭ, Ānanḍa, and Chiṭ which is unconditioned and pure. I am the Sachchiḍānanḍa that is eternal, enlightened and pure. I am ever of the nature of the eternal S'esha (serpent-time). I am ever beyond all. My nature is beyond form. My form is supreme ākās'. My nature is of the bliss of earth. I am ever without speech. My nature is the all-seat (foundation of all). I am ever replete with consciousness, without the attachment of body, without thought, without the modifications of chiṭṭa, the sole essence of Chiḍāṭma, beyond the visibility of all and of the form of vision. My nature is ever full. I am ever fully contented, the all, and Brahman, and the very consciousness; I am 'I'. My nature is of the earth. I am the great Āṭmā and the supreme of the supreme; I appear sometimes as different from myself; sometimes as possessing a body, sometimes as a pupil and sometimes as the basis of the worlds. I am beyond the three periods of time, am worshipped by the Veḍas, am determined by the sciences and am fixed in the chiṭṭa. There is nothing left out by me, neither the earth nor any other objects here. Know that there is nothing which is out of myself. I am Brahmā, a Siḍḍha, the eternally pure, non-dual one, Brahman, without old age or death. I shine by myself; I am my own Āṭmā, my own goal, enjoy myself, play in myself, have my own spiritual effulgence, am my own greatness, and am used to play in my own Āṭmā, look on my own Āṭmā and am in myself happily seated. I have my own Āṭmā as the residue, stay in my own consciousness, and play happily in the kingdom of my own Āṭmā. Sitting on the real throne of my own Āṭmā, I think of nothing else but my own Āṭmā. I am Chiḍrūpa alone, Brahman alone, Sachchiḍānanḍa, the secondless, the one replete with bliss and the sole Brahman and ever without anything, have the bliss of my own Āṭmā, the unconditioned bliss, and am always Āṭma-Ākās'. I alone am in the heart like Chiḍāḍiṭya (the consciousness-sun). I am content in my own Āṭmā, have no form, or no decay, am without the number one, have the nature of an unconditionod and emancipated one, and I am subtler than ākās'; I am without the existence of beginning or end, of the nature of the all-illuminating, the bliss greater than the great, of the sole nature of Saṭ, of the nature of pure Moksha, of the nature of truth and bliss, full of spiritual wisdom and bliss, of the nature of wisdom alone, and of the nature of Sachchiḍānanḍa. Āll this is Brahman alone. There is none other than Brahman and that is 'I'.

"I am Brahman that is Saṭ, and bliss, and the ancient. The word 'thou' and the word 'that' are not different from me. I am of the nature of consciousness. I am alone the great S'iva. I am beyond the nature of existence. I am of the nature of happiness. Ās there is nothing that can witness me, I am without the state of witness. Being purely of the nature of Brahman, I am the eternal Āṭmā. I alone am the Āḍis'esha (the primeval S'esha).[1] I alone am the S'esha. I am without name and form, of the nature of bliss, of the nature of being unperceivable by the senses, and of the nature of all beings; I have neither bondage nor salvation. I am of the form of eternal bliss. I am the primeval consciousness alone, the partless and non-dual essence, beyond reach of speech and mind, of the nature of bliss everywhere, of the nature of fullness everywhere, of the nature of earthly bliss, of the nature of contentment everywhere, the supreme nectary essence, and the one and secondless Saṭ, (*viz.*,) Brahman. There is no doubt of it. I am of the nature of all-void. I am the one that is given out by the Veḍas. I am of the nature of the emancipated and emancipation, of Nirvāṇic bliss, of truth and wisdom, of Saṭ alone and bliss, of the one beyond the fourth, of one without fancy, and ever of the nature of Āja (the unborn). I am without passion or faults. I am the pure, the enlightened, the eternal, the all-pervading and of the nature of the significance of Om, of the spotless, and of Chiṭ. I am neither existing nor non-existing. I am not of the nature of anything. I am of the nature of the actionless. I am without parts. I have no semblance, no manas, no sense, no buḍḍhi, no change, none of the three bodies, neither the waking, dreaming, or dreamless sleeping states. I am neither of the nature of the three pains nor of the three desires. I have neither

[1] Sesha, meaning remainder is the serpent representing time.

s'ravaṇa nor manana in Chiḍāṭma in order to attain salvation. There is nothing like me or unlike me. There is nothing within me. I have none of the three bodies.

"The nature of manas is unreal, the nature of buḍḍhi is unreal, the nature of aham (the 'I') is unreal; but I am the unconditioned, the permanent and the unborn. The three bodies are unreal, the three periods of time are unreal, the three guṇas are unreal, but I am of the nature of the Real and the pure. That which is heard is unreal, all the Veḍas are unreal, the S'āsṭras are unreal, but I am the Real and of the nature of Chiṭ. The Mūrṭis (Brahmā, Vishṇu, and Ruḍra having limitation) are unreal, all the creation is unreal, all the ṭaṭṭvas are unreal, but know that I am the great S'aḍās'iva. The master and the disciple are unreal, the manṭra of the Guru is unreal, that which is seen is unreal, but know me to be the Real. Whatever is thought of is unreal, whatever is lawful is unreal, whatever is beneficial is unreal, but know me to be the Real. Know the Purusha (ego) to be unreal, know the enjoyments to be unreal, know things seen and heard are unreal as also the one woven warp-wise and woof-wise, *viz.*, this universe; cause and non-cause are unreal, things lost or obtained are unreal. Pains and happiness are unreal, all and non-all are unreal, gain and loss are unreal, victory and defeat are unreal. All the sound, all the touch, all the forms, all the taste, all the smell, and all ajñāna are unreal. Everything is always unreal—the mundane existence is unreal—all the guṇas are unreal. I am of the nature of Saṭ.

"One should cognize his own Āṭmā alone. One should always practise the manṭra of his Āṭmā. The manṭra (Ahambrahmāsmi) 'I am Brahman' removes all the sins of sight, destroys all other manṭras, destroys all the sins of body and birth, the noose of Yama, the pains of duality, the thought of difference, the pains of thought, the disease of buḍḍhi, the bondage of chiṭṭa, all diseases, all griefs and passions instantaneously, the power of anger, the modifications of chiṭṭa, saṅkalpa, crores of sins, all actions and the ajñāna of Āṭmā. The manṭra 'I am Brahman' gives indescribable bliss, gives the state of ajada (the non-inertness or the undecaying) and kills the demon of non-Āṭmā. The thunderbolt 'I am Brahman' clears all the hill of not-Āṭmā. The wheel 'I am Brahman' destroys the asuras of not-Āṭmā. The manṭra 'I am Brahman' will relieve all (persons). The manṭra 'I am Brahman' gives spiritual wisdom and bliss. There are seven crores of great manṭras and there are vraṭas (vows) of (or yielding) hundred crores of births. Having given up all other manṭras, one should ever practise this manṭra. He obtains at once salvation, and there is not even a particle of doubt about it. Thus ends the third chapter of the Ṭejobinḍu-Upanishaḍ."

Chapter IV

The Kumāra asked the great Lord: "Please explain to me the nature of Jīvanmukṭi (embodied salvation) and viḍehamukṭi (disembodied salvation)." To which the great S'iva replied: "I am Chiḍāṭmā. I am Para-Āṭmā. I am the Nirguṇa, greater than the great. One who will simply stay in Āṭmā is called a Jīvanmukṭa. He who realises: 'I am beyond the three bodies, I am the pure consciousness and I am Brahman,' is said to be a Jīvanmukṭa. He is said to be a Jīvanmukṭa, who realises: 'I am of the nature of the blissful and of the supreme bliss, and I have neither body nor any other thing except the certitude "I am Brahman" only'. He is said to be a Jīvanmukṭa who has not at all got the 'I' in myself, but who stays in Chinmāṭra (absolute consciousness) alone, whose interior is consciousness alone, who is only of the nature of Chinmāṭra, whose Āṭmā is of the nature of the all-full, who has Āṭmā left over in all, who is devoted to bliss, who is undifferentiated, who is all-full of the nature of consciousness, whose Āṭmā is of the nature of pure consciousness, who has given up all affinities (for objects), who has unconditioned bliss, whose Āṭmā is tranquil, who has got no other thought (than Itself), and who is devoid of the thought of the existence of anything. He is said to be a Jīvanmukṭa who realises: 'I have no chiṭṭa, no buḍḍhi, no ahaṅkāra, no sense, no body at any time, no prāṇas, no Māyā, no passion and no anger, I am the great, I have nothing of these objects or of the world, and I have no sin, no characteristics, no eye, no manas, no ear, no nose, no tongue, no hand, no waking, no dreaming, or causal state in the least or the fourth state.' He is said to be a Jīvanmukṭa, who realises: 'All this is not mine, I have no time, no space, no object, no thought, no snāna (bathing), no sanḍhyās (junction-period ceremonies), no deity, no place, no sacred places, no worship, no spiritual wisdom, no seat, no relative, no birth, no speech, no wealth, no virtue, no vice, no duty, no auspiciousness, no Jīva, not even the three worlds, no salvation, no duality, no Veḍas, no mandatory rules, no proximity, no distance, no knowledge, no secrecy, no Guru, no disciple, no diminution, no excess, no Brahmā, no Vishṇu, no Ruḍra, no moon, no earth, no water, no vāyu, no ākās', no agni, no clan, no lakshya (object aimed at), no mundane existence, no meditator, no object of meditation, no manas, no cold, no heat, no thirst, no hunger, no friend, no foe, no illusion, no victory, no past, present, or future,. no quarters, nothing to be said or heard in the least, nothing to be gone (or attained) to, nothing to be contemplated, enjoyed or remembered, no enjoyment, no desire, no yoga, no absorption, no garrulity, no quietude, no bondage, no love, no joy, no instant joy, no hugeness, no smallness, neither length nor shortness, neither increase nor decrease, neither aḍhyāropa (illusory attribution) nor apavāḍa (withdrawal of that conception) no oneness, no manyness, no blindness, no dullness, no skill, no flesh, no blood, no lymph, no skin, no marrow, no bone, no skin, none of the seven ḍhāṭus, no whiteness, no redness, no blueness, no heat, no gain, neither importance nor non-importance, no delusion, no perseverance, no mystery, no race, nothing to be abandoned or received, nothing to be laughed at, no policy, no religious vow, no fault, no bewailments, no happiness, neither knower nor knowledge nor the knowable, no Self, nothing belonging to you or to me, neither you nor I, and neither old age nor youth nor manhood; but I am certainly Brahman. "I am certainly Brahman. I am Chiṭ, I am Chiṭ".' He is said to be a Jivanmukṭa who cognizes: 'I am Brahman alone, I am Chiṭ alone, I am the supreme.' No doubt need be entertained about this; 'I am Hamsa itself, I remain of my own will, I can see myself through myself, I reign happy in the kingdom of Āṭmā and enjoy in myself the bliss of my own Āṭmā.' He is a Jīvanmukṭa who is himself, the foremost and the one undaunted person who is himself the lord and rests in his own Self.

"He is a Viḍehamukṭa who has become Brahman, whose Āṭmā has attained quiescence, who is of the nature of Brāhmic bliss, who is happy, who is of a pure nature, and who is a great mouni (observer of silence). He is a Viḍehamukṭa who remains in Chinmāṭra alone without (even) thinking thus: 'I am all Āṭma, the Āṭma that is equal (or the same) in all, the pure, without one, the non-dual, the all, the self only, the birthless and the deathless—I am myself the undecaying Āṭma that is the object aimed at, the sporting, the silent, the blissful, the beloved and the bondless salvation—I am Brahman alone—I am Chiṭ alone.' He is a Viḍehamukṭa who having abandoned the thought: 'I alone am the Brahman' is filled with bliss. He is a Viḍehamukṭa who having given up the certainty of the existence or non-existence of all objects is pure Chiḍānanḍa (the consciousness-bliss), who having abandoned (the thought): 'I am Brahman' (or) 'I am not Brahman' does not mingle his Āṭmā with anything, anywhere or at any time, who is ever silent with the silence of Saṭya, who does nothing, who has gone beyond guṇas, whose Āṭmā has become the All, the great, and the purifier of the elements, who does not cognize the change of time, matter, place, himself or other differences, who does not see (the difference of) 'I,' 'thou,' 'this' or 'that,' who being of the nature of time is yet without it, whose Āṭmā is void, subtle and universal, but yet without (them), whose Āṭmā is divine and yet without Ḍevas, whose Āṭmā is measurable and yet without measure, whose Āṭmā is without inertness and within every one, whose Āṭmā is devoid of any saṅkalpa, who thinks always: 'I am Chinmāṭra, I am simply Paramāṭman, I am only of the nature of spiritual wisdom, I am only of the nature of Saṭ, I am afraid of nothing in this world,' and who is without the conception of Ḍevas, Veḍas and sciences, 'All this is consciousness, etc.,' and regards all as void. He is a Viḍehamukṭa who has realised himself to be Chaiṭanya alone, who is remaining at ease in the pleasure-garden of his own Āṭmā, whose Āṭmā is of an illimitable nature, who is without the conception of the small and the great, and who is the fourth of the fourth state and the supreme bliss. He is a Viḍehamukṭa whose Āṭmā is nameless and formless, who is the great spiritual wisdom of the nature of bliss, and of the nature of the state beyond ṭurya, who is neither auspicious nor inauspicious, who has yoga as his Āṭmā, whose Āṭmā is associated with yoga, who is free from bondage or freedom, without guṇa or non-guṇa, without space, time, etc., without the witnessable and the witness, without the small or the great, and without the cognition of the universe or even the cognition of the nature of Brahman, but who finds his spiritual effulgence in his own nature, who finds bliss in himself, whose bliss is beyond the scope of words and mind, and whose thought is beyond the beyond. He is said to be a Viḍehamukṭa who has gone beyond (or mastered quite) the modifications of chiṭṭa, who illumines such modifications, and whose Āṭmā is without any modifications at all. In that case, he is neither embodied nor disembodied. If such a thought is entertained (even), for a moment, then he is surrounded (in thought) by all. He is a Viḍehamukṭa whose external Āṭmā invisible to others is the supreme bliss aiming at the highest veḍānṭa, who drinks of the juice of the nectar of Brahman, who has the nectar of Brahman as medicine, who is devoted to the juice of the nectar of Brahman, who is immersed in that juice,who has the beneficent worship of the Brāhmic bliss, who is not satiated with the juice of the nectar of Brahman, who realises Brāhmic bliss, who cognizes the S'iva bliss in Brāhmic bliss, who has the effulgence of the essence of Brāhmic bliss, who has become one with it, who lives in the household of Brāhmic bliss, has mounted the car of Brāhmic bliss, who has an imponderable Chiṭ being one with it, who is supporting (all), being full of it, who associates with me having it, who stays in Āṭmā having that bliss and who thinks: 'All this is of the nature of Āṭmā, there is nothing else beside Āṭmā, all is Āṭmā, I am Āṭmā, the great Āṭmā, the supreme Āṭmā, and Āṭmā of the form of bliss.' He who thinks: 'My nature is full, I am the great Āṭmā, I am the all-contented and the permanent Āṭmā. I am the Āṭmā pervading the heart of all, which is not stained by anything, but which has no Āṭmā; I am the Āṭmā whose nature is changeless, I am the quiescent Āṭmā; and I am the many Āṭmā.' He who does not think this is Jīvāṭmā and that is Paramāṭmā, whose Āṭmā is of the nature of the emancipated and the non-emancipated, but without emancipation or bondage, whose Āṭmā is of the nature of the dual and the non-dual one, but without duality and non-duality; whose Āṭmā is of the nature of the All and the non-All, but without them; whose Āṭmā is of the nature of the happiness arising from objects obtained and enjoyed, but without it; and who is devoid of any saṅkalpa—such a man is a Viḍehamukṭa. He whose Āṭmā is partless, stainless, enlightened, Purusha, without bliss, etc., of the nature of nectar, of the nature of the three periods of time, but without them; whose Āṭmā is entire and non-measurable, being subject to proof though without proof; whose Āṭmā is the eternal and the witness, but without eternality and witness; whose Āṭmā is of the nature of the secondless, who is the self-shining one without a second, whose Āṭmā cannot be measured by viḍyā and aviḍyā but without them; whose Āṭmā is without conditionedness or unconditionedness, who is without this or the higher worlds, whose Āṭmā is without the six things beginning with s'ama, who is without the qualifications of the aspirant after salvation, whose Āṭmā is without gross, subtle, causal, and the fourth bodies, and without the anna, prāṇa, manas, and vijñāna sheaths; whose Āṭmā is of the nature of ānanḍa (bliss) sheath, but without five sheaths; whose Āṭmā is of the nature of nirvikalpa, is devoid of saṅkalpa, without the characteristics of the visible or the audible, and of the nature of void, owing to unceasing samāḍhi, who is without beginning, middle, or end; whose Āṭmā is devoid of the word Prajñāna, who is without the idea 'I am Brahman,' whose Āṭmā is devoid (of the thought) of 'thou art', who is without the thought 'this is Āṭmā', whose Āṭmā is devoid of that which is described by Om, who is above the reach of any speech or the three states, and is the indestructible and the Chiḍāṭmā, whose Āṭmā is not the one which can be known by Āṭmā and whose Āṭmā has neither light nor darkness. Such a personage is a Viḍehamukṭa. Look only upon Āṭmā; know It as your own. Enjoy your Āṭmā yourself, and stay in peace. O six-faced one, be content in your own Āṭmā, be wandering in your own Āṭmā, and be enjoying your own Āṭmā. Then you will attain Viḍehamukṭi."

CHAPTER V

The Sage named Niḍāgha addressed the venerable Ṛbhu: "O Lord please explain to me the discrimination of Āṭmā from non-Āṭmā." The Sage replied thus:

"The furthest limit of all vāk (speech) is Brahman; the furthest limit to all thoughts is the Guru.[1] That which is of the nature of all causes and effects but yet without them, that which is without saṅkalpa, of the nature of all bliss and the auspicious, that which is the great one of the nature of bliss, that which illuminates all luminaries and that which is full of the bliss of nāḍa (spiritual sound), without any enjoyment and contemplation and beyond nāḍas and kalās (parts)—that is Āṭmā, that is the 'I', the indestructible. Being devoid of all the difference of Āṭmā and non-Āṭmā, of heterogeneity and homogeneity, and of quiescence and non-quiescence—that is the one Jyoṭis at the end of nāḍa. Being remote from the conception of Mahā-vakyārṭha (*i. e.*, the meaning of Maha-vākyas) as well of 'I am Brahman,' being devoid of or without the conception of the word and the meaning, and being devoid of the conception of the destructible and indestructible—that is the one Jyoṭis at the end of nāḍa. Being without the conception 'I am the partless non-dual essence' or 'I am the blissful,' and being of the nature of the one beyond all—that is one Jyoṭis at the end of nāḍa. He who is devoid of the significance of Āṭmā (*viz.*, motion) and devoid of Sachchiḍānanḍa—he is alone Āṭmā, the eternal. He who is undefinable and unreachable by the words of the Veḍas, who has neither externals nor internals, and whose symbol is either the universe or Brahman—he is undoubtedly Āṭmā. He who has no body, nor

[1] Herein is given the hint as to the difference of functions between an Ishta-ḍevaṭā and a Guru.

is a Jīva made up of the elements and their compounds, who has neither form nor name, neither the enjoyable nor the enjoyer, neither Saṭ nor asaṭ, neither preservation nor regeneration, neither guṇa nor non-guṇa—that is undoubtedly my Āṭmā. He who has neither the described nor description, neither s'ravaṇa nor manana, neither Guru nor disciple, neither the world of the Ḍevas nor the Ḍevas nor Āsuras, neither duty nor non-duty, neither the immaculate nor non-immaculate, neither time nor non-time, neither certainty nor doubt, neither manṭra nor non-manṭra, neither science nor non-science, neither the seer nor the sight which is subtle, nor the nectar of time—that is Āṭmā. Rest assured that not-Āṭmā is a misnomer. There is no manas as not-Āṭmā. There is no world as not-Āṭmā. Owing to the absence of all saṅkalpas and to the giving up of all actions, Brahman alone remains, and there is no not-Āṭmā. Being devoid of the three bodies, the three periods of time, the three guṇas of Jīva, the three pains and the three worlds, and following the saying 'All is Brahman,' know that there is nothing to be known through the absence of chiṭṭa; there is no old age through the absence of body; no motion through the absence of legs; no action through the absence of hands; no death through the absence of creatures; no happiness through the absence of buḍḍhi; no virtue, no purity, no fear, no repetition of manṭras, no Guru nor disciple. There is no second in the absence of one. Where there is not the second, there is not the first. Where there is truth alone, there is no non-truth possible; where there is non-truth alone, there is no truth possible. If you regard a thing auspicious as inauspicious, then auspiciousness is desired (as separate) from inauspiciousness. If you regard fear as non-fear, then fear will arise out of non-fear. If bondage should become emancipation, then in the absence of bondage will be no emancipation. If birth should imply death, then in the absence of birth, there is no death. If 'thou' should imply 'I,' then in the absence of 'thou' there is no 'I'. If 'this' should be 'that,' 'this' does not exist in the absence of 'that'. If being should imply non-being, then non-being will imply being. If an effect implies a cause, then in the absence of effect, there is no cause. If duality implies non-duality, then in the absence of duality, there is no non-duality. If there should be the seen, then there is the eye (or sight); in the absence of the seen, there is no eye. In the absence of the interior, there is no exterior. If there should be fullness, then non-fullness is possible. Therefore (all) this exists nowhere. Neither you nor I, nor this nor these exist. There exists no (object of) comparison in the true one. There is no simile in the unborn. There is (in it) no mind to think. I am the supreme Brahman. This world is Brahman only. Thou and I are Brahman only. I am Chinmāṭra simply, and there is no not-Āṭmā. Rest assured of it. This universe is not (really at all). This universe is not (really) at all. It was nowhere produced and stays nowhere. Some say that chiṭṭa is the universe. Not at all. It exists not. Neither the universe nor chiṭṭa nor ahaṅkāra nor Jīva exists (really). Neither the creation of Māyā nor Māyā itself exists (really). Fear does not (really) exist. Actor, action, hearing, thinking, the two samāḍhis, the measurer, the measure, ajñāna and aviveka—none of these exists (truly) anywhere. Therefore the four moving[1] considerations and the three kinds of relationship exist not. There is no Gaṅgā, no Gayā, no Seṭu (bridge), no elements or anything else, no earth, water, fire, vāyu, and ākās' anywhere, no Ḍevas, no guardians of the four quarters, no Veḍas, no Guru, no distance, no proximity, no time, no middle, no non-duality, no truth, no untruth, no bondage, no emancipation, no Saṭ, no asaṭ, no happiness, etc., no class, no motion, no caste, and no worldly business. All is Brahman only and nothing else—all is Brahman only and nothing else. There exists then nothing (or statement) as that 'consciousness alone is'; there is (then) no saying such as 'Chiṭ is I'. The statement 'I am Brahman' does not exist (then); nor does exist (then) the statement: 'I am the eternally pure'. Whatever is uttered by the mouth, whatever is thought by manas, whatever is determined by buḍḍhi, whatever is cognized by chiṭṭa—all these do not exist. There is no Yogin or

[1] The four moving considerations (of veḍānṭa) are subject (Brahman), object, relationship, and the qualified person.

yoga then. All are and are not. Neither day nor night, neither bathing nor contemplating, neither delusion nor non-delusion—all these do not exist then. Know that is no not-Āṭmā.

"The Veḍas, Sciences, Purāṇas, effect and cause, Īs'vara and the world and the elements and mankind—all these are unreal. There is no doubt of it. Bondage, salvation, happiness, relatives, meditation, chiṭṭa, the Ḍevas, the demons, the secondary and the primary, the high and the low—all these are unreal. There is no doubt of it. Whatever is uttered by the mouth, whatever is willed by saṅkalpa, whatever is thought by manas—all these are unreal. Whatever is determined by the buḍḍhi, whatever is cognized by chiṭṭa, whatever is discussed by the religious books, whatever is seen by the eye and heard by the ears, and whatever exists as Saṭ, as also the ear, the eye, and the limbs—all these are unreal. Whatever is described as such and such, whatever is thought as so-and-so, all the existing thoughts such as 'thou art I', 'that is this,' and 'He is I,' and whatever happens in moksha, as also all saṅkalpas, delusion, illusory attribution, mysteries and all the diversities of enjoyment and sin—all these do not exist. So is also not-Āṭmā. Mine and thine, my and thy, for me and for thee, by me and by thee—all these are unreal. (The statement) that Vishṇu is the preserver, Brahmā is the creator, Ruḍra is the destroyer—know that these undoubtedly are false. Bathing, utterings of manṭras, japas (religious austerities) homa (sacrifice), study of the Veḍas, worship of the Ḍevas, manṭra, ṭanṭra, association with the good, the unfolding of the faults of guṇas, the working of the internal organ, the result of aviḍyā, and the many crores of mundane eggs—all these are unreal. Whatever is spoken of as true according to the verdict of all teachers, whatever is seen in this world and whatever exists—all these are unreal. Whatever is uttered by words, whatever is ascertained, spoken, enjoyed, given or done by anyone, whatever action is done, good or bad, whatever is done as truth—know all these to be unreal. Thou alone art the transcendental Āṭmā and the supreme Guru of the form of ākās', which is devoid of fitness (for it) and of the nature of all creatures.

Thou art Brahman ; thou art time ; and thou art Brahman, that is ever and imponderable. Thou art everywhere, of all forms, and full of consciousness. Thou art the truth. Thou art one that has mastered the siḍḍhis, and thou art the ancient, the emancipated, emancipation, the nectar of bliss, the God, the quiescent, the diseaseless, Brahman the full, and greater than the great. Thou art impartial, Saṭ and the ancient knowledge, recognised by the words 'Truth, etc'. Thou art devoid of all parts. Thou art the ever-existing—thou appearest as Brahmā, Ruḍra, Inḍra, etc.—thou art above the illusion of the universe—thou shinest in all elements—thou art without saṅkalpa in all—thou art known by means of the underlying meaning of all scriptures; thou art ever content and ever happily seated (in thyself) ; thou art without motion, etc. In all things, thou art without any characteristics ; in all things thou art contemplated by Vishṇu and other Ḍevas at all times ; thou hast the nature of Chiṭ, thou art Chinmāṭrā unchecked, thou stayest in Āṭmā itself, thou art void of everything and without guṇas, thou art bliss, the great, the one secondless, the state of Saṭ and asaṭ, the knower, the known, the seer, the nature of Sachchidānanḍa, the lord of Ḍevas, the all-pervading, the deathless, the moving, the motionless, the all and the non-all with quiescence and non-quiescence, Saṭ alone, Saṭ commonly (found in all), of the form of Niṭya-Siḍḍha (the unconditioned developed one), and yet devoid of all siḍḍhis. There is not an atom which thou dost not penetrate; but yet thou art without it. Thou art devoid of existence and non-existence as also the aim and object aimed at. Thou art changeless, decayless, beyond all nāḍas, without kāla or kāshta (divisions of time) and without Brahmā, Vishṇu, and S'iva. Thou lookest into the nature of each and art above the nature of each. Thou art immersed in the bliss of Self. Thou art the monarch of the kingdom of Self, and yet without the conception of Self. Thou art of the nature of fullness and incompleteness. There is nothing that thou seest which is not in thyself. Thou dost not stir out of thy nature. Thou actest according to the nature of each. Thou art nothing but the nature of each. Have no doubt 'thou art I'.

13

"This universe and everything in it, whether the seer or the seen, resembles the horns of a hare (or are illusory). Earth, water, agni, vāyu, ākās', manas, buḍḍhi, ahaṅkāra, ṭejas, the worlds and the sphere of the universe, destruction, birth, truth, virtue, vice, gain, desires, passion, anger, greed, the object of meditation, wisdom, guru, disciple, limitation, the beginning and end, auspiciousness, the past, present, and future, the aim and the object of aim, mental restraint, inquiry, contentment, enjoyer, enjoyment, etc., the eight parts of yoga, yama, etc., the going and coming (of life), the beginning, middle and end, that which can be taken and rejected, Hari, S'iva, the organs, manas, the three states, the twenty-four ṭaṭṭvas, the four means, one of the same class or different classes, Bhūḥ and other worlds, all the castes and orders of life with the rules laid down for each, manṭras and ṭanṭras, science and nescience, all the Veḍas, the inert and the non-inert, bondage and salvation, spiritual wisdom and non-wisdom, the enlightened and the non-enlightened, duality and non-duality, the conclusion of all Veḍānṭas and S'āsṭras, the theory of the existence of all souls and that of one soul only, whatever is thought by chiṭṭa, whatever is willed by saṅkalpa, whatever is determined by buḍḍhi, whatever one hears and sees, whatever the guru instructs, whatever is sensed by all the organs, whatever is discussed in mīmāmsā, whatever is ascertained by nyāya (philosophy) and by the great ones who have reached the other side of the Veḍas, the saying 'S'iva destroys the world, Vishṇu protects it, and Brahmā creates it', whatever is found in the purāṇas, whatever is ascertained by the Veḍas, and is the signification of all the Vedas—all these resemble the horns of a hare. The conception 'I am the body' is spoken of as the internal organ; the conception 'I am the body' is spoken of as the great mundane existence; the conception 'I am the body' constitutes the whole universe. The conception 'I am the body' is spoken of as the knot of the heart, as non-wisdom, as the state of asaṭ, as nescience, as the dual, as the true Jīva and as with parts, is certainly the great sin, and is the disease generated by the fault of thirst after desires. That which is saṅkalpa, the three pains, passion, anger, bondage, all the miseries, all the faults and the various forms of time—know these to be the result of manas. Manas alone is the whole world, the ever-deluding, the mundane existence, the three worlds, the great pains, the old age and others, death and the great sin, the saṅkalpa, the Jīva, the chiṭṭa, the ahaṅkāra, the bondage, the internal organ and earth, water, agni, vāyū, and ākās'. Sound, touch, form, taste, and odour, the five sheaths, the waking, the dreaming, and dreamless sleeping states, the guardians of the eight quarters, Vasus, Ruḍras, Ādiṭyas, the seen, the inert, the pairs and non-wisdom—all these are the products of manas. Rest assured that there is no reality in all that is saṅkalpa. The whole world, the guru, disciple, etc., do not exist, yea, do not exist. Thus ends the fifth chapter of this Upanishaḍ."

CHAPTER VI

Ṛbhu continued again: "Know everything as Sachchinmaya (full of Saṭ and consciousness). It pervades everything. Sachchiḍānanḍa is non-dual, decayless, alone and other than all. It is 'I'. It alone is ākās' and 'thou'. It is I. There is (in it) no manas, no buḍḍhi, no ahaṅkāra, no chiṭṭa, or the collection of these—neither 'thou' nor I, nor anything else nor everything. Brahman alone is. Sentence, words, Veḍas, letters, beginning, middle, or end, truth, law, pleasure, pain, existence, māyā, prakṛṭi, body, face, nose, tongue, palate, teeth, lip, forehead, expiration and inspiration, sweat, bone, blood, urine, distance, proximity, limb, belly, crown, the movement of hands and feet, S'āsṭras, command, the knower, the known, and the knowledge, the waking, dreaming and dreamless sleeping and the fourth state—all these do not belong to me. Everything is Sachchinmaya interwoven. No attributes pertaining to body, elements and spirit, no root, no vision, no Ṭaijasa, no Prājña, no Virāt, no Sūṭrāṭma, no Īs'vara, and no going or coming, neither gain nor loss, neither the acceptable nor the rejectable, nor the censurable, neither the pure nor the impure, neither the stout nor the lean, no sorrow, time, space, speech, all, fear, duality, tree, grass or mountain, no meditation, no siḍḍhi of yoga, no Brāhmaṇa, Kshaṭṭriya or Vais'ya, no bird or beast, or limb, no greed, delusion, pride, malice, passion, anger or others, no woman, S'ūḍra, castes or others, nothing that is eatable or enjoyable, no increase or decrease, no belief in the Veḍas, no speech, no worldliness or unworldliness, no transaction, no folly, no measure or measured, no enjoyment or enjoyed, no friends, son, etc., father, mother, or sister, no birth or death, no growth, body or 'I', no emptiness or fullness, no internal organs or mundane existence, no night, no day, no Brahmā, Vishṇu, or S'iva, no week, fortnight, month, or year, no unsteadiness, no Brahmaloka, Vaikuṇtha, Kailāsa and others, no Swarga, Inḍra, Agniloka, Āgni, Yamaloka, Yama, vāyuloka, guardians of the world, three worlds—Bhūḥ, Bhuvaḥ, Svaḥ, Pāṭāla or surface of earth, no science, nescience, māyā, prakṛṭi, inertness, permanency, transience, destruction, movement, running, object of meditation, bathing, manṭra or object, no adorable object, anointment or sipping with water, no flower, fruit, sandal, light waved before god, praise, prostrations or circumambulation, no entreaty, conception of separateness even, oblation of food, offered food, sacrifice, actions, abuse, praise, Gāyaṭrī and sanḍhi (period of junction, such as twilight, etc.), no mental state, calamity, evil desire, bad soul, chaṇḍāla (low caste person) pulkasa, unbearableness, unspeakableness, kirāṭa (hunter), kaiṭava (demon), partiality, partisanship, ornament, chief, or pride, no manyness, no oneness, durability, triad, tetrad, greatness, smallness, fullness, or delusion, no kaiṭava, Benares, ṭapas, clan, family, sūṭra, greatness, poverty, girl, old woman or widow, no pollution, birth, introvision or illusion, no sacred sentences, identity, or the siḍḍhis, aṇimā, etc.

"Everything being consciousness alone, there is no fault in anything. Everything being of the nature of Saṭ alone, is Sachchiḍānanḍa only. Brahman alone is everything and there is nothing else. So 'That' is 'I', 'That' is 'I'. 'That' alone is 'I'. 'That' alone is 'I'. 'That' alone is 'I'. The eternal Brahman alone is 'I'. I am Brahman alone without being subject to mundane existence. I am Brahman alone without any manas, any buḍḍhi, organs or body. I am Brahman alone not perceivable. I am Brahman alone and not Jīva. I am Brahman alone and not liable to change. I am Brahman alone and not inert. I am Brahman alone and have no death. I am Brahman alone and have no prāṇas. I am Brahman alone and greater than the great. This is Brahman. Great is Brahman. Truth is Brahman. It is all-pervading. Time is Brahman. Kāla is Brahman. Happiness is Brahman. It is self-shining. One is Brahman. Two is Brahman. Delusion is Brahman. S'ama and others are Brahman. Badness is Brahman. Goodness is Brahman. It is of the form of restraint, quiescence, the all-pervading and the all-powerful. The Loka (world) is Brahman. Guru is Brahman. Disciple is Brahman. It is Saḍās'iva. (That which) is before is Brahman. (That which will be) hereafter is Brahman. Purity is Brahman. Āuspiciousness and inauspiciousness are Brahman. Jīva always is Brahman. I am Sachchiḍānanḍa. Āll are of the nature of Brahman. The universe is said to be of the nature of Brahman. Brahman is itself. There is no doubt of it. There is nothing out of itself. The letter Om of the form of consciousness is Brahman alone. Everything is itself. I alone am the whole universe and the highest seat, have crossed the guṇas and am greater than the great, the supreme Brahman, Guru of Gurus, the support of all and the bliss of bliss. There is no universe besides Āṭmā. The universe is of the nature of Āṭmā. There is nowhere (or no place) without Āṭmā. There is not even grass different from Āṭmā. There is not husk different from Brahman. The whole universe is of the nature of Āṭmā. Āll this is of the nature of Brahman. Asaṭ is not of the nature of Brahman. There is not a grass different from Brahman. There is not a seat different from Brahman; there is not a Guru different from Brahman; there is not a body different from Brahman. There is nothing different from Brahman like I-ness or you-ness. Whatever is seen in this world, whatever is spoken of by the people, whatever is enjoyed everywhere—all these are asaṭ (unreal) only. The differences arising from the actor, action, qualities, likes, taste and gender—all these arise from asaṭ and are (but) pleasurable.

The differences arising from time, objects, actions, success or defeat and whatever else—all these are simply asaṭ. The internal organ is asaṭ. The organs are asaṭ. Ȧll the prāṇas, the collections of all these, the five sheaths, the five deities, the six changes, the six enemies, the six seasons, and the six tastes, are asaṭ. I am Sachchiḍānanḍa. The universe is rootless. I am Ȧṭmā alone, Chiṭ and Ȧnanḍa. The scenes of mundane existence are not different. I am the Truth of the nature of Ȧnanḍa and of the nature of the imponderable Chiṭ. Ȧll this is of the nature of jñāna.

"I am the secondless, having jñāna and bliss. I am of the nature of an illuminator of all things. I am of the nature of all non-being. I alone shine always. Therefore how can I with such a nature become asaṭ? That which is called 'thou' is the great Brahman of the nature of the bliss of consciousness and of the nature of chiṭ having chiḍākās' and chiṭ alone as the great bliss. Ȧṭmā alone is 'I'. Asaṭ is not 'I'. I am Kūtasṭha, the great guru and Sachchiḍānanḍa alone. I am this born universe. No time, no universe, no māyā, no prakṛṭi (in me). I alone am the Hari. Personally, I alone am the Saḍās'iva. I am of the nature of pure consciousness. I am the enjoyer of pure saṭṭva. I am the only essence full of chiṭ. Everything is Brahman and Brahman alone. Everything is Brahman and is chiṭ alone. I am of the nature of the all-latent and the all-witness. I am the supreme Ȧṭmā, the supreme Jyoṭis, the supreme wealth, the supreme goal, the essence of all veḍānṭas, the subject discussed in all the S'āsṭras the nature of yogic bliss, the ocean of the chief bliss, the brightness of all wisdom, of the nature of chief wisdom, the brightness of the fourth state and the non-fourth but devoid of them, the indestructible chiṭ, truth, Vāsuḍeva, the birthless, and the deathless Brahmā, Chiḍākās', the unconditioned, the stainless, the immaculate, the emancipated, the utterly emancipated, the soulless, the formless and of the nature of the non-created universe.

"The universe which is assumed as truth and non-truth does not really exist. Brahman is of the nature of eternal bliss and is even by itself. It is endless, decayless, quiescent and of one nature only. If anything is other than myself, then it is as unreal as the mirage in an oasis. If one should be afraid of the son of a barren woman, or if a powerful elephant be killed by means of the horns of a hare, then the world (really is). If one (person) can quench his thirst by drinking the waters of the mirage, or if one should be killed by the horns of a man, then the universe really is. The universe exists always in the true Ganḍharva city (merely unreal). When the blueness of the sky really exists in it, then the universe really is. When the silver in mother-of-pearl can be used in making an ornament, when a man is bitten by (the conception of) a snake in a rope, when the flaming fire is quenched by means of a golden arrow, when milky food is obtained in the (barren) forest of Vinḍhya (mountains), when cooking can take place by means of the fuel of (wet) plantain trees, when a female (baby) just born begins to cook, when curds resume the state of milk, or when the milk (milked) goes back through the teats of a cow, then will the universe really be. When the dust of the earth shall be produced in the ocean, when the maddened elephant is tied by means of the hair of a tortoise, when (mountain) Meru is shaken by the thread in the stalk of a lotus, when the ocean is bound by its rows of tides, when the fire flames downwards, when flame shall become (really) cold, when the lotus shall grow out of flaming fire, when Inḍranīla (sapphire) arises in the great mountains, when Meru comes and sits in the lotus-eye, when a mountain can become the offspring of a black bee, when Meru shall shake, when a lion is killed by a gnat, when the three worlds can be found in the space of the hollow of an atom, when the fire which burns a straw shall last for a long time, when the objects seen in a dream shall come in the waking state, when the current of a river shall stand still (of itself), when the delivery of a barren woman shall be fruitful, when the crow shall walk like a swan, when the mule shall fight with a lion, when a great ass shall walk like an elephant, when the full moon shall become a sun, when Rāhu (one of the nodes) shall abandon the sun and the moon, when a good crop shall arise out of the waste (burnt) seeds, when the poor shall enjoy the happiness of the rich, when the lions shall be conquered by the bravery of dogs, when the heart of Jñānīs is known by fools, when the ocean is drunk by the dogs without any remainder, when the pure ākās' shall fall upon men, when heaven shall fall on the earth, when the flower in the sky shall emit fragrance, when a forest appearing in pure ākās' shall move, and when reflection shall arise in a glass simply (without mercury or anything else in its back), then the world really is. There is no universe in the womb of Āja (the unborn Brahman)—there is no universe in the womb of Āṭmā. Duality and non-duality, which are but the results of differentiation, are really not. All this is the result of māyā. Therefore, there should be Brahma-Bhāvanā. If misery should arise from the conception of 'I am the body,' then it is certain 'I am Brahman.' The knot of the heart is the wheel of Brahman, which cuts asunder the knot of existence. When doubt arises in one, he should have faith in Brahman. That non-dual Brahman, which is eternal and of the form of unconditioned bliss, is the guard of Āṭmā against the chief of the form of not-Āṭmā. Through instances like the above is established the nature of Brahman. Brahman alone is the all-abode. Ābandon the name even of the universe. Knowing for certain 'I am Brahman,' give up the 'I'. Everything disappears as the flower from the hands of a sleeping person. There is neither body nor karma. Everything is Brahman alone. There are neither objects, nor actions, nor the four states. Everything which has the three characteristics of vijñāna is Brahman alone. Ābandoning all action, contemplate 'I am Brahman,' 'I am Brahman'. There is no doubt of this. I am Brahman of the nature of chiṭ. I am of the nature of Sachchiḍānanḍa.

"This great science of S'aṅkara should never be explained to any ordinary person, to an atheist or to a faithless, ill-behaved or evil-minded person. It should be, after due examination, given to the high-souled ones whose minds are purified with devotion to their gurus. It should be taught for a year and a half. Leaving off thoroughly and entirely the practice recommended by the (other) Upanishaḍs, one should study the Ṭejobinḍu-Upanishaḍ always with delight. By once studying it, he becomes one with Brahman. Thus ends the sixth chapter. Thus ends the Upanishaḍ."

BRAHMOPANISHAḌ[1]

OF

KṚSHṆA-YĀJURVEḌA

[This Upanishaḍ is intended to give a complete and clear idea of the nature of Āṭmā, that has four avasṭhās (states of consciousness) and four seats, for the better consummation of the nirguṇa ḍhyāna.]

Om. S'aunaka Mahās'ala questioned the holy Sage Pippalāḍa of the Aṅgiras goṭra thus: "In this beautiful Brahmapura of body, the fit residence of divine beings, how are (the deities of) vāk, etc., located? How do they function? To whom belongs this power? He to whom this power belongs, what is He?"

Pippalāḍa then having deeply considered, imparted to him the Brahmaviḍyā (divine wisdom), that most excellent of all things. "It is prāṇa (*i.e.*,) Āṭmā. It is Āṭmā that exercises this power. It is the life of all Ḍevas. It is their death and (their) life. Brahman that shines pure, nishkala, resplendent, and all-pervading, in this divine Brahmapura (of body), rules (all). The Jīva (identifying himself with) the inḍriyas, rules them like a spider. The spider throws out from a single thread out of his body a whole web, and draws it into himself by that same thread; so prāṇa, whenever it goes, draws after it the objects of its creation (vāk, etc.). During sushupṭi, (the prāṇa) goes to its seat (Brahman) through the nādis of which is the ḍevaṭā, like an eagle, that making air as the means of communication, reaches his abode. They say, as ḍevaḍaṭṭa, though beaten (during sushupṭi) by a stick, etc., does not move, so also the actor does not suffer or enjoy for the

[1] In this Upanishaḍ, the Southern Indian edition begins later on but the other portions also are given as being fuller.

merits or demerits of religious actions. Just as a child obtains happiness without desiring for it (in play), so also ḍevaḍaṭṭa obtains happiness in sushupṭi. He certainly knows, (being) Param-Jyotis, and the person desiring jyoṭis, enjoys bliss in the contemplation of jyoṭis. Then he comes back to the dream-plane by the same way, like a caterpillar. It remaining on a blade of grass, first puts forward its foot on another blade in front, conveys its body to it, and having got a firm hold of it, then only leaves the former and not before. So this is the jāgraṭa state. As this (ḍevaḍaṭṭa) bears at the same time eight skulls, so this jāgraṭa, the source of Ḍevas and Veḍas, clings to a man like the breasts in a woman. During the jāgraṭa avasṭhā, merit and demerit are postulated of this Ḍeva (power); he is capable of great expansion and is the inner mover. He is khaga (bird), karkata (crab), pushkara (ākās'), prāṇa, pain, parāpara, Āṭmā and Brahman. This deity causes to know. He who knows thus obtains Brahman, the supreme, the support of all things, and the Ksheṭrajña. He obtains Brahman, the supreme, support of all things, and the Ksheṭrajña.

[1] "The Pursuha has four seats—navel, heart, neck, and head. There Brahman with the four feet specially shines. Those feet are jāgraṭa, svapna, sushupṭi, and ṭurya. In jāgraṭa he is Brahmā, in svapna Vishṇu, in sushupṭi Ruḍra, and in ṭurya the supreme Akshara. He is Āḍiṭya, Vishṇu, Īs'vara, Purusha, prāṇa, jīva, agni, the resplendent. The Para-Brahman shines in the midst of these. He is without manas, ear, hands, feet, and light. There the worlds are no worlds, Ḍevas no Ḍevas, Veḍas no Veḍas, sacrifices no sacrifices, mother no mother, father no father, daughter-in-law no daughter-in-law, chaṇḍāla no chaṇḍāla, paulkasa no paulkasa, s'ramaṇa no s'ramaṇa, hermits no hermits; so one only Brahman shines as different. In the Hṛḍayākās' (ākās' in the heart) is the Chiḍākās'. That is Brahman. It is extremely subtle. The Hṛḍayākās' can be known. This moves in it. In Brahman, everything is strung. Those who thus know the Lord know everything. In him the Ḍevas, the worlds, the Piṭṛs and the Ṛshis do not rule. He who has awakened knows everything.

[1] **The South Indian Edition begins here.**

All the Ḍevas are in the heart; in the heart are all the prāṇas: in the heart are prāṇa, jyoṭis and that three-plied holy thread. In the heart in Chaiṭanya, it (prāṇa) is. [1] Put on the yajñopavīṭa (holy thread), the supreme, the holy, which came into existence along with the Prajāpaṭi, which gives long life and which is very excellent; let this give you strength and ṭejas. The wise man having shaved his head completely, should throw away the external thread. He should wear, as the holy thread, the supreme and indestructible Brahman. It is called sūṭra, because sūchanāṭ (indicating) (that the Āṭmā is in the heart). Sūṭra means the supreme abode. He who knows that sūṭra is a vipra (brāhmaṇa), he has crossed the ocean of the Veḍas. On that sūṭra (thread), everything is strung, like the beads on the thread. The yogin, well versed in yoga and having a clear perception of Truth, should wear the thread. Practising the noble yoga, the wise man should abandon the external thread. He who wears the sūṭra as Brahman, he is an intelligent being. By wearing the sūṭra, he is not polluted. They whose sūṭra is within, whose yajñopavīṭa is jñāna—they only know the sūṭra, and, they only wear the yajñopavīṭa in this world. Those whose tuft of hair is jñāna, who are firmly grounded in jñāna and whose yajñopavīṭa is jñāna, consider jñāna only as supreme. Jñāna is holy and excellent. He whose s'ikhā (tuft of hair) is jñāna like the s'ikhi (flame of agni)—he, the wise one, only wears a true s'ikhā; others wear a mere tuft of hair. Those brāhmaṇas and others who perform the ceremonies prescribed in the Veḍas—they wear this thread only as a symbol of their ceremonies. Those who know the Veḍas say that he only is a true brāhmaṇa who wears the s'ikhā of jñāna and whose yajñopavīṭa is the same (jñāna). This yajñopavīṭa (Yajña means Vishṇu or sacrifice and Upavīṭa is that which surrounds; hence that which surrounds Vishṇu) is supreme and is the supreme refuge. He who wears that really knows—he only wears the sūṭra, he is Yajña (Vishṇu) and he only knows Yajña (Vishṇu). One God hidden in all things, pervades all things and is the Inner Life of all things. He awards the fruits

[1] This manṭra is repeated whenever the holy thread is newly worn.

of karma, he lives in all things, he sees all things without any extraneous help, he is the soul of all, there is nothing like him, and he is without any guṇas (being secondless). He is the great wise one. He is the one doer among the many actionless objects. He is always making one thing appear as several (by māyā). Those wise men who see him in buḍḍhi, they only obtain eternal peace. Having made Āṭmā as the (upper) araṇi (attritional piece of wood) and Praṇava the lower araṇi, by constant practice of ḍhyāna one should see the concealed deity. As the oil in the sesamum seed, as the ghee in the curds, as the water in the rivers, and as the fire in the araṇi, so they who practise truth and austerities see Him in the buḍḍhi. As the spider throws out and draws into itself the threads, so the jīva goes and returns during the jāgraṭa and the svapna states. The heart is in the form of a closed lotus-flower, with its head hanging down; it has a hole in the top. Know it to be the great abode of All. Know that during jāgraṭa it (jīva) dwells in the eye, and during svapna in the throat; during sushupṭi, it is in the heart and during ṭurya in the head. [1](Because buḍḍhi unites) the Praṭyagāṭma with the Paramāṭma, the worship of sanḍhyā (union) arose. So we should perform sanḍhyāvanḍana (rites). The sanḍhyāvanḍana performed by ḍhyāna requires no water. It gives no trouble to the body or the speech. That which unites all things is the sanḍhyā of the one-staffed (sannyāsins). Knowing That from which speech and mind turn back without being able to obtain it and That which is the bliss of jīva, the wise one is freed. The secret of Brahmaviḍyā is to reveal the real nature of the Āṭmā, that is all-pervading, that is like ghee in the milk, that is the source of āṭmaviḍyā and ṭapas and to show that everything is in essence one.

"So ends the Brahmopanishaḍ."

---

[1] The five sentences from here relating to Sanḍhyā are not to be found in the South Indian Edition.

VAJRASŪCHI[1]-UPANISHAḌ

OF

SĀMAVEḌA

I NOW proceed to declare the vajrasūchi—the weapon that is the destroyer of ignorance—which condemns the ignorant and praises the man of divine vision.

There are four castes—the brāhmaṇa, the kshaṭriya, the vais'ya, and the s'ūḍra. Even the smṛṭis declare in accordance with the words of the veḍas that the brāhmaṇa alone is the most important of them.

Then this remains to be examined. What is meant by the brāhmaṇa? Is it a jīva? Is it a body? Is it a class? Is it jñāna? Is it karma? Or is it a doer of ḍharma?

To begin with: is jīva the brāhmaṇa? No. Since the jīva is the same in the many past and future bodies (of all persons), and since the jīva is the same in all of the many bodies obtained through the force of karma, therefore jīva is not the brāhmaṇa.

Then is the body the brāhmaṇa? No. Since the body, as it is made up of the five elements, is the same for all people down to chaṇḍālas,[2] etc., since old age and death, ḍharma and aḍharma are found to be common to them all, since there is no absolute distinction that the brāhmaṇas are white-coloured, the kshaṭriyas red, the vais'yas yellow, and the s'ūḍras dark, and since in burning the corpse of his father, etc., the stain of the murder of a brāhmaṇa, etc., will accrue to the son, etc., therefore the body is not the brāhmaṇa.

[1] Lit., the diamond-needle-Upanishaḍ.
[2] The lowest class of persons among the Hinḍūs.

Then is a class the brāhmaṇa? No. Since many great Ṛshis have sprung from other castes and orders of creation —Ṛshyaśṛṅga was born of deer; Kauśika, of Kuśa grass; Jāmbuka of a jackal; Vālmīki of valmīka (an ant-hill); Vyāsa of a fisherman's daughter; Gauṭama, of the posteriors of a hare; Vasishtha of Ūrvaśi[1]; and Āgasṭya of a water-pot; thus have we heard. Of these, many Ṛshis outside the caste even have stood first among the teachers of divine Wisdom; therefore a class is not the brāhmaṇa.

Is jñāna the brāhmaṇa? No. Since there were many kshaṭriyas and others well versed in the cognition of divine Truth, therefore jñāna is not the brāhmaṇa.

Then is karma the brāhmaṇa? No. Since the prārabḍha[2], sañchiṭa[3], and āgami[4] karmas are the same for all beings, and since all people perform their actions as impelled by karma, therefore karma is not the brāhmaṇa.

Then is a doer of ḍharma (virtuous actions) the brāhmaṇa? No. Since there are many kshaṭriyas, etc., who are givers of gold, therefore a doer of virtuous actions is not the brāhmaṇa.

Who indeed then is brāhmaṇa? Whoever he may be, he who has directly realised his Āṭmā and who is directly cognizant, like the myrobalan in his palm, of his Āṭmā that is without a second, that is devoid of class and actions, that is free from the faults of the six stains[5] and the six changes, [6]that is of the nature of truth, knowledge, bliss, and eternity, that is without any change in itself, that is the substratum of all the kalpas, that exists penetrating all things that pervades everything within and without as ākāś, that is of nature of undivided bliss, that cannot be reasoned about and that is known only by direct cognition. He who by the reason of having obtained his wishes is devoid of the faults of thirst after worldly objects and passions, who is the possessor of the qualifications beginning

[1] One of the celestial nymphs dancing in the court of Inḍra.
[2] The kārmic affinities generated by us in our former lives, the fruit of which is being enjoyed in our present life.
[3] The kārmic affinities generated by us in our former lives and collected together to be enjoyed in our future lives.
[4] The affinities generated by us in our present life to be enjoyed hereafter.
[5] The six stains—hunger, thirst, grief, confusion, old age, and death.
[6] Birth, existence, etc.

with s'ama[1], who is free from emotion, malice, thirst after worldly objects, desire, delusion, etc., whose mind is untouched by pride, egoism, etc., who possesses all these qualities and means—he only is the brāhmaṇa.

Such is the opinion of the vedas, the smṛṭis, the iṭihāsa and the purāṇas. Otherwise one cannot obtain the status of a brāhmaṇa. One should meditate on his Āṭmā as Sachchiḍānaḍa, and the non-dual Brahman. Yea, one should meditate on his Āṭmā as the Sachchiḍānanḍa Brahman. Such is the Upanishaḍ.

[1] Sama, ḍama, uparaṭi, ṭiṭikshā, samāḍhāna, and sraḍḍhā.

S'ĀRĪRAKA-UPANISHAḌ[1]

OF

KṚSHṆA-YĀJURVEḌĀ

OM. The body is a compound of pṛṭhivī (earth) and other mahābhūṭas (primordial elements, as āpas or water, agni or fire, vāyu or air, and ākās'). (In the body), that which is hard is (of the essence of) earth; that which is liquid is (of the essence of) water; that which is hot is (of the essence of) fire; that which moves about is (of the essence of) vāyu; that which is perforated is (of the essence of) ākās'. The ear and others are the jñānenḍriyas (organs of sense). The ear is of the essence of ākās', the skin of the essence of vāyu, the eye of the essence of fire, the tongue of the essence of water, and the nose of the essence of earth; sound, touch, form, taste, and odour being respectively the objects of perception for these organs. These arose respectively out of the primordial elements, beginning with earth. The mouth, the hands, the legs, the organs of excretion and the organs of generation are the karmenḍriyas (or organs of action). Their functions are respectively talking, lifting, walking, excretion, and enjoyment. Antaḥkaraṇa (or the internal organ) is of four kinds—manas, buḍḍhi, ahaṅkāra, and chiṭṭa. Their functions are respectively saṅkalpa-vikalpa, (or will-thought and doubt), determination, egoism, and memory. The seat of manas is the end of the throat, that of buḍḍhi the face, that of ahaṅkāra the heart, and that of chiṭṭa the navel. The bone, skin, nādis, nerves, hair, and flesh are of the essence of earth. Urine,

[1] This Upanishaḍ treats of Sarira or the body.

phlegm, blood, s'ukla (or sperm), and sweat are of the essence of water. Hunger, thirst, sloth, delusion, and (desire of) copulation are of the essence of fire. Walking, scratching, opening and closing the gross eyes, etc., are of the essence of vāyu. Desire, anger, avarice, delusion, and fear are of the essence of ākās'. Sound, touch, form, taste, and odour are the properties of earth : sound, touch, form, and taste are the properties of water : sound, touch, and form, are the properties of fire : sound and touch are the properties of vāyu : sound alone is the property of ākās'. There are three guṇas (or qualities), sāṭṭvika, rājasa, and ṭāmasa. Non-killing, veracity, not stealing, continence, non-covetousness, refraining from anger, serving the guru, purity (in mind and body), contentment, right conduct, abstinence from self-praise, freedom from pompousness, firm conviction in the existence of God, and not causing any injury to others—all these are to be known as sāṭṭvika-guṇas chiefly. I am the actor, I am the enjoyer, I am the speaker, and I am the egoistic—such are said by knowers of Brahman to be rājasa-guṇas. Sleep, sloth, delusion, desire, copulation, and theft are said by expounders of the Veḍas to be ṭāmasa-guṇas. Those having saṭṭva-guṇa (go) up (*viz.*, to higher spheres)—those having rājasa-guṇa (stay) in the middle (*viz.*, the sphere of earth)—those having ṭāmasa-guṇa (go) down (*viz.*, to hell, etc.). Perfect (or divine) knowledge is of sāṭṭvika-guṇa; knowledge of ḍharma is of rājasa-guṇa, and mental darkness is of ṭāmasa. Jāgraṭa (waking state), svapna (dreaming state), sushupṭi (dreamless sleeping state), and ṭurya (the fourth state beyond these three) are the four states. Jāgraṭa is (the state) having (the play of) the fourteen organs, the organs of sense (five), the organs of action (five), and the four internal organs. Svapna is (the state) associated with the four internal organs. Sushupṭi is (the state) where the chiṭṭa is the only organ. Ṭurya is that state having jīva alone. Regarding jīvāṭmā and Paramāṭmā (enjoying the three states) of a person with opened eyes, with closed eyes, and with eyes in an intermediate state with neither, jīva is said to be the Ksheṭrajña (the lord of the body). The organs of sense (five), the organs of action (five), prāṇas (five), manas, and buḍḍhi—all these seventeen are said to constitute the sūkshma or liṅga (*viz.*, subtle) body. Manas, buḍḍhi, ahaṅkāra, ākas', vāyu, fire, water, and earth—these are the eight prakṛṭis (or matter) : ear, skin, eye, tongue, nose the fifth, the organs of excretion, the organs of secretion, hands, legs, speech the tenth, sound, form, touch, taste, and odour are the fifteen modifications (of the above eight prakṛṭis). Therefore the ṭaṭṭvas are twenty-three. The twenty-fourth is avyakṭa (the undifferentiated matter) or praḍhāna. Purusha is other than (or superior to) this. Thus is the Upanishaḍ.

GARBHA-UPANISHAḌ[1]

KṚSHNĀ-YĀJURVEḌĀ

Oм. The body is composed of the five (elements); it exists in
the five (objects of sense, etc.); it has six supports: it is associated with the six guṇas; it has seven ḍhāṭus (essential ingredients)
and three malas (impurities); it has three yonis (wombs) and is
formed of four kinds of food.

Why is the body said to be composed of five? Because
there are five elements in this body (*viz.*), pṛṭhivī, āpas, agni,
vāyu, and ākāś. In this body of five elements, what is the pṛṭhivī
element? what āpas? what agni? what vāyu? and what
ākāś? Pṛṭhivī is said to be that which is hard; āpas is said to
be that which is liquid; agni is said to be that which is hot;
vāyu is that which moves; ākāś is that which is full of holes
(or tubes[2]). Of these, pṛṭhivī is seen in supporting (objects),
āpas in cohesion, ṭejas (or agni) in making forms visible, vāyu
in moving, ākāś chiefly in avakāś'a (*viz.*, giving space). (Then
what are the five objects of sense, etc.?) The ear exists in
sound, the skin in touch, the eye in forms, the tongue in taste,
and the nose in odour. (Then) the mouth (exists) in speech, the
hand in lifting, the feet in walking, the anus in excreting, and
the genitals in enjoying. (Then) through buḍḍhi, one knows
and determines; through manas, he thinks and fancies; through
chiṭṭa, he recollects; through ahaṅkāra, he feels the idea of ' I '.
Thus these perform their respective functions.

---

[1] The Upanishaḍ treating of embryo, etc.
[2] The Sanskrit word 'sushira' means perforated or tubular.

Whence the six supports? There are six kinds of rasas (essences or tastes)—sweet, sour, saltish, bitter, astringent, and pungent. The body depends upon them while they depend upon the body. There are six changes of state (*viz.*), the body exists, is born, grows, matures, decays, and dies. And there are also six chakras (wheels) depending on the ḍhāmāni (nerves), (*viz.*), mūlāḍhāra, svāḍhishthāna, maṇipūraka, anāhaṭa, vis'uḍḍhi, and ājñā. Also the guṇas are six—kāma (passion) and others and s'ama (mental restraint) and others; there being properly—association (with the former) and devotion (to the latter). Then there are seven kinds of sounds, (*viz.*), shadja (sa), ṛshabha (ri), gānḍhāra (ga), maḍhyama (ma), pañchama (pa), ḍaivaṭa (ḍa), and nishāḍa (ni), which are stated to be seven agreeable and disagreeable ones; and there are seven kinds of ḍhāṭus having seven colours, (*viz.*), s'ukla (white), rakṭa (red), kṛshṇa (dark-blue or indigo), ḍhūmra (blue), pīṭa (yellow), kapila (orange-red), and pāṇdara (yellowish white). In whomsoever these substances arise and increase, the rasa (essence) is the cause of the one following and so on (as stated below). (These) rasas are six in number; from the rasas (probably chyme) arises blood: from blood, flesh; from flesh, fat; from fat, bones; from bones, marrow; and from marrow, s'ukla (the male seminal fluid). From the union of s'ukla and s'oṇiṭa (the female vital energy), occurs garbha (conception in the womb). Being stationed in the heart, it is led. In the heart of persons, (there is) an internal agni; in the seat of agni, there is bile; in the seat of bile, there is vāyu; in the seat of vāyu, is hṛḍya (heart or Āṭmā).

Through having connection at the ṛṭu (season) fit for raising issues, it (the embryo formed in the womb) is like water in the first night; in seven nights, it is like a bubble; at the end of half a month, it becomes a ball. At the end of a month, it is hardened; in two months, the head is formed; in three months, the region about the feet; and in the fourth month, the region about the stomach and the loins and also ankle is formed; in the fifth month, the back (or spinal) bone; in the sixth, the face of the nose, eyes, and ears; in the seventh, it becomes united with Jīva (Āṭmā); in the eighth month, it becomes full (of all organs); in the ninth, it becomes fatty. S'ukla belongs to men and s'oṇiṭa to women. Each (by itself) is neutral (or is powerless). (But in their combination) a son is born when the father's seed preponderates. A daughter is born when the mother's seed preponderates. Should both be equal, a eunuch is born. Since females have more of passion, on account of their deriving more pleasure (than males from sexual union), a greater number of females are born. Action corresponds to the mental state (of the actor). Hence the child (born) takes after (the thought of) the parents. From parents with minds full of anxieties (at the time of union) are born the blind, the lame, the hunchback, the dwarf, and the limbless. (From impregnation) during the eclipses of the sun and the moon, children are born with defective limbs. Increase or decrease, similarities or dissimilarities of bodies arise (in children) through the influence of time, place, action, ḍravya (substance), and enjoyment. From a well-conducted intercourse (or union), the child being born with the form of the father possesses, his qualities, just as the image in a glass reflects truly the original. When s'ukla bursts into two through the interaction (or blowing against one another) of the vāyu of both s'ukla and s'oṇiṭa, then twins (of the same sex) are born. In the same manner when the reṭas (the seminal fluids), *viz.*, (s'ukla and s'oṇiṭa) of both the parents burst into two, then mixed progeny (male and female) is the result. Among mankind, five embryos (only can be formed at a pregnancy in the womb). A womb with one embryo is common. There are some with two. Those with three are only to be found (as rarely) as one in a thousand. Where there is a frequent pouring (of seminal fluid into the womb), a greater number of limbs is produced (in the child). When the pouring (within the womb) is only once, then the child becomes dried up (or contracted). By pouring (within) more than once, couples are (sometimes) born.

Then, (*viz.*, in the ninth month), this (in the body) made of the five elements and able to sense odour, taste, etc., through ṭejas (spiritual fire), etc., which is also made up of the five elements—this cognizes the indestructible Omkāra through its deep wisdom and contemplation. It cognizes as the one letter

(Om). Then there arise in the body the eight prakṛṭis[1] and the sixteen vikāras (changes). Through the food and drink of the mother transmitted through her nādis, the child obtains prāṇa. In the ninth month, it is full of all attributes.

It then remembers its previous births, finds out what has been done and what has not been done, and discriminates between actions, right and wrong. (Then it thinks thus :) " Many thousands of wombs have been seen by me, many kinds of food have been tasted (by me), and many breasts have been suckled (by me). All parts of the world have been my place of birth, as also my burning-ground in the past. In eighty-four lakhs[2] of wombs, have I been born. I have been often born and have often died. I have been subject to the cycle of re-births very often. I have had birth and death, again birth and death, and again birth (and so on). There is much suffering whilst living in the womb. Delusion and sorrow attend every birth. In youth are sorrow, grief, dependence on others, ignorance, the non-performance of what is beneficiall laziness, and the performance of what is unfavourable. In adult age, (the sources of sorrow are) attachment to sensual objects and the groaning under the three kinds[3] of pain. In old age anxiety, disease, fear of death, desires, love of self, passion, anger, and non-independence—all these produce very great suffering. This birth is the seed of sorrow, and being of the form of sorrow is unbearable. I have not attained the ḍharma of nivṛṭṭi, (*viz.*, the means of overcoming the cycle of re-birth) nor have I acquired the means of yoga and jñāna. Alas ! I am sunk in the ocean of sorrow and find no remedy for it. Fie on ajñāna l fie on ajñāna ! fie on the troubles caused by passion and anger ; fie on the fetters of samsāra (the mundane existence) ! I shall attain wisdom from a guru. If I get myself freed from the womb, then I shall practise sāṅkhya yoga which is the cause of the extinction of all evil and the bestower

[1] The eight prakṛtis are mūlaprakṛṭi, mahaṭ, ahaṅkāra, and the five elements ; the sixteen vikāras are the five organs of sense, the five organs of action, the five prāṇas, and anṭahkaraṇa.

[2] The Hinḍūs believe in so many number of wombs to be born on the earth.

[3] Those that arise from the body, the elements, and the ḍevas.

of the fruit of emancipation. If I get myself freed from the womb, I shall seek refuge in Mahes'vara (the great Lord) who is the cause of the extinction of all evil and bestower of the (four[1]) ends of life. If I get myself freed from the womb, then I shall seek refuge in that Lord of the world who is the Chiḍāṭmā of all s'akṭis and the cause of all causes. If I get myself freed from the womb, then I shall seek refuge in that supreme Lord Bhargaḥ (S'iva or light) who is pas'upaṭi (the lord of pas'us or souls), Ruḍra, Mahāḍeva (the great Ḍeva) and the Guru of the world. If I get myself freed from the bondage of the womb, I shall perform great penances. If I get myself freed from the passage of the womb, I shall worship Vishṇu in my heart who is the bestower of nectar, who is bliss, who is Nārāyaṇa, and who never decays. I am now confined in my mother's womb; and were I freed from its bonds, I shall please the divine Vāsuḍeva without diverting my mind from Him. I am burnt through actions, good and bad, committed by me alone before for the sake of others, whilst those who enjoyed the fruits thereof have disappeared. Through non-belief (unspirituality), I formerly gave up all fear (of sin) and committed sins. I now reap their fruits. I shall become a believer hereafter[2]."

Thus does the Jīva (Āṭmā) within the (mother's womb) contemplate again and again the many kinds of miseries (it had undergone), and remembering always the miseries of the cycle of re-births, becomes disgusted (with the material enjoyments of the world), often fainting in the inmost centre (*viz.*, heart) of all creatures at (the idea of) his aviḍyā, desire, and karma. Then this being, who had entered many hundreds of female wombs of beings (in the previous births), comes to the mouth of the womb wishing to obtain release. Here being pressed by the yanṭra (neck of the uterus), it suffers much trouble. Moreover it is much affected by prasūṭi (delivery) vāyu. As soon as it is born, it comes in contact with the vaishṇavī vāyu and ceases to remember anything of the past;

[1] They are kāma (passion), ārtha (acquisition of wealth), ḍharma (performance of duty), and moksha (salvation).

[2] The reason why it remembers them seems to be that the jīvāṭmā is in the pineal gland then, prior to its coming down.

it also ceases to see far and to be the cognizer of the real. Coming into contact with the earth, it becomes fierce-eyed and debased. The evil of the eye after it is rubbed with (or cleaned by) water vanishes; and with it, vanishes memory of birth and death, good and bad actions and their affinities. Then how does he understand vāyu, bile, and s'leshma (phlegm)? When they are in their proper state, they produce health: with their disturbance, diseases are generated. It should be known that one becomes capable of knowing through a proper quantity of bile; through having a little more or a little less of it, he comes to know more. When the bile is changed (otherwise), he becomes changed and acts like a mad man. And that bile is agni. Āgni influenced by karma is kindled by vāyu, the source (or seat) of virtue and vice, as fuel is kindled within (by fire) from without (by the wind).

And of how many kinds is that agni? It has three bodies, three reṭas (seeds or progeny), three puras (cities), three ḍhāṭus, and three kinds of agni threefold. Of these three, Vais'vānara is bodiless. And that agni becomes (or is subdivided into) Jñānāgni (wisdom-fire), Ḍars'anāgni (eye-fire), and Koshthāgni (digestive fire). Of these Jñānāgni pertains to the mind; Ḍars'anāgni pertains to the senses; and Koshthāgni pertains to ḍahara and daily cooks (or digests) equally whatever is eaten, drunk, licked, or sucked through prāṇa and apāna. Ḍars'anāgni is (in) the eye itself and is the cause of vijñāna and enables one to see all objects of form. It has three seats, the (spiritual) eye itself being the (primary) seat, and the eyeballs being the accessory seats. Ḍakshiṇāgni is in the heart, Gārhapaṭya is in the belly, and in the face is Āhavanīya. (In this sacrifice with the three agnis), the Purusha is himself the sacrificer; buḍḍhi becomes his wife; sanṭosha (contentment) becomes the ḍīkshā (vow) taken; the mind and the organs of the senses become the sacrificial vessels; the karmenḍriyas (organs of action) are the sacrificial instruments. In this sacrifice of the body, the several ḍevas who become the ṛṭvijas (sacrificial priests) perform their parts following the master of the sacrifice, (*viz.*, the true individuality), wherever he goes. In this (sacrifice), the body is the sacrificial place, the skull of the head is the fire-pit, the hairs are the kus'a grass; the mouth is the anṭarveḍi (raised platform in sacrifice); kāma (or passion) is the clarified butter; the period of life is the period of sacrifice; nāḍa (sound) produced in ḍahara (heart) is the sāmaveḍa (recited during the sacrifice); vaikharī is the yajus (or yajurveḍa hymns); parā, pas'yanṭi, and maḍhyamā[1] are the ṛks (or ṛgveḍa hymns); cruel words are the aṭharvas (aṭharvaveḍa hymns) and khilas (supplementary texts of each veḍa); true words are the vyāhṛṭis[2]. Life, strength, and bile are the pas'us (sacrificial creatures) and death is avabhṛṭa (the bath which concludes the sacrifice). In this sacrifice, the (three) fires blaze up and then according to (the desires of) the wordly, the ḍevas bless him. All who are living (in this world) are the sacrificers. There is none living who does not perform yajña (sacrifice). This body is (created) for yajña, and arises out of yajña and changes according to yajña. If this yajña is continued in a direction changed (from the right course, or is abused), then it leads to an ocean of misery.

In this body, there are sixteen side-teeth, having each a membrane (as its root) and fifteen openings. It (the body) is measured by ninety-six digits. There are in it fourteen nādi seats and 108 joints. There are seventy-two tubes seats with seventy-two nādis between them, of which three are important, *viz.*, idā, piṅgalā, and sushumnā, the fourth is purīṭaṭi, and jīvaṭa the fifth. Above jīvaṭa is bile and near bile is Purīṭaṭi. Above the navel, two digits to the left of it, is seated the source of bile. The food taken in is divided into three parts—urine, fæces, and sāra (the essence or chyme). The urine dividing itself into two, spreads to the left below the navel. The fæces is in the right side and is of seven kinds. The sāra is of five kinds and spreads itself over the body. Hence the semen and blood are produced from food and drink. In this body, vāyu which is moving as prāṇa is the Sūṭrāṭma. Through it, one inspires and expires and moves (his limbs). Without it, no limb of the body will be

[1] Vaikharī and the three others are the different stages of nāḍa (sound).
[2] Vyāhṛṭis are parts of the Gāyaṭrī Manṭra, *viz.*, Bhūḥ, Bhuvaḥ, Suvaḥ.

animated. Through vāyu, the current of blood is driven into the nādis from the chakra (plexus) of the heart, and those which can be touched (on the body) are easily discernible. The juicy essences (of food) which arise out of digestion enter the womb which is suspended in the stomach of the mother and coming near the child's head nourishes the child's prāṇa through the sushumnā (on the head or pineal gland). Sushumnā is the Brahma-nādi. Prāṇa and others are found there. It (prāṇa) descends lower and lower as the time of birth approaches and settles in the heart when the child is born. Through yoga, it should be brought from the middle of the eyebrows to the end of sushumnā (*viz.*, the pineal gland), when he becomes the cognizer of the Real like the child in the womb. In the body of this nature, Āṭmā is latent and deathless, and is the witness and Purusha. It lives in this body, being enveloped (by māyā). Prāṇī (or the jīva having prāṇa) has abhimāna (identification with the body) on account of aviḍyā. Ajñāna which surrounds it is the seed; the anṭaḥkaraṇa (internal organ) is the sprout and the body is the tree. In this tree (of body), there are eight crores of hairs, eighty hundreds of joints, nine hundreds of tendons, eight palams of heart[1], twelve palams of tongue, one prasṭha (or two palams) of bile; one ādhaka of phlegm, one kudupa (or $^1/_4$ prasṭha) of s'ukla and two prasṭhas of marrow. One should consider everything as evanescent, like the child in the womb (with its prāṇa, etc.,) stationed in the sushumnā (of the head). Then he becomes freed and gets no more body. If not, an ignorant man becomes subject to the cycle of re-births, etc., is exposed like a worm to the drink of urine and fæces, and undergoes in this body the sufferings of hell. Therefore knowing all this, one should be averse to worldly objects. Thus ends the moksha-s'āsṭra of Pippalāḍa—thus ends the moksha-s'āsṭra of Pippalāḍa. Thus ends the Upanishaḍ.

---

[1] Eight palams are $^3/_5$ of a lb. (avdp.)

ṬĀRASĀRA-UPANISHAḌ[1]

OF

S'UKLA-YAJURVEḌA

Om. Bṛhaspaṭi asked Yājñavalkya: "That which is called Kurukshetra is the place of the sacrifice of the Ḍevas and the spiritual seat of all beings. Therefore where should one go in order that he may cognize Kurukshetra, the place of the sacrifice of the Ḍevas and the spiritual seat of all beings?" (To which Yājñavalkya replied:) "Avimukṭa[2] is Kurukshetra, the place of the sacrifice of the Ḍevas and of the study of Brahman, because it is there that Ruḍra initiates one into the Ṭāraka[3] Brahman when prāṇa (life) goes out. Through this, one becomes immortal and the enjoyer of moksha. Therefore one should always be in the midst of that place avimukṭa, and should never leave, O reverend sir, avimukṭa." Thus said Yājñavalkya.

Then Bhāraḍvāja asked Yājñavalkya: "What is ṭāraka? what is that which causes one to cross (this mundane existence)." To which Yājñavalkya replied: "Om-Namō-Nārāyaṇāya is the ṭāraka. It should be worshipped as Chiḍāṭma. Om is a single syllable and of the nature of Āṭmā. Namaḥ is of two syllables and is of the nature of prakṛṭi (matter). Nārāyaṇāya is of five syllables and is of the nature of Parabrahman. He who knows this becomes immortal. Through Om, is Brahmā produced; through *Na* is Vishṇu produced; through *Ma* is Ruḍra produced; through *Nā* is Īs'vara produced; through *Rā* is the Āṇda-Virāt (or Virāt of the universe) produced; through *Ya* is

[1] This Upanishaḍ treats of the sāra (essence) for ṭāra (crossing).

[2] It is one of the many names given to Benares.

[3] Ṭāraka is Om—from *ṭr*, to cross.

Purusha produced; through *Nā* is Bhagavān (Lord) produced; and through *Ya* is Paramāṭmā produced. This Ashṭākshara (eight syllables) of Nārāyaṇa is the supreme and the highest Purusha. Thus is the Ṛgveḍa with the first foot (or half). That which is Om is the indestructible, the supreme, and Brahman. That alone should be worshipped. It is this that is of the eight subtle syllables. And this becomes eight, being of eight forms. Ā is the first letter; U is the second; M is the third; Binḍu is the fourth; Nāḍa is the fifth; Kalā is the sixth; Kalāṭīṭa (that beyond kalā) is the seventh; and that which is beyond these is the eighth. It is called Ṭāraka, because it enables one to cross this mundane existence. Know that Ṭāraka alone is Brahman and it alone should be worshipped." The (following) verses may be quoted here: "From the letter Ā came Brahmā named Jāmbavān (the bear[1]). From the letter U came Upenḍra[2], named Hari. From the letter M came S'iva, known as Hanumān[3]. Binḍu is named Īs'vara and is S'aṭrughna, the Lord of the discus itself. Nāḍa should be known as the great Lord named Bharaṭa and the sound of the conch itself. From Kalā came the Purusha himself as Lakshmaṇa and the bearer of the earth. Kalāṭīṭa is known as the goddess Sīṭā Herself. That which is beyond is the Paramāṭmā named S'rī-Rāma and is the highest Purusha. All this is the explanation of the letter Om, which is the past, the present, and future, and which is other than these (*viz.*,) ṭaṭṭva, manṭra, varṇa, (colour), ḍevaṭā (deity), chhanḍas (metre), ṛk, kāla, s'akṭi, and sṛshti (creation). He who knows this becomes immortal. (Thus is) Yajurveḍa with the second foot."

Then Bhāraḍvāja asked Yājñavalkya: "Through what manṭra is Paramāṭmā pleased and shows his own Āṭmā (to persons)? Please tell this." Yājñavalkya replied:

"(1st Manṭra:) Om. He who is S'rī-Paramāṭmā, Nārāyaṇa, and the Lord described by (the letter) Ā and is Jāmbavān (the bear) and Bhūḥ, Bhuvaḥ, and Suvaḥ: Salutation to Him."

[1] As the bear, Brahmā incarnated according to the 'Rāmāyaṇa'.

[2] As Upenḍra, Vishṇu incarnates in the lower ṭala as well in the legs in man.

[3] Hanumān is the incarnation of vāyu, one of the elements of Siva.

"(2nd Manṭra :) He who is Paramāṭmā, Nārāyaṇa, and the Lord described by (the letter) U and is Upenḍra (or) Hari and Bhūḥ, Bhuvaḥ, and Suvaḥ: Salutation to Him.

"(3rd Manṭra :) Om. He who is S'rī-Paramāṭmā, Nārāyaṇa, and the Lord described by (the letter) M and is of the form of S'iva (or), Hanumān and Bhūḥ, Bhuvaḥ, and Suvaḥ: Salutation to Him.

"(4th Manṭra :) Om. He who is S'ri-Paramāṭmā, Nārāyaṇa, the Lord of S'aṭrughna[1] of the form of Binḍu and the Bhuḥ, Bhuvaḥ, and Suvaḥ: Salutation to Him.

"(5th Manṭra :) Om. He who is S'ri-Paramāṭmā, Nārāyaṇa, and the Lord, and is Bharaṭa[1] of the form of Nāḍa and the Bhūḥ Bhuvaḥ, and Suvaḥ: Salutation to Him.

"(6th Manṭra :) Om. He who is S'ri-Paramāṭmā, Nārāyaṇa, and the Lord, and is Lakshmaṇa of the form of Kalā and the Bhūḥ, Bhuvaḥ, and Suvaḥ: Salutation to Him.

"(7th Manṭra :) Om. He who is S'ri-Paramāṭmā, Nārāyaṇa, and the Lord, and is Kalāṭīṭa, the Goddess Sīṭa, of the form of Chiṭ and the Bhūḥ, Bhuvaḥ, and Suvaḥ: Salutation to Him.

"(8th Manṭra :) Om. He who is S'ri-Paramāṭmā, Nārāyaṇa, and the Lord that is beyond that (Kalāṭīṭa), is the supreme Purusha, and is the ancient Purushoṭṭama, the eternal, the immaculate, the enlightened, the emancipated, the true, the highest bliss, the endless, the secondless, and the all-full—that Brahman is myself. I am Rāma and the Bhūḥ, Bhuvaḥ, and Suvaḥ: Salutation to Him."

He who has mastered this eightfold manṭra is purified by Agni; he is purified by Vāyu; he is purified by the sun; he is purified by S'iva; he is known by all the Ḍevas. He attains the fruit of reciting Iṭihāsas, Purāṇas, Ruḍra (Manṭras), a hundred thousand times. He who repeatedly remembers (or recites) the Ashtākshara (the eight-syllabled manṭra) of Nārāyaṇa gains the fruit of the recitation of Gāyaṭrī a hundred thousand times or of Praṇava (Om) a myriad of times. He purifies (his ancestors) ten (degrees) above and (his descendants) ten

[1] Bharaṭa is rather the incarnation of discus or consciousness and Saṭrughna, that of conch—*viz.*, ākāśic sound.

(degrees) below. He attains the state of Nārāyaṇa. He who knows this (attains the state of Nārāyaṇa).

Like the eye (which sees without any obstacle) the things spread (in the sky), the wise ever see this supreme seat of Vishṇu. Brāhmaṇas who are spiritually awake praise in diverse ways and illuminate the supreme abode of Vishṇu. Thus is the Upanishaḍ. (Thus is) the Sāmaveḍa with the third foot.

NĀRĀYAṆA-UPANISHAḌ

OF

KṚSHṆA-YĀJURVEḌĀ

OM. Then Nārāyaṇa, the supreme Purusha desired. "I shall create offspring." From Nārāyaṇa emanates prāṇa, manas, the several organs of sense and action, ākās', vāyu, agni, āpas and pṛṭhivī that supports all. From Nārāyaṇa emanates Brahmā. From Nārāyaṇa emanates Ruḍra. From Nārāyaṇa emanates Inḍra. From Nārāyaṇa emanates Prajāpaṭi (the divine progenitor). From Nārāyaṇa emanates the twelve āḍiṭyas, ruḍras, vasus, and all the chhanḍas (Veḍas). From Nārāyaṇa only do (all these) proceed. Through Nārāyaṇa do (they) prosper. In Nārāyaṇa (they) are absorbed. The Ṛgveḍa teaches this.

Then Nārāyaṇa is eternal. Brahmā is Nārāyaṇa, S'iva is Nārāyaṇa, Inḍra is Nārāyaṇa, Kāla (time) is Nārāyaṇa, Ḍik (space) is Nārāyaṇa, the intermediate quarters also are Nārāyaṇa; that which is above is Nārāyaṇa, that which is below is Nārāyaṇa, that which is in and out is Nārāyaṇa, the whole universe which existed and will exist is Nārāyaṇa. Nārāyaṇa is the only one that is stainless, sinless, changeless, and unnameable, and that is pure and divine. There is no second. Whoever knows Him thus, becomes Vishṇu Himself. The Yajurveḍa teaches this.

One should utter "Om" first, then "namaḥ," and then "Nārāyaṇāya." "Om" (is) a single syllable; "Namaḥ" contains two syllables: "Nārāyaṇāya contains five syllables. This is the sentence known as the Ashtākshara[1] of Nārāyaṇa.

[1] The eight syllables.

Whoever studies this Ashtākshara of Nārāyaṇa and recites it constantly, attains full life and supremacy over men, enjoys the pleasures of royalty and becomes the master of all souls. He attains moksha; yea, he attains moksha. The Sāmaveḍa teaches this.

The Yogin having pronounced (the name of) Him who is complete bliss, who is Brahma-purusha and who is of the nature of Praṇava (Om)—a combination of Ā, U, and M—is released from the bondage of birth and mundane existence. He who practises the manṭra "Om-Namo-Nārāyaṇāya" reaches Vaikuṇtha (the abode of Vishṇu). It is this lotus (heart). It is replete with vijñāna: It has the brilliancy of lightning. The son of Ḍevākī is Brahmaṇya[1]. Maḍhusūḍana is Brahmaṇya. Nārāyaṇa who pervades all elements, who is one only, who is the cause Purusha and who is causeless, is known as Parabrahman. The Aṭharvaṇa Upanishaḍ teaches this.

Whoever recites (this Upanishaḍ) in the morning destroys the sins committed the night (before). Whoever recites it in the evening destroys the sins committed during the day. Whoever recites morning and evening becomes free from sins, however sinful he may be. Whoever recites (it) in the noon facing the sun is freed from all the five[2] great sins as well as from the minor ones. He derives the good effects of the recitation of all the Veḍas. Whoever knows thus attains Sāyujya of Nārāyaṇa (*viz.*, is absorbed in the essence of Nārāyaṇa). He attains Sāyujya of Nārāyaṇa. Thus is the Upanishaḍ.

---

[1] Means Vishṇu or Brahmā devoted to Ṭapas, Veḍas, Truth, and Jñāna.

[2] They are theft of gold, drinking alcohol, the murder of a Brāhman, and unlawful union with the guru's wife and association with them.

KALISANṬĀRAṆA UPANISHAḌ[1]

OF

KṚSHṆA-YAJURVEḌA

At the end of Ḍvāpara yuga, Nāraḍa[2] went to Brahmā and addressed him thus: "O Lord, how shall I, roaming[3] over the earth, be able to cross Kali?" To which Brahmā thus replied: "Well asked. Hearken to that which all S'ruṭis (the Veḍas) keep secret and hidden, through which one may cross the samsāra (mundane existence) of Kali. He shakes off (the evil effects of) Kali through the mere uttering of the name of the Lord Nārāyaṇa, who is the primeval Purusha." Again Nāraḍa asked Brahmā: "What is the name?" To which Hiraṇyagarbha (Brahmā) replied thus: (the words are:) "1. Harē, 2. Rāma, 3. Harē, 4. Ramā, 5. Rāma, 6. Rāma, 7. Harē, 8. Harē; 9. Harē 10. Kṛshṇa, 11. Harē, 12. Kṛshṇa, 13. Kṛshṇa, 14. Kṛshṇa 15. Harē, 16. Harē. These sixteen names (words) are destructive of the evil effects of Kali. No better means than this is to be seen in all the Veḍas. These (sixteen names) destroy the āvaraṇa (or the centripetal force which produces the sense of individuality) of jīva surrounded by the sixteen kalās (rays). Then like the

[1] This Upanishaḍ treats of the means of crossing Kali completely: Nāraḍa having asked the question in Ḍvāpara yuga—the third of the four yugas.

[2] Nāraḍa is called Kali-Kāraka or the generator of kali or strife and discord. If Nāraḍa is himself the strife-maker, why should he go to Brahmā for the means of crossing Kali? Nāraḍa being himself an adjuster of the laws of karma, this Upanishaḍ gives the means of getting over strife, etc., in this Kali-age when the whole of nature is thrown off its balance by the depraved tendencies of men. The jiva has sixteen kalās, corresponding to which sixteen manṭras or words are given.

[3] The story is that he was cursed by Ḍaksha to roam over the worlds with a lute in his hand (*viz.*, to adjust the laws of harmony).

sphere of the sun which shines fully after the clouds (screening it) disperse, Parabrahman (alone) shines."

Nāraḍa asked: "O Lord, what are the rules to be observed with reference to it?" To which Brahmā replied that there were no rules for it. Whoever in a pure or an impure state, utters these always, attains the same world of, or proximity with, or the same form of, or absorption into Brahmā.

Whoever utters three and a half kotis[1] (or thirty-five millions) times this manṭra composed of sixteen names (or words) crosses the sin of the murder of a Brāhmaṇa. He becomes purified from the sin of the theft of gold. He becomes purified from the sin of cohabitation with a woman of low caste. He is purified from the sins of wrong done to piṭṛs, ḍevas, and men. Having given up all ḍharmas, he becomes freed at once from all sins. He is at once released from all bondage. That he is at once released from all bondage is the Upanishaḍ.

---

[1] This number can be reached by uttering the manṭra completely within one year if uttered at the rate of a lakh per day: and within ten years if uttered at the rate of 10,000 per day; and within 100 years if uttered at the rate of 1,000 *per diem*.

BHIKSHUKA[1]-UPANISHAḌ

OF

S'UKLA-YAJURVEḌA

AMONG bhikshus (religious mendicants) who long for moksha (salvation), there are four[2] kinds, *viz.*, Kutīchaka, Bahūḍaka, Hamsa, and Paramahamsa. Gauṭama, Bharaḍvāja, Yājñavalkya, Vasishtha and others belong to the first kind. They take eight mouthfuls (of food daily) and strive after moksha alone through the path of yoga. The second kind carry three (bamboo) staves (tied together) and a waterpot, and wear tuft of hair (s'ikhā), sacred thread (yajñopavīṭa) and red-coloured cloth. They take eight mouthfuls of food in the house of Brahmarṣhis, abstain from flesh and alcohol and strive after emancipation alone through the path of yoga. Then the Hamsas should live not more than a night in a village, five nights in a town, and seven nights in a sacred place, partaking daily of cow's urine and cow's dung, observing Chānḍrāyaṇa[3] and striving after moksha alone through the path of yoga. Paramahamsas like Samvarṭaka, Āruṇī, S'weṭakeṭu, Jadabharaṭa, Ḍaṭṭāṭreya, S'uka, Vāmaḍeva, Hārīṭaka and others take eight mouthfuls and strive after moksha alone through the path of yoga. They live clothed or naked at the foot of trees, in ruined houses, or in burning grounds. With

[1] One who lives on bhikshā or alms. Hence a religious mendicant.

[2] In Nāraḍaparivrājaka Upanishaḍ there are stated to be six kinds.

[3] A religious expiatory ceremony regulated by the moon's age diminishing the daily consumption of food daily by one mouthful for the dark half of the month beginning with fifteen at the full moon until it is reduced to one at the new moon and then increasing it in like manner during the fortnight of the moon's increase.—WILSON.

them, there are no dualities as ḍharma and aḍharma, gain and loss, and purity and impurity. They look upon gold and stone and clod of earth with the same eye (of indifference), live on alms, begging from all without any distinction of caste and look upon everything as Āṭmā alone. Being (naked) as nature made them, being free from the sense of duality and from covetousness, being engaged in pure contemplation (s'ukladhyāna), meditating on Āṭmā, and begging at stated times, simply to keep the body and soul together, they reside in ruined houses, temples, straw-huts, ant-hills, the foot of trees, potteries, the places of agnihoṭra, the sand in the bed of rivers, mountain-caves, cavities, the hollows of trees, waterfalls, and sṭhaṇdila (the level square piece of ground prepared for sacrifice). Having advanced far in the path of Brahman, and being pure in mind, they quit this body through the methods prescribed for Paramahamsa Sannyāsins. These are the Paramahamsas. Such is the Upanishaḍ.

NARAḌAPARIVRĀJAKA-UPANISHAḌ

OF

AṬHARVAṆAVEḌA

UPAḌES'A I

OM. Once upon a time, Nārada, the ornament of Parivrājakas (roaming ascetics), after roaming over all worlds and cleansing, through merely by looking at the places of pilgrimage able to impart rare religious merits, observed, with a mind that had attained purity, without hate, quiescent and patient, and indifferent towards all (objects), the forest of Naimis'a (the modern Nimsār), filled with Ṛshis that were engaged in the contemplation of Reality and had attained the greatness of the ordained bliss; (there) through the recitation of stories about Hari (Vishṇu), associated with the musical motes of Sa, Ri, Ga, Ma, Pa, Ḍha, and Ni (of the gamut), able to impart indifference to objects and to make one look down upon the universe, and instilling divine devotion, fixed and movable (or mental and bodily), he entered (the forest), fascinating the crowds of beings human, animal, Kimpurushas[1], celestials, Kinnaras,[2] Āpsaras (Houris), and Uragas[3] (collected there). (Thereupon the) great Ṛshis S'āunaka and others who had been engaged for twelve years in saṭṭra sacrifice well-skilled in the recitation of Veḍas, the knowers of all, and the good practisers of ṭapas, observed Nāraḍa the son of Brahmā and the devotee of the Lord, and having

[1] A higher being with the form of a horse but with a human head.

[2] A higher being with a human form but with the head of a horse.

[3] A semidivine serpent with a human face.

risen up, paid due respect to him. Then having with due respect requested him to sit down, they also seated themselves and addressed him thus: "O Lord, son of Brahmā, what is the means of salvation for us? It is meet that it should be communicated (to us)." Thus addressed, Nāraḍa replied to them thus: "One born in a good family and fit to go through the forty-four samskāras, upanayana and others, should, under a teacher to whom he is devoted, study, after the recitation of the Veḍa of his own s'ākhā (division), all the different branches of knowledge; then should fulfil, according to the rules ordained, for twelve years the observance of Brahmacharya (celibacy), such as the service of the guru, etc.; then for twenty-five years the ās'rama (order of life) of a gṛhasṭha (householder), and for twenty-five years the ās'rama of a vānaprasṭha (forester). After thus practising well the fourfold celibacy,[1] the sixfold[2] householder's life, and the fourfold[3] forester's life, and having performed all the duties thereof, he should acquire the fourfold[4] means of salvation; thus the sannyāsin who gives up the desires along with the karmas of mind, speech, and body in this samsāra as well as the vāsanā towards the threefold desire (of son, wife, and wealth), and being without malice and endowed with quiescence and patience, undisturbed in the order of life of Paramahamsa, quits the body in the contemplation of Reality, is an emancipated person. Such is the Upanishaḍ."

UPAḌES'A II

All the Ṛshis, S'aunaka and others addressing Lord Nāraḍa said thus: "O Lord, please tell us the rules of sannyāsa." At which, seeing them, Nāraḍa replied: "It is but meet that we should know the whole truth from the mouth of Brahmā

[1] The four Brahmacharyas are: (1) Gāyaṭri; (2) Prājāpaṭya; (3) Vaiḍika; (4) Naishtika.

[2] The six Gṛhasṭhas are: (1) Vārṭāvṛtti; *viz.*, Agriculture; (2) Sālīnavṛṭṭi; (3) Yāyāvara; (4) Ghorasannyāsin; etc.

[3] The four Vānaprasṭhas are: (1) Auḍumbara; (2) Vaikhānasa; (3) Samprakshāli; (4) Pourṇama.

[4] They are Viveka, Vairagya, etc.

Himself." After the saṭṭra sacrifice was completed, he took the ṛshis along with him to saṭyaloka; and after duly making prostrations to and eulogising Brahmā engaged in meditation upon Brahman, he along with others was duly seated under the orders of Brahmā. Then Nāraḍa addressed Brahmā thus: "Thou art guru; thou art father; thou art the knower of the secret of all learning; thou art the knower of all; thou shalt therefore tell me one secret. Who else but thee is fit to tell the secret dear unto me? It is this. Please tell us the rules of the real sannyāsa (asceticism)."

Thus prayed to by Nāraḍa, Brahmā surveyed all in the four quarters; and after meditating for one muhūrṭa (48 minutes), and assuring himself that the inquiry was truly for the purpose of escaping from the pain of samsāra, Brahmā eyeing Nāraḍa, said thus: "The mystery that was imparted before by Virāṭ-Purusha of illimitable form according to the *Purusha-Sūkṭa-Upanishaḍ* is now being divulged to you. It is very mysterious. It is fit to be hearkened to with great attention. O Nāraḍa, one born in a good family and obedient to his parents, should, after the performance of upanayana according to the rules, find a virtuous guru that is other than his father, is of good custom and habits, of faith, born of good family, a knower of Veḍas, a lover of S'āsṭras, of (good) qualities and free from duplicity. Having made prostrations and rendered useful service to him, he should respectfully acquaint him with his intention. Having studied all departments of knowledge and rendered service for twelve years, he should, under his (the guru's) orders, marry a girl fit for his family and dear unto him. Then having performed for twenty-five years the karmas incidental to a householder and attained the status of a Brāhmaṇa that has performed sacrifices and the rest, he should beget a son with the only desire of perpetuating the family. After thus spending twenty-five years in the performance of household ḍharma, he should bathe thrice daily for twenty-five years and take only one meal in the fourth period; he should live alone in the forest, after giving up his previous wanderings in city and village; and without desire for fruit, should perform the karmas incidental to that (forester's) order of life, and be without desire for objects seen and heard. Being skilled in the forty samskāras, he should be devoid of desire for all, have a purified mind, have burnt up desire, jealousy, envy and egoism, and have developed the four means of salvation. Then he becomes fit for sannyāsa. Such is the Upanishaḍ."

UPAḌES'A III

Then Nāraḍa addressed the grandfather thus:

"O Lord, by whom, after attaining the qualifications of sannyāsa, is it fit to be taken?" To which Brahmā replied: "After first expounding the qualifications of sannyāsa, the rules of sannyāsa will then be stated. Hearken carefully. A eunuch, the outcaste, the maimed, the lewd, the deaf, the youth, the dumb, the heretic, the discus-bearer, the Liṅga-wearer, the vaikhānasa (forester), the Haraḍhvaja (carrier of S'iva's flag), the reciter of Veḍas for hire, the bald-headed, one without (sacrificial) fire—all these, even though they have attained vairāgya are unfit for sannyāsa. Even though they have become sannyāsins, they are unfit to be initiated into the mahāvākyas (sacred veḍic sentences). The Paramahamsa sannyāsin stated before (as fit to take sannyāsa) is the one qualified. It is stated in the smṛṭis that he is a parivrāt who is not afraid of others, as others are not afraid of him. The eunuch, the limbless, the blind, the youth, the sinful, the outcaste, the doọr-keeper, the vaikhānasa, the Haraḍhvaja, the chakrī (discus-bearer), the Liṅgī (Liṅga-wearer), the heretic, the bald-headed, one without fire (sacrifice), one that had undergone sannyāsa twice or thrice, the reciter of Veḍas for hire—all these are not fit for regular sannyāsa but only for āṭura-sannyāsa (*viz.*, sannyāsa taken while a person is afflicted, etc.). What is the opinion of āryas (Hinḍūs) on the (fit) time for āṭura-sannyāsa (being taken)? The time when prāṇa (life) is about to rise (out of the body) is called āṭura. The time other than it is incapable of conferring (upon one) the path of salvation and is not āṭura. Even in āṭura-sannyāsa, the wise should according to rules, initiate themselves into sannyāsa after reciting the manṭras again and again in the course of respective manṭras. There is no difference between regular and āṭura-sannyāsa in the manṭras to be uttered at the time of taking sannyāsa. There is no karma without manṭras; (hence) karma needs manṭras. Anything done without manṭra cannot be termed karma. Hence manṭras should not be given up. Any karma done without manṭra is like an offering made in ashes. Through the conciseness (of the performance) of the karmas, it is stated to be āṭura-sannyāsa.

"Therefore, O Muni, the recitation of manṭras is stated to be in āṭura-sannyāsa. One who is always duly doing agnihoṭra (fire-sacrifice) should, when he quits (the house) for foreign places through indifference, perform the prājāpaṭya sacrifice in water and then take up sannyāsa. After completing in water the observances of karma through the mind, or the recitation of manṭras, the wise man should attain sannyāsa. Else he becomes a fallen man. When, in the mind, indifference to all objects arises, then men should long after sannyāsa, (that being the best time for it); otherwise they are fallen. One who attains vairāgya should take sannyāsa. One who does not, should remain at home. That vile twice-born with desire, should he take sannyāsa, reaches hell. That Brāhmaṇa who is a celibate, who has under control his tongue, sexual organ, stomach, and hand may become a sannyāsin without undergoing the ceremony of marriage. Having known samsāra as one without sāra (or essence) and not having undergone any marriage on account of the desire to know the sāra (or essence of God), they become sannyāsins on account of the practice of the supreme vairāgya. The characteristic of pravṛṭṭi (path) is the performance of karma; that of nivṛṭṭi is jñāna. Therefore placing jñāna in the forefront, the wise man should take up sannyāsa. When the reality of the eternal Parabrahman is understood, then he should take up one ḍaṇḍa (staff) and abandon the holy thread and tuft of hair. Then he becomes fit to eat the alms-food (of sannyāsa), having become devoted to Paramāṭmā, indifferent to those that are not-Paramāṭmā and freed from all desires. He becomes fit to be the eater of alms-food who preserves the same countenance when he is beaten, as when he is worshipped or prostrated to. He becomes fit to be the eater of alms-food who is of the firm certitude that he is no other than the non-dual and indestructible Brahman, otherwise named Vāsuḍeva. He in whom are existent s'ānṭi (control of the organs), s'ama (control of mind), purity (of mind and body), saṭya (truth), sanṭosha (contentment), ārjava (straightforwardness), poverty, and non-ostentatiousness should be in the order of life of kaivalya (sannyāsa). When one does not, through actions, mind, or speech, commit any sinful action to any being, then he becomes fit for eating alms-food. Having become quiescent (through the control of the mind), having practised the ten kinds of ḍharmas, having, according to rules, studied veḍānṭa, and having paid the three debts (to ḍevas, ṛshis, and piṭṛs), one should take up sannyāsa. Courage, fortitude, the control of the body, honesty, purity of (mind and body), control of the (inner) organs, shame, knowledge, truth, and absence of anger—these ten are the characteristics of ḍharma. One who does not look back (with pleasure) upon past enjoyments, nor forward into the future, and one who does not rejoice in the present, is fit to become a sannyāsin. One who is able to control within, the inner organs and without, the external organs, may be in the order of life of kaivalya. One who while in life is not affected by pleasures and pains, as the body is unaffected by them after death, may be in the order of life of kaivalya.

"An ascetic of the Paramahamsa (order) shall wear two loin-cloths, one ragged cloth, and one staff. Nothing more is ordained (in his case). Should he through desire wear more than these, he will fall into the hell of raurava and be born into the womb of an animal. Having stitched together old and clean cloths into one and having coloured it with red (ochre), he should wear it as his upper cloth. He may be with one cloth or even without it. He should roam about alone with the sole vision (of Brahman), devoid of desires; but he may be in one place alone in the rainy season. Having quite abandoned his family, including son and wife, veḍānṭa, sacrifice, and the sacred thread, the ascetic should wander incognito.

Having given up all faults, such as passion, anger, pride, desire, and delusion, the parivrāt (ascetic) should become one that owns nothing. He is a muni who is devoid of love and hate, who regards equally a clod of earth, stone, or gold, who does no injury to any living creature, and is freed from all. That ascetic reaches salvation who is associated with Āṭmajñāna, who is freed from ostentation and egoism, from doing injury and tale-bearing. Through attraction to the senses, he becomes subject to fault, there is no doubt: through their control, he gains perfection. Lust when enjoyed is never gratified. Just as fire increases with the oblation (of ghee, etc., poured into it) so also lust waxes strong (with enjoyment). It should be known that that man who does not rejoice or grieve through hearing, touching, eating, seeing, or smelling is a jiṭenḍriya (conqueror of the organs). He whose speech and mind are well brought under control attains, completely and always, all the fruits of veḍānṭa.

"That Brāhmaṇa who is always afraid of respect as poison and always longs after disrespect as nectar, sleeps soundly and rises happily even though he is treated with disrespect. He moves about happily in this world. The one who treats him with disrespect perishes. All cruel words should be endured. None should be treated with disrespect. On account of bodily relationship, none should be made inimical. No anger should be directed in turn towards one who is angry. Soft words (only) should be spoken, even when (violently) pulled by another. No untrue words should be uttered, even should afflictions arise to the seven gates (of the body). One desirous of bliss should dwell in this universe through the aid of Āṭmā alone, intent upon Āṭmā, free from desires, and without the desire of blessing (others). He becomes fit for salvation through the control of the organs, the destruction of love and hate and non-injury to beings. He should abandon (all identification with) this feeble, perishable, and impure body of five elements whereof the bones are the pillars, which is strung by the nerves, coated over with flesh and blood, covered up by the skin, is of bad odour, full of urine and fæces is ever haunted by dotage and miseries and is the seat of all ills. If an ignorant man be fond of this body firmly knit together with flesh, blood, pus, fæces, and urine, nerves, fat, and bones, he would, *a fortiori*, be fond of hell. That (identification of the body with the Self) is alone the seat of the Kālasūṭra hell. That is alone the Mahā-Vīchi-Vāgura (hell). That is alone the Asipaṭravanas'reṇi (hell). Such an idea of the body being the Self should be strenuously abandoned, though all should perish. That love of the body is not fit to be felt by one intent upon his welfare, just as a low-caste woman eating dog's flesh is unfit to be touched.

"One (fit to reach salvation), after leaving all meritorious actions to those dear to him and all sins to those not dear, attains the eternal Brahman through ḍhyāna-yoga. Such a man, through the ordinances, gives up little by little all associations, and being freed from all pairs of opposites, remains in Brahman alone. On account of the accomplishment (of salvation), he should be moving about alone and without any help. He who having understood the effect of being alone never derogates from it, is never left in want. The bowl, the foot of the tree, the tattered robe, the state of being without help, the equality of vision in all these are the characteristics of the emancipated one. One intent upon the welfare of all beings, with a quiescent mind, having the three-knotted staff and bowl, and ever devoted to the One (Brahman), after taking up sannyāsa, may enter a village. Such one is a bhikshu (alms-taker). Should two unite, it is called miṭhuna (a pair or union); with three, it becomes a grāma (or village); with more, it is a nagara (or city). No city or village, or, miṭhuna should be made, and an ascetic who commits these three (offences) falls from his duty. Through such intercourse (of ascetics), all kinds of talks connected with the king and alms, friendship, tale-bearing, and malice occur between them. There is no doubt of it.

"He (the ascetic) should be alone and desireless. He should not converse with anybody. The ascetic should ever be uttering the word Nārāyaṇa in each sentence. Being alone, he should be meditating upon Brahman in all mental, spoken, and bodily actions. He should neither rejoice at dying or living. He should be anticipating the time when life will close. He should not be glad of dying; nor should he be glad of living. He should be biding his time like a hireling (for his pay). Ān ascetic who plays the part of the dumb, the eunuch, the lame, the blind, the deaf, and the idiot is emancipated through the (above six) means. There is no doubt of this. He who has not fondness for eating, saying that this is good and that is bad, who speaks only words that are beneficial, true, and moderate is said to be the dumb. He is a eunuch who is no more affected by the sight of a sixteen years old girl than of a new-born female baby or a hundred-years old woman. He who does not move about for more than the distance of a yojana for alms or for the calls of nature is a lame man. That parivrāt (ascetic) is said to be a blind man, who whether sitting or walking, has his vision extended to no more than four yokes' distance on the ground. He is said to be deaf who, though hearing words, beneficial or non-beneficial, pleasant or painful to the mind, is as if he does not hear them. That clever ascetic is said to be an idiot who is ever in a state of sleep, as it were, having his organs non-agitated by objects, even though near. He should never observe the following six—the scenes of dancing, etc., gambling, lovely women, eatables, enjoyables, and women in their monthly course.

"The ascetic should never in thought even think of others with the six (*viz.,*) love, hate, pride, deceit, treachery, and the illusion (of confounding them). To the ascetics, the following six are sinful: cot, white cloth, the stories of women, love towards women, sleep during the day, and vehicles. He who is engaged in Āṭmic contemplation should carefully avoid a long journey. He should ever practise the upanishaḍic viḍyā tending to salvation. The ascetic need not bathe daily. He need not observe upavāsa (fast). He need not be one that had studied Veḍas. He need not be one that is able to produce a commentary (lecture). He should daily observe acts without sin, deceit, or falsehood. He who, having withdrawn the organs within, like a turtle its limbs (within its shell), is with the actions of the organs and the mind annihilated, without desires, without possessing any object as his own, without dualities, without prostrations, without the oblations to piṭṛ ḍevaṭās (they being with desires), without mine or I, without awaiting anything, without the desire to be happy, and living in places where men do not live—he alone is emancipated. There is no doubt of this.

" A celibate, or householder, or forester, who is (ever) vigilant, has karma, devotion, and knowledge and is independent, after understanding his peculiar tendency and having become indifferent (to his order of life), may become an householder after ending the celibate life, or may from the householder's life enter the life of a forester, and then the life of an ascetic; or from the life of a celibate, or householder, or forester may (directly) enter that of an ascetic. The moment vairāgya arises in him, he may become an ascetic that moment, whether he is with vraṭa (religious observance) or not, is snāṭaka[1] or not, or with a discontinued fire-sacrifice or not. On account of that, some perform Prājāpaṭya-sacrifice alone; or Āgneya-sacrifice may be performed. Is not agni, prāṇa? Through this alone, one should perform that sacrifice only which is connected with the three ḍhāṭus. The three ḍhāṭus are saṭṭva, rajas, and ṭamas alone. With the manṭra, अयं ते योनिर्ऋत्विजो यतो जातो अरोचथाः । तं जानन्नग्न आरोहाथा नो वर्धया रयिं ॥, agni (fire) should be taken in. Thus it is said (in the S'ruṭis): एष वा अग्नेर्योनिर्यः प्राणः, प्राणं गच्छ स्वां योनिं गच्छ स्वाहा ॥ The agni from āhavanīya should be brought and taken in as before (with the manṭras above mentioned). Should such an agni be not obtainable, the homa (oblation) should be done in water with the manṭra, आपो वै सर्वा देवतास्सर्वाभ्यो देवताभ्यो जुहोमि स्वाहा । After performing homa, the water should be taken in and sipped. After uttering the manṭra, साज्यं हविरनामयं मोक्षदं, he abandons the tuft of hair in the head, the holy thread, father, son, wife, karma, veḍic study and manṭra and becomes an ascetic. The S'ruṭis say that a knower of Āṭmā should be engaged in meditation upon Brahman, through the three mantras tending to salvation."

Then Nāraḍa asked Brahmā thus: " How can one, without the holy thread, be a Brāhmaṇa?" To which Brahmā replied "The wise should, after shaving (the head) together with the

[1] A celibate who has completed his first Āsrama.

tuft of hair, cast off the holy thread. He should wear, as his sūṭra (thread), the indestructible and supreme Brahman. On account of (sūchanāṭ) its being an indication, it (thread) is called sūṭra. Sūṭra is the Paramapaḍa (supreme seat). He by whom that sūṭra is known is Brāhman. That sūṭra (thread of Brahman) in which is strung the whole universe like beads on a sūṭra (string), should be worn by the yogin that has known yoga and ṭaṭṭva. The wise man that is in supreme yoga should abandon the outer sūṭra (thread). He who wears (in his heart) this sūṭra of Brāhmic Reality is alone Brāhmaṇa. Through wearing this higher sūṭra, it becomes not a rejected one, not an impure one. Those only whose sūṭra is internal, having the holy thread as jñāna are the real knowers of the sūṭra; they are said to possess the yajñōpavīṭa (holy thread). To those whose s'ikhā (tuft of hair) is jñāna, whose holy thread is jñāna, and whose meditation is upon jñāna, jñāna alone is supreme. It is said that jñāna alone is able to purify. That wise man alone who possesses the jñāna-s'ikhā like the s'ikhā (flame) of agni (fire) is said to possess s'ikhā (tuft of hair). Those that have mere s'ikhā are no s'ikhīs. The Brāhmaṇas and others that are entitled to perform the veḍic karmas are allowed to wear the (external) thread, only as an auxiliary to the karmas. It is only veḍic. The knowers of Brahman know that all Brāhmaṇya (the state of Brahman) accrues to him only that has the jñānamaya s'ikhā (knowledge-tuft of hair) and the ṭanmaya (That or Brahman-ful) upavīṭa (holy thread).

"Having known it, a Brāhmaṇa should take up sannyāsa. Such a sannyāsin, should be, in order to bear the bodily afflictions, with one cloth, bald-headed and without having anything as being required (for his use); or according to rules, he may be (naked) as nature made his body, and should abandon his son, friend, wife, trustworthy relatives, etc., as well as all karmas and love for the universe, the loin-cloth, staff, and covering. Enduring all pairs of opposites without cold or heat, happiness or grief, fame or disgrace, without the six changes, I-ness, malice, pride, ostentation, jealousy, slander of others, love and hate, pleasure and pain, passion, anger, greed and delusion and regarding his body as a mere carcase, without thinking of all the things, internal and external, that are other than Self. Without prostrations, without the worship of ḍevas and piṭṛs and without praise or condemnation, he should wander about of his own accord. He should not receive gold and others. For him, there is no invocation or dismissal (of deities), manṭra or non-manṭra, meditation or worship, aim or non-aim, others or not-others; without having another's or (his own) settled place of residence, and having a firm conviction, he should be in a desolate house or at the foot of trees, or in a temple, a plenteous turfed spot, a potter's place or that of agnihoṭra or sacrifice, river, tank, sand-heap, subterranean vault, cave, mountain-rill, the place prepared for sacrifice or forest; or like the naked personages, S'veṭaketu, Ṛbhu, Niḍāgha, Jadabharaṭa, Ṛshabha, Ḍurvāsas, Samvarṭaka, Sanaṭsujāṭa, Vaiḍeha (Janaka), Vaṭasiḍḍha, S'uka, Vāmaḍeva, Ḍattāṭreya, Raivaṭaka, and Goraksha, he should roam about as nature made him, without being recognised and without any means of discovery of his course of life, like a lad, or an insane man, or a ghost, with the actions of a madman though not mad, after discarding in water the three-knotted staff, the stringed sling (bag), vessel, bowl, waist-string, loin-cloth, stick, and cloth. He should ever be engaged in Āṭmic deliberation. Being in his natural state without being affected by the pairs, without receiving anything, being ever settled firmly in the Brāhmic path, having a pure mind, eating the food that is obtained without asking, in the palm as vessel, or in another's vessel in order to merely protect the body at the tim-required, being of equal mind whether the object is gained or not, without having aught of his own, always meditating upon Brahman, being with Āṭma-nishthā, having eradicated all actions, virtuous and sinful, and having given up all—that one who ever utters Brahma-Praṇava, that "I am Brahman" alone, with the blissful and non-dual jñāna, and after rising above the three bodies (to Brahman), like the analogy of the wasp and the worm,[1] gives up the body as a

[1] Referring to the idea of the worm becoming the wasp, with the latter's frequent stinging.

sannyāsin, is said to have done all his work (in this world). Such is the Upanishaḍ."

UPAḌEŚA IV

"One who after giving up the world, the Veḍas, the objects and the organs is in Āṭmā alone, attains the supreme abode. A good ascetic should not make known his caste, name, goṭra (clan), etc., his place and time, the Veḍas, etc. studied by him, his family, age, history, observance, and conduct. He should neither converse with women nor remember the women he had seen. He should give up all stories connected with women. He should not even see the figure of a woman in a picture. The mind of an ascetic who through delusion adopts the above four things connected with women is necessarily affected and thereby perishes. The following are prohibited (in his case): Thirst, malice, falsehood, deceit, greed, delusion, the pleasant and the unpleasant, manual work, lecture, yoga, kāma (passion), desire, begging, I-ness, mine-ness, the obstinacy of curing diseases, penance, pilgrimage and the accomplishment of fruits of manṭras, and medicines. He who performs these interdicted things, goes into a debased state. A muni who has moksha as his supreme seat should address such respectful words as "Please come, please go, please stay, and welcome" to one, even though he be his intimate friend. He should neither receive presents, etc., nor ask for them to be given to oṭhers. Even in dream, an ascetic should never direct a person (to do work for him). Even should he witness or hear of the happiness or grief of his wife, brother, son, and other relatives, he should not be affected thereby. He should abandon all joy and sorrow.

"To the ascetics controlling their mind, the following are their svaḍharmas (own duties): Harmlessness, truth, honesty, celibacy, non-coveting, humility, high-spiritedness, clearness of mind, steadiness of mind, straightforwardness, non-attachment (to any), service to the guru, faith, patience, bodily restraint, mental restraint, indifference, firm and sweet words, endurance, compassion, shame, jñāna, vijñāna, yoga, moderate food, and courage. That paramahamsa of an ascetic in the order of life of a sannyāsin who is without dualities, always follows the pure saṭṭvaguṇa and sees all equally, is no other than the actual Nārāyaṇa Himself. He may live one day in a village and five days in a city, but five months in the wintry season. Āt other times he should live in other places (such as forest, etc.). He should not live in a village for two days (even); should he do so, desires and the rest will arise in him and thereby he becomes fit for hell. He should live like a (harmless) worm on the earth with his mind under control and with no settled place of residence, at the end of the village where there are no persons. He may live in the same place in the wintry season. He should roam about on the earth with one or no cloth, with the one vision (of Brahman) alone, with no desires (of objects), with no condemnation of the actions of the wise and with meditation. That yogin of an ascetic should go about, observing the duties of his order of life, and with the eyes cast on the earth, in pure places. He should not roam about in night, midday or the two twilight periods in which are places void or difficult to be waded through or likely to injure living creatures. He may live for one day in a village, for three days in a town, for two days in a hamlet and for five days in a city. He may live in the wintry season (longer) in one place surrounded fully by water. The ascetic should regard all creatures as Self and dwell upon earth like the blind, the hunchback, the deaf, the insane, and the dumb. The bahūḍaka and the forester should bathe thrice a day. In the case of hamsa, one bath only is ordained; but none in the case of a paramahamsa. In the case of the one having one staff, seven things are ordained, *viz.*, silence, yoga-posture, yoga, endurance, solitariness, desirelessness, and equal vision over all. Bathing being not prescribed for a paramahamsa, he should abandon all the modifications of the mind only; what is the difference between the worms and the men that rejoice over this ill-smelling body which is but a collection of skin, flesh, blood, nerves, fat, marrow, bone, offal and urine? What is the body but a collection of all, phlegm, etc.? Ānd what are the qualities, the vāsana of the body, effulgence, beauty, etc.? (They are opposed to one another.) The ignorant man that is fond of this body, which is but a compound of flesh, blood, the ill-smelling urine and offal, nerve, fat and bone, will be fond of hell too. Though there is no difference between the women's secret parts that cannot be described by words and an (ever) oozing tubular wound, yet through the difference of the mind, (men are deluded). Such men are said to be without prāṇa, (*viz.*, dead) though alive. Prostrations to those that sport in that piece of flesh which is rent in twain and tainted with the breaking of the wind, etc. What more revolting thing is there than this?

" To the wise, there is nothing to do, no sign (of identification). The muni who is without 'mine' and fear, with quiescence, without duality and eating leaf (alone), should ever be in meditation with either loin-cloth or no cloth. A yogin who is thus in meditation becomes fit to be Brahman. Though he may have some signs (of identification to pass under this order of life or that), such signs are useless for gaining moksha. The cause of salvation is jñāna alone. He is a (true) brāhmaṇa who cannot be identified as saṭ (good person) or asaṭ, knower of religious books or not, follower of good conduct or bad conduct. Therefore that learned man who is without signs, a knower of ḍharma, engaged in the actions of Brahman and a knower of the secret mysteries, should roam about, incognito. He should go about on this earth without any caste or order of life and without being (even) doubted (regarding his identity) by any beings, like the blind, the idiot, or the mute. Then (even) the angels become fond of him who has a quiescent mind. It is the dictate of the Veḍas that the sign (of non-identification) itself is Kaivalya."

Then Nāraḍa asked the Grandfather about the rules of sannyāsa. To which Brahmā assented and said: " Before either the āṭura or regular sannyāsa is taken, kṛchchhra penance should be done and then the eight s'rāḍḍhas. In each of the (eight) s'rāḍḍhas, two brāhmaṇas should be fed, in lieu of Vis'veḍevas called Saṭyavasu and the (Ṭrimūrṭis called) Brahmā, Vishṇu, and Mahes'vara, in Ḍevas'rāḍḍha first; then in Ṛshi-s'rāḍḍha in lieu of Ḍevarṣhi, Rājarṣhi, and Manushyarṣhi; then in Ḍivyas'rāḍḍha, in lieu of Vasu, Rudra, and Āḍiṭyas; then in manushyas'rāḍḍha in lieu of Sanaka, Sananḍana, Sanaṭkumāra, and Sanaṭsujāṭa; then in bhūṭas'rāḍḍha, in lieu of the five great elements, pṛṭhivī, etc., eye and other organs and the four kinds of collections of bhūṭas; then in Piṭṛs'rāḍḍha, in lieu of father, grandfather and great-grandfather; then in māṭṛs'rāḍḍha, in lieu of mother, mother's father and mother's grandfather; and then in Āṭmas'rāḍḍha, in lieu of himself, his father and grandfather or of himself, grandfather and great-grandfather, should his father be alive. He should perform the eight s'rāḍḍhas in one day, or eight days, with the manṭras of his s'ākhā in one yājñapaksha or eight yājñapakshas. Then he should worship and feed the brāhmaṇas according to the rules contained in piṭṛyajña. Then offering the piṇdas (balls of rice to the piṭṛs), he should gladden the brāhmaṇas with the ṭāmbūla (nut and betel, etc.,) presents and dismiss them. Then for the accomplishment of the remaining karmas, he should pluck off seven hairs; then again for finishing the rest of the karmas, he should hold seven or eight hairs and have the head shaved. Except his arm-pit and secret parts, he should have the hairs of his head, whiskers and mustache and nails shaved. After shaving, he should bathe and perform the evening sanḍhyā, uttering Gāyaṭrī a thousand times. Then performing brahmayajña, he should establish his own fire and acting up to his s'ākhā, should perform the oblation of ghee according to what is said therein till the ājya portion with those (manṭras beginning with) Āṭmā, etc.; he should eat thrice the fried rice-powder, and then sipping the water, he should maintain the fire; then seated north of the fire on a deer-skin, he should be engaged in the study of Purāṇas; without sleeping, he should bathe at the end of the four yāmas and after cooking the oblation of (rice) in the fire, he should offer it to the fire in sixteen oblations according to (the manṭras of) Purusha-Sūkṭa. Then having done virajā-homa and sipped water, he should close it with the gift (to brāhmaṇas) of cloth, golden vessel, and cows along with presents of money and then dismiss Brahmā (who had been invoked). With the prescribed manṭra, he should attract Āgni (fire) unto himself. Âfter meditating upon and coming round and prostrating before the fire, he should dismiss it. Then in the morning performing sanḍhyā and uttering Gāyaṭrī a thousand times, he should make upasṭhāna (worship) to the sun. Then descending into water up to the navel, he should make arghya (water-offering) to the guardians of the eight quarters; then he should give leave to Gāyaṭrī, making Sāviṭrī enter into vyāhṛṭi.

The manṭra prescribed for this should be uttered through the mind and voice in high, middling, and low tones. With the manṭra, अभयं सर्वभूतेभ्यो मत्तः सर्वं प्रवर्तते । the water should be sipped and having taken the water with the two hands, it should be dropped on the east. Having uttered स्वाहा, he should pluck his hair (yet left) and uttering the prescribed manṭra and having torn off the sacred thread and taken it in the hand with water, should utter ओं भूः 'go to the ocean' and cast them down as oblation in water:—ओं भूः संन्यस्तं मया । ओं भुवः संन्यस्तं मया । ओं स्वः संन्यस्तं मया ॥ Having uttered thrice and saturated thrice (the water) with (the influence of) the manṭra, he should sip the water; and then uttering the manṭras ओं भूः, etc., he should cast aside in water the cloth and waist-cord. Having thought himself to be the abdicator of all karmas, he, being in the meditation of his own Reality as nature made him, should go as before northwards with hands upraised. Should he be a sannyāsin learned (in the Veḍas, etc.), he should get himself initiated into Praṇava from his teacher and go about at his own free will with the thought of there being none other but his Self, and feeding his body with fruits, leaves and water, live in mountains, forest and temples. That lover of salvation who after sannyāsa roams about naked in all places with his heart full of the enjoyment of Âṭmic bliss, with the fruit of avoidance of karmas and maintaining his life with fruits, juice, barks, leaves, roots and water should abandon his body in mountain caves, uttering the Praṇava. But an aspirant after wisdom, should he become a sannyāsin, should, after walking a hundred steps, be addressed by the teacher and other Brāhmans thus: "O Mahābhāga (very fortunate person), stay,

stay, wear the staff, cloth and bowl, come to the teacher in order to learn the meaning of Praṇava manṭra vākya". He should then take up the waist-cord, loin-cloth, red-coloured cloth and bowl. A bamboo staff which is not injured from top to bottom, equal, beautiful, and not spotted with black, should be worn by him, after sipping the water and uttering the manṭra prescribed for the purpose. Then the bowl should be taken up, after uttering the manṭra with the Praṇava preceding it:—ओं जगज्जीवनं जीवनाधारभूतं मातेव मा मन्त्रयस्व सर्वदा सर्व सौम्य ॥ Then after first uttering (the manṭra) गुह्याच्छादनं कौपीनं ओं । शीतवातोष्णत्राणकरं देहैकरक्षणं वस्त्रं ओं ॥ he should take up the waist-cord, loin-cloth and cloth with the āchamana (sipping of water) preceding it.

"Thus consecrated with yoga and thinking that he had done all that should be done, he should be firm in the observances of his order of life. Thus is the Upanishaḍ."

UPAḌES'A V

Then Nārada said to the Grandfather thus:—

"You said that sannyāsa was the liberator of all karmas. Now you say again that the sannyāsin is one that should be in the observance of his ās'rama (order of life). (How to reconcile the two?)" To which the Grandfather replied thus: "To the jīva possessing the body, there are three avasṭhās—the waking, the dreaming, and the dreamless sleeping with ṭurya (the fourth). Those beings of Purushas that are subject to these avasṭhās follow the observances, incidental to them, of karma, jñāna and vairāgya." Nāraḍa said: "O Lord, if so, what are the differences of different orders of sannyāsa? And what are the differences of their observances? Please tell us truly."

Therefore the differences of sannyāsas, and the differences of observances were related for the sake of Nāraḍa by Brahmā, after assenting to his (Nāraḍa's) question thus:—

"Truly sannyāsa is of one kind only. On account of ajñāna, inability and non-performance of karmas (of persons), it is divided into three and then into four, thus: vairāgya-sannyāsa, jñāna-sannyāsa, jñānavairāgya-sannyāsa and karma-sannyāsa.

The vairāgya-sannyāsin is one who becomes an ascetic after being in a vicious condition of lust, etc., and then, becomes disgusted with the objects through his former good karmas. Ā jñāna-sannyāsin is one who becomes an ascetic with the four means of salvation, after controlling the organs through book-wisdom, and becoming familiar with the experiences of the world of virtue and vice, after abandoning anger, jealousy, envy, ahaṅkāra and all sannyāsa productive of identification, after giving up the three vāsanās of the body, books and world, which are of the form of desires for women, wealth and earth, and after thinking that the whole of the universe should be given up, like vomited food. Ā jñānavairāgya-sannyāasin is one who becomes an ascetic as nature made him, after practising and enjoying all, and having the body alone remaining, through jñāna and vairāgya, in the realisation of the Reality. Ā karma-sannyāsin is one who, though he has no vairāgya, becomes an ascetic by regularly passing from one ās'rama to another, from the celibate, to the householder and then to the forester. Ā vairāgya-sannyāsin is one who becomes an ascetic from the celibate order (directly), being as nature made him.

"(There is another fourfold classification.) The four kinds are: vidvaṭ-sannyāsa, jñāna-sannyāsa, vividishā-sannyāsa and karma-sannyāsa. In karma-sannyāsa, there are two (sub-) divisions, nimiṭṭa (causal) and animiṭṭa (non-causal). Āṭura-sannyāsa (on account of the cause of approaching death, disease, etc.), is nimiṭṭa-sannyāsa. The krama (regular) sannyāsa is animiṭṭa. Āṭura-sannyāsa is on account of defective karmas. When sannyāsa is taken at the time of death, it is called nimiṭṭa. Animiṭṭa is that when one becomes duly a sannyāsin when the body is strong, (after being convinced) that all created things are subject to destruction, that body and others should be given up, that all Āṭmās (souls)—each one shining in the pure Ākās', dwelling in all, moving in the anṭariksha (middle world) as of the form of vāyu, in the sacrificial pit as of the form of fire, in the moon, in all men, in the supreme angels, in the form of truth, in ākās', in the form of the conch, pearl, fish, etc., in water, in the form of grain, etc., on earth, in the form of the limbs of Veḍas, in the form of the rivers from the mountains, in the form of truth and the great one—are no other than Brahman and that others are but perishable.

"There are six classes of sannyāsins—kutīchaka, bahūḍaka, hamsa, paramahamsa, ṭurīyāṭīṭa and avaḍhūṭa. Kutīchaka is one who wears the tuft of hair, holy thread, staff, bowl, loin-cloth and tattered cloth, who worships mother, father, and teacher, who has potsherd and sling, who is uttering manṭras, who takes food in one and the same place, who wears, vertically, the white earth (on the forehead as sect-mark) and who has a staff. Bahūḍaka is one who, like kutīchaka, wears the tuft of hair, tattered cloth, etc., as well as the three (sect-) marks, but who eats eight morsels of food through getting alms. The hamsa is one who wears matted hair and the three vertical sect-marks and eats the alms-food without any limit (as to the morsel) and wears the bare loin-cloth only. The paramahamsa is he who is without tuft of hair and holy thread, begs food in one day from five houses, has one loin-cloth, wears one red cloth alone and sacred ashes and has given up all. The ṭurīyaṭīṭa is one who either may take fruits, eating them with his mouth like cows, or if he is an eater of food, may beg food from three houses. The naked man having the body alone has the bodily actions (quiescent), like the dead body. Such an one is the ṭurīyāṭīṭa. The avaḍhūṭa is he who is without any rules, gets his food (in his mouth), following the course of the boa constrictor,[1] from all persons except persons of ill-repute and outcastes, and is ever engaged in the realisation of the Real. Should the āṭura-sannyāsin be alive (after taking sannyāsa), he should take up regular sannyāsa. The rules to be observed in the case of the (three), kutīchaka, bahūḍaka and hamsa are the same as for the orders of life from the celibate to the sannyāsin. For the three, paramahamsa upwards, they have no waist-cord, loin-cloth, cloth, bowl and staff. They may get food from all castes and should be as nature made them. Such are the rules.

[1] The snake, or boa constrictor, is said to remain in one place only on account of its huge body, taking any food that may come to its mouth as it is lying there.

"At the time of the sannyāsa, the recitation of the Vedas should be made till the mind is cleared; and after casting aside in water the waist-cord, loin-cloth, staff, cloth, bowl, etc., he should roam about. He should be without even the slightest tattered cloth. He should neither utter anything other than Praṇava, nor talk nor hear. He should not study logic or grammar. He should not talk many words; they will but pain his vocal organ. He should not converse with people through the vocal organ. He should not talk in other language (than Samskṛṭ). He has no worship of God and no witnessing of festivals; he should be free from pilgrimage. The other rules of ascetics are: The kutīchaka should beg alms in one house only; for the bahūḍaka, eight morsels in eight houses; for the hamsa, there is no limit; for paramahamsa, he should beg with his hand as the vessel in five houses; for the ṭurīyāṭīṭa, he should eat fruits with his mouth like cows; (for avaḍhūṭa), he should take food like a boa constrictor in all castes. The ascetic should not dwell in one place for many days. He should not make prostrations to any one. Among the ṭurīyāṭīṭa and avaḍhūṭa (ascetics), even though one is junior, he should not make prostrations to another, a senior who has known the Reality. He should not swim with his hands and cross the river. He should not climb up a tree, nor get into a carriage. Nothing should be purchased or sold (by him). No exchange should be made, no ostentation for him. There is nothing for the ascetic to do. If there is anything for him to do, he will perish. Therefore the only thing he is qualified to do is reflection, etc.

"To the āṭuras and kutīchakas, the world they attain is bhūrloka and bhuvarloka; to the bāhūḍakas, swargaloka; to the hamsas, ṭapoloka; to the paramahamsas, saṭyaloka. To the ṭurīyāṭīṭa and avaḍhūta, Kaivalya in Āṭmā according to the analogy of the wasp and the worm through the realisation of Reality. It is the command of the Veḍas that whatever form one thinks of at the last (death) moment and before leaving the body is attained by him and no other. Knowing it thus, he should not be a practiser of anything but the realisation of Reality.

Through the observance of any other, he goes to the world of that other. To one that has attained jñāna-vairāgya, his salvation is in the Self, as there is no other observance for him. The same one (Āṭmā) alone is styled Vis'va in the waking state, Ṭaijasa in the dreaming state and Prājña in the dreamless sleeping state. Through the difference of states, there is the difference of the agent presiding over them. To the fourteen organs (the ten organs of sense and actions and the four organs of the mind in these states,) the outer and inner vṛṭṭis (modifications) are the material cause. There are four vṛṭṭis, *viz.*, manas, buḍḍhi, ahaṅkāra and chiṭṭa. Through the differences of actions of the vṛṭṭis, there arise the differences of separate functions. When (the presiding agent is) in the eyes, there is the waking state; in the throat, the dreaming state; in the heart, the dreamless sleeping state; and in the head, the ṭurya (or fourth) state. Knowing these and that the ṭurya is the indestructible, one should not hear or see anything in the waking state, as if he were in dreamless sleeping state. To such a one who does not apparently know them, even the dreaming state forms the same (dreamless sleeping) state. Such a one is termed Jīvanmukṭa. All the Veḍas say that there is salvation to such a one.

" To the ascetic, there should be no desire of this world or the higher. Then he will be one that will practise accordingly. Through the practices of (the study of) books foreign to the realisation of Reality, he becomes a useless person like a camel bearing saffron paint. To him, there is no entry into yoga books, no study of sāṅkhya books, no practise of manṭra or ṭanṭra. Should there be any entry into other books (than the one treating of Reality), then it will be like an ornament to a dead body. Like a cobbler, he should be beyond karma and knowledge and unfit for salutation and repeating the names of the Lord. He will duly get the benefit of the karmas (of his order of life). Having given up all like the foam (separating itself) from the castor oil, having the mental staff which controls the mind clinging to objects, having the hand as the vessel (for eating) and having the quarters alone as the cloth, the ascetic should go about like a lad, idiot, or ghost. He should neither desire to live nor die. Like a coolie abiding his appointed time (of pay), the ascetic should bide his time (of death). One who lives by taking alms without (the qualifications of) patience, wisdom, vairāgya and the qualifications beginning with s'ama (control of mind) is the spoiler of the order of life of an ascetic. There is no salvation obtained through the mere assumption of the staff or making the head bald or other disguise or through ostentatious observances. That man who has jñāna as his staff is said to be the ēkaḍaṇḍī (one having Brahman alone as the staff). An ascetic who, having merely a wooden staff without jñāna, eats all (indiscriminately) in all places, goes to the terrible hells called Mahāraurava. (The sense of) greatness in his case is likened by the ṛshis to the pig's dung. Having given it up, he should move about like a worm. Food and cloth without being begged for by him should be obtained involuntarily through the will of others. A naked (ascetic) may bathe at the wish of another. A man who practises the the meditation upon Self in the dreaming state as in the waking is said to be the foremost and first of Brahmavāḍins. He should neither grieve for things not obtained, nor rejoice at things obtained. With the organs not attached to objects, he should be engaged in the sole protection of life. He should always look down upon the gains obtained with much respect (shown to him). Through the gains obtained with much respect, the ascetic though released becomes bound. What is meant by the protection of life, is this: When the fire (of the hearth in a house) had been extinguished and all have taken food, he may go to the houses of caste people that are fit for taking alms from. The yogin who has his hand only as his alms-bowl should not often take alms. He may take (food) standing or sitting; so in the middle (of taking food), he may sip water. Those who have pure mind should not over-step the limits like the ocean. The great ones do not give up their self-restraint like the sun. When the muni takes, like a cow, the food with the mouth only (without the use of the hand), he becomes of equal vision to all beings. Then he becomes fit for salvation. He may, for alms, go from a forbidden house to a non-forbidden one. He should go (for alms) to a house where the door is ajar, but not to a house where it is closed. The muni who has a dusty body, an uninhabited house or the foot of a tree as his abode, without anything dear or not dear to him, sleeping where the sun sets, without any fire-worship, without any settled place and with patience and the organs under control, should live without any desire in any place obtained. He who after going to the forest dwells with jñāna as the sacrifice and the organs under his mastery and awaits his time (of death), is fit to be of the nature of Brahman. A muni who goes about with no cause for instilling fear into all beings need never have any fear from them. One without any abhimāna (identification with body) or egoism or dualities or doubt, never is angry, never hates, never lies through the vocal organ. That person who, having visited all sacred places, does not do any injury to any living creature and gets alms at the proper time, is fit to be of the nature of Brahman. He should not associate with a forester or householder. He should conduct himself in such manner as not to be known to others. He should not be glad of anything. He should roam about on earth like a worm, according to the direction pointed out by the sun. He should not do or cause to do works tending to (his) fame or pains or people's benefit. He should not be inclined towards vicious books. He should not live dependent upon any. He should give up all over-disputatious reasoning. He should not join any party (fighting with another). He should not take any disciples. He should not study many books. He should not discourse. Neither should he commence any works. Without any distinguishing characteristics and without letting others know his opinions, that wise man, or muni, ever intent upon the Brāhmic vision, should exhibit himself to people like an idiot, or a lad, or a mute person. He should neither do nor talk anything. He should not think of a good or bad thing. Rejoicing in That within himself, the muni should go about like an idiot. He should roam about alone without associating with any, and with the senses under control. The clever jñānī sporting in Āṭmā, ever delighting in Āṭmā, looking upon all with equal vision like an Āṭma-jñānī, and playing like a child, should wander about like an idiot. That learned man versed in Brahma-viḍyā should talk like a madman. He should follow the observances of cows (by eating with the mouth, causing no trouble to anybody). A good jñānī whether pushed, disregarded, slighted, beaten, or hindered by the vicious, or burnt by their acts, or having urine and fæces thrown upon him by them, or afflicted in various other ways, should always think well of them though pained, and thus make them lift themselves through their own Selves. A yogin whether praised or afflicted by others, never thinks of it in order to reach a superior state in yoga. A yogin who is slighted by people, attains a higher state in yoga. A yogin never goes against the actions of the virtuous. He is the same whether people slight him or do not desire his association. He should do all that is right through the actions of mind, speech and body to all beings born out of the embryo or the egg, etc. He should harbour no malice against any and give up all clinging to things. The ascetic after giving up passion, anger, pride, desire, delusion and other faults should be without fear. Eating alms-food, preserving silence, ṭapas, special meditation, a good jñāna, and vairāgya—these are said, in the opinion (of the great), to be the ḍharma of the ascetic. Wearing the red cloth, and being ever in ḍhyāna-yoga, he should live either at the foot of a tree, outside the village, or in the temple. Daily he should live upon begging. He should not eat one food alone (from one only). Till the mind becomes pure, the learned man should thus be moving about. Then when the mind is purified, he may be anywhere as a parivrājaka. Seeing Janārḍana in and out everywhere, preserving silence, being without stain like vāyu, roaming everywhere, being equal in happiness and pains, and with patience, eating whatever comes to hand, equally regarding without any hate brāhmaṇa, cow, horse, beasts and others, meditating through the mind upon Vishṇu that is Paramāṭmā and Īs'vara, thinking ever of Brāhmic bliss and thinking himself to be Brahman alone—such a one having known thus, regarding the staff to be no other than the certitude of the mind as above, having no desire, being naked and having abandoned all samsāra through the actions ever done through the mind, speech, and body, attains salvation, according to the analogy of the wasp and the worm, through the practice of the realisation of Reality without ever seeing the universe. Such is the Upanishaḍ."

UPAḌES'A VI

Nāraḍa addressing Brahmā asked: "O Lord! You said of abhyāsa (practice) according to the analogy of wasp and the worm. What is that practice?"

To which the Grandfather replied thus:—

"One (*viz.*, an ascetic) should live with true speech and jñāna-vairāgya and with the body alone as the remaining (possession). Know jñāna alone as the body, vairāgya alone as prāṇa, s'ānṭi (mental control) and ḍānṭi (bodily control) as the eyes, manas alone as the face, buḍḍhi alone as kalā (parts of effulgence), the twenty-five ṭaṭṭvas as the limbs, the avasṭhās as the five great elements, karma, bhakṭi, jñāna, and vairāgya as the branches (or parts) and that the waking, dreaming, dreamless sleeping, and ṭurya avasṭhās and the fourteen organs as being of the nature of a pillar planted in the mud. Though such is the case, the man who masters these through his buḍḍhi like a boatman regarding the boat immersed in the mire, or the elephant-driver regarding the elephant (under his control), and has known that all else beside Self is illusory and destructible and become indifferent, should ever utter: 'I am Brahman alone.' He should not know anything as other than Self. A Jīvanmukṭa who lives thus is a doer of that which should be done. He should not discourse that he is other than Brahman. But he should ever be discoursing: 'I am Brahman'. From the waking, dreaming and dreamless sleeping states, he should reach the ṭurya state and then ṭuryāṭīṭa (the state beyond ṭurya). The waking state is in the day; the dreaming in the night and the dreamless sleeping in the midnight. Each avasṭhā (or state) has its sub-states. The functions of the fourteen organs, eye and others mutually dependent are the following: The eyes perceive forms; the ears, sounds; the tongue perceives tastes; the nose, odours; the vocal organ speaks; the hand lifts; the leg walks; the anus excretes; the sexual organ enjoys; the skin feels; the buḍḍhi perceives objects, being under the control of the organs; through buḍḍhi, he understands; through chiṭṭa, he thinks; through ahaṅkāra, he says 'I'. All these should be abandoned. Through the identification with the house (the body), he, like a householder, becomes a jīva thinking that the body is itself.

"The jīva is dwelling in this body. When he is in the eastern petal (of the heart), he is inclined to virtuous actions; in the south-eastern petal, to sleep and laziness; in the southern petal, to cruel actions; in the south-western petal, to sinful actions; in the western petal, to love of sport (or to flirt); in the north-western petal, to travelling; in the northern petal, to peace of mind; in the north-eastern petal, to jñāna; in (the middle of) the pericarp, to vairāgya; in the filament, to Āṭma-deliberation. Such are the different aspects to be understood (in the heart). The first living avasṭhā (of jīva) is the waking; the second is the dreaming; the third is the dreamless sleeping; the fourth ṭurya; that which is not these four is ṭuryāṭīṭa. The one Lord alone that is witness and without qualities appears (as many) through the differences of Vis'va, Ṭaijasa, Prājña, and Ṭatasṭha (the neutral). One should (always) utter: 'I am Brahman alone.' Else in the waking state, (he is) in the four states of the waking state and others:[1] in the dreaming state, (he is) in the four states of the dreaming state and others; in the dreamless sleeping state, (he is) in the four states of the dreamless sleeping and others; in the ṭurya, (he is) in the four states of ṭurya and others; to the ṭuryāṭīṭa that is nirguṇa, such states are not. There is only one witness in all the states of Vis'va, Ṭaijasa and Prājña, who is presiding over the gross, the subtle and the causal

[1] Probably "others" refer to the subdivisions of the dreaming; so also of other states.

(bodies). Is Ṭatasṭha the seer? or is he not? As (to Ṭatasṭha), there is the property of seeing; the jīva that is affected by the egoism, etc., of agency and enjoyment is not the seer. The one other than jīva (*viz.*, Ṭatasṭha) is not concerned (with egoism, etc.). If it is said that the jīva is not so (concerned with egoism), then it is not a fact. Through the abhimāna of the jīva, there is the abhimāna of the body. And (conversely) through the abhimāna of the body, there is the abhimāna of the jīva. The state of the jīva is as a screen (to screen Brahman) like (the pot and house in) the pot-ākās' and the house-ākās'. Through such a screen, he reaches self-realisation through the manṭra—'Hamsa-So'ham'[1] having the characteristics of inspiration and expiration. Having known thus, if he should give up the identification with the body, then he does not identify himself with the body (*i.e.*, not attain the state of jīva). Such a one is stated to be Brahman. Having given up abhimāna and anger, being content with moderate food, having conquered the organs and having controlled the avenues (of the organs), one should make the mind enter into meditation. The yogin who has always controlled (his mind and organs) should ever diligently commence his meditation in empty places, caves and forests. The knower of yoga who is bent upon accomplishing the end should never be engaged in giving feasts to Brāhmaṇas, in s'rāḍḍha sacrifices, etc., or in going to places of pilgrimages, festivals or crowds. The well-controlled yogin should go about as if people had treated him with disrespect. He should not go against the actions of the wise. That great ascetic is said to be a ṭridaṇdin (or having a three-knotted staff) who holds firmly the three-ḍaṇda (control) of mind, speech, and body. That ascetic is said to be a supreme person who begs alms-food of worthy brāhmaṇas, when smoke has ceased and fire has been extinguished (in their houses). Is he not a degraded ascetic who, though holding the staff and begging food, is without vairāgya and is not intent upon the observances of his order? He is an ascetic—not any other—who does

[1] With Hamsa, there is the inspiration, and with So'ham, there is the expiration.

not go to the house where he expects to find special alms or which he already visited. He is said to transcend all castes and orders of life who realises the self-shining supreme Ṭaṭṭva that is without body and organs, the all-witness, the real vijñāna that is of the form of bliss. To the Āṭmā that is of the nature of jñāna, such an idea as: 'the order of life, etc., is mine,' being generated out of māyā in this body, can never exist. He who knows thus through veḍānṭa is beyond all castes and orders of life. He from whom all castes and orders of life slip away through Āṭmic vision, transcends them all and remains in Āṭmā alone. That person is said by knower of the meaning of the Veḍas to be aṭivarṇās'ramī (beyond caste and order of life) who after crossing all castes and orders of life abides in Āṭmā alone. Therefore, O Nāraḍa, the castes and orders of life which are foreign (to Āṭmā) are attributed falsely, by the ignorant, to Āṭmā. O Nāraḍa, for those that are Brahma-jñānīs, there are no rules ordained nor prohibited; there is nothing to be given up or not; similarly nothing else (for them). Having attained indifference to all objects even up to Brahmā's seat, having destroyed (or done away with) all fondness for everything, as for son, relatives, wife, etc., and having faith in the path of salvation, and through love of veḍānṭa-jñāna, he should approach a guru who is a knower of Brahman with gift (in his hand). Having an equilibrated mind, he should satisfy the guru for a long time through service, etc., and learn with a steady firm mind the meaning of the sentences of the Veḍas. Then being devoid of 'I' and 'mine' and of all attractions, and having attained peace of mind, etc., he sees Āṭmā in himself. Through observing the faults of samsāra, there arises indifference. There is no doubt that sannyāsa arises in one who becomes disgusted with samsāra. The aspirant after salvation who is called paramahamsa should, through the hearing, etc., of veḍānṭa, practise Brahma-jñāna, which is the direct and chief means of salvation. In order to attain Brahma-jñāna, the one named paramahamsa should possess the qualities of the control of mind and body, etc. He should always be a practiser of veḍānṭa, being master of the mind, the body and the organs, being without fear and egoism, with a firm mind, without the pairs (of opposites), without attaching himself to any, having a worn-out loin-cloth, and being bald-headed or naked. He should have the great intelligence of the knower of veḍānṭa, a yogin without 'I' and 'mine' and being equal and friendly to friends and other beings. That jñānī alone and none else is able to cross samsāra who has his mind at peace. With the grace of the guru towards him, he should live with him for one year. He should be careful to observe yama (restraint) and niyama (religious observance). At the end of that (year), he should attain the supreme jñāna-yoga, and roam about on this earth without going against ḍharma; (or) at the end of one year, he should give up the three orders of life and attain the chief ās'rama (of sannyāsa), as well as the supreme jñāna-yoga. Then, taking leave of the guru, he should wander over the earth, having given up association (with wife, etc., as well as auger, and being content with moderate food and having controlled the senses. The householder who does not perform karma, and the ascetic who performs karma—both become fallen through their perverse doings. Each becomes intoxicated through seeing women. Each becomes intoxicated through drinking alcohol. Therefore women, mere sight of whom is poison, should be shunned at a distance. Such things as conversation and proximity with, and sight of, women, dancing, singing, using violence against persons, and disputatious arguments should be given up. Therefore, O Nāraḍa, to such a one, there is neither bath nor muttering of manṭras nor worship nor homa, nor means of accomplishment, nor any karma of fire-sacrifice, etc., nor worshipping with flowers, etc., nor karmas to the piṭṛs nor pilgrimages, nor religious observances, nor ḍharmas, nor aḍharmas, nor any rules of observance, nor any other worldly karmas. He should give up all karmas and worldly observances. That yogin of an ascetic who is a learned person, having his intelligence directed towards Reality, should never injure any worm or insect, bird or tree. O Nāraḍa, roam through the world with vision ever directed inwards, with purity, with mind under control, with a mind that is full of Brahman and all attraction given up within. The muni that goes about alone, does (or should) not dwell in countries where there is no king. (In his case), there is neither praise nor prostration, nor the propitiation of ḍevas or piṭṛs. Thus the ascetic who has his abode changeful (in body), or changeless (in Âṭmā), should be content with whatever he gets. Thus is the Upanishaḍ."

UPAḌES'A VII

The Grandfather, after eulogizing Nāraḍa who asked about the observance of ascetics, replied thus:—

"The ascetic that has attained indifference (to objects), should stay in one and the same place in the rainy season (for four months), and then for (the remaining) eight months should wander alone. Then also the ascetic should not stay in one and the same place for more than a day. Like a deer that does not stay in one place on account of fear, he should not stay in one place. He should not create an attraction (in his mind) that may serve aṣ an obstacle to his going about. He should not cross a stream (by swimming) with his hand, nor ascend a tree, nor witness the festival of a God, nor partake of regal food, nor do the external worship of God. Having discarded all things other than the Self, he should be with his body emaciated by taking food (from each house) like the bees (from each flower). He should not increase the fat (in the body); he should discard ghee like blood. Regarding such royal food as flesh, sandal-coating, etc., as offal, the different tastes as the degraded caste, the cloth as a defiled vessel, the oil-bath as sexual union, the gladdening of a friend as urine, desires as cow's flesh, the country known to him as the outcastes' place, gold and women as cobra or deadly poison, the place of assembly as the burning ground, the capital of the town as the hell called Kumbhīpāka, and royal food as balls of rice offered to the dead, he should be without any worship of God other than the Self; and having given up all the actions of the world and his own country, and ever thinking of the bliss of his Self like the bliss arising from the discovery of a lost object, forgetting his country and the fondness for his body, and knowing that his body should be slighted like a carcase, he should dwell away from son, relations and native place, like a thief released from prison. Taking whatever comes to him without effort, ever intent upon the realisation, through meditation, of Brahma-Praṇava, being freed from all karmas, having burnt up all passion, anger, greed, delusion, pride, malice, etc., having transcended the three guṇas, being without the six human infirmities,[1] without the six changes,[2] speaking the truth and being opposed to all savoury things, he should live for one day in a village, five days in a town, five days in a sacred place, and five days in sacred waters. With no settled place of residence and with a firm mind, he should dwell alone in mountain caves without uttering falsehood. Two persons should not join together. Should three join, there is created a village thereby; with four, is formed a city. Therefore he should live alone in a village. In it, the ascetic should not give scope to his fourteen organs. Having attained wealth of vairāgya through the non-dissipated jñāna, and having deliberated within himself that there is none other than the Self, he should attain Jīvanmukṭi, having seen the Reality everywhere. Till prārabḍha karma is over, he should understand the four kinds of svarūpa[3] (in Ṭaṭṭvamasi) and should live in the realisation of Reality, till his body falls (a prey to death).

"To the kutīchaka there is (prescribed) a bath three times daily; to the bahūḍaka, twice; to the hamsa, once; to the paramahamsa there is the mental bath; to the ṭuryāṭīṭa, there is the holy-ashes bath; to the avaḍhūṭa, there is the wind as the bath. For the kutīchaka, there is the vertical sect-mark; for the bahūḍaka, there is the three-lined (horizontal) sect-mark; for the hamsa, both; for the paramahamsa, there is the holy-ashes sect-mark; for the ṭuryāṭīṭa, there is the spot-sect-mark; for the

[1] The six human infirmities are hunger, thirst, grief, delusion, dotage, and death.

[2] The six changes are birth, existence, growth, transformation, decrease, and annihilation.

[3] "Ṭaṭ" has its two aspects of the word and its meaning which is Nirguṇa. In "Tvam" also there are two, *viz.*, the disciple and the jīva.

avaḍhūṭa or for the ṭuryāṭīṭa and avaḍhūṭa, there is none. For the kutīchaka, shaving takes place once in two months; for the bahūḍaka, once in four months; for the hamsa and paramahamsa, none, or if wanted, once in a year; for the ṭuryāṭīṭa and avaḍhūṭa, none at all. The kutīchaka should take the food in one (place only); the bahūḍaka should take alms (in many places); for the hamsa and paramahamsa, the hand is the vessel; the ṭuryāṭīṭa, should take food with the mouth as the cow; for the avaḍhūṭa, it is like the action of the boa constrictor (opening the mouth and taking whatever comes into it). For the kutīchaka, there are two cloths; for the bahūḍaka, there is one cloth; for the hamsa there is a piece of cloth; and the paramahamsa should be naked or have only a loin-cloth; in the case of the ṭuryāṭīṭa and avaḍhūṭa, they should be as nature made them. For the hamsa and paramahamsa, there is (prescribed) a deer-skin, and for no others. For the kutīchaka and bahūḍaka, there is the worship of the divine (image); for the hamsa and paramahamsa, there is mental worship; for the ṭuryāṭīṭa and avaḍhūṭa, there is the idea that they alone are Brahman. The kutīchaka and bahūḍaka are entitled to manṭras and japas; the hamsa and paramahamsa, to ḍhyāna (meditation); the ṭuryāṭīṭa and avaḍhūta are entitled to none; but they are entitled to the initiation of the sacred sentences of the Veḍas; so also the paramahamsa. The kutīchaka and bahūḍaka are not entitled to initiate others; for them, there is (the uttering of) the mental praṇava; for the hamsa and paramahamsa, there is the internal praṇava (in the heart); for the ṭuryāṭīṭa and avaḍhūṭa, there is the Brahma-praṇava (always). For the kuṭīchaka and bahūḍaka, there is s'ravaṇa (hearing and study); for the hamsa and paramahamsa, there is manana (thinking and remembering); for the ṭuryāṭīṭa and avaḍhūṭa there is nidiḍhyāsana (profound meditation ever). For all these, there is necessarily the meditation upon Āṭmā. Thus the aspirant after salvation should ever be uttering the Praṇava which enables one to cross samsāra, and be living as a Jīvanmukṭa. Thus the ascetic, according to each one's capacity, should ever be seeking the means to attain Kaivalya. Such is the Upanishaḍ."

UPAḌES'A VIII

Then Nārada asked Parameshthī (Brahmā) to enlighten him, who had surrendered himself to Him, about samsāra-ṭāraka (or that ṭāraka or Praṇava which lifts one out of samsāra).

Assenting to which, Brahmā began thus: "Omkāra that is Brahman is the vyashti (individual) and the samashti (cosmic). What is the individual? What is the cosmic? Brahma-praṇava is of three kinds, sambāra- (destructive) praṇava, sṛshti- (creative) praṇava, and ubhayāṭmaka (belonging to both) praṇava, as being of two forms, internal and external. (It is also eight:) Ānṭaḥ-praṇava, Vyāvahārika-praṇava, bāhya-praṇava, ārsha-praṇava, ubhayāṭmaka or virāt-praṇava, sambāra-praṇava, brahma-praṇava, and arḍhamāṭrā praṇava. Om is Brahman. Know that the manṭra of the one-syllabled Om is Praṇava. It has the eight differences of akāra, ukāra, makāra, arḍhamāṭrā, nāḍa, binḍu, kalā, and s'akṭi. Know it is not four (alone). Ākāra is associated with ten thousand limbs; ukāra, with one thousand limbs; makāra with one hundred limbs; arḍhamāṭrā is of the nature of endless limbs. That which is saguṇa (associated with guṇas) is virāt- (preservation) praṇava; that which is nirguṇa (not associated with guṇas) is sambāra- (or destruction) praṇava; that which is associated with guṇas and is not so associated, is uṭpaṭṭi- (or origination) praṇava. Pluṭa (the elongated accent) is virāt: pluṭapluṭa is sambāra. The virāt-praṇava is of the form of sixteen māṭrās and is above the thirty-six ṭaṭṭvas. The sixteen māṭrās are thus: Ākāra is the first māṭrā; ukāra is the second; makāra is the third; arḍhamāṭrā is the fourth; nāḍa is the fifth; bindu is the sixth; kalā is the seventh; kalāṭīṭa is the eighth; s'ānṭi is the ninth; s'ānṭyaṭīṭa is the tenth; nnmanī is the eleventh; manonmanī is the twelfth; purīṭaṭi is the thirteenth; ṭanumaḍhyamā is the fourteenth; paṭi is the fifteenth; parā is the sixteenth. Then (again) having sixty-four māṭrās and their division into the two, Prakṛṭi and Purusha and resolving themselves into the one hundred and twenty-eight differences of māṭrās, it becomes saguṇa and nirguṇa. Though Brahma-praṇava is one only, it is the substratum of all, the support of the whole universe, of the form of all aksharas (letters), time, Vedas, and S'iva. This Omkāra should be sought after, that is mentioned in the Vedas of the nature of the Upanishads. Know that this Omkāra is the Āṭmā that is indestructible during the three periods of time, past, present, and future, able to confer salvation and eulogized by Brahma-sound (Vedas). Having experienced this one Om as immortal and ageless, and having brought about the Brahma-nature in this body, become convinced that your Āṭmā, associated with the three bodies, is Parabrahman. Through Vis'va and others (*viz.*, Ṭaijasa, Prājña, and Ṭurya) in order, the realisation of Parabrahman should be attained, since Āṭmā is of four kinds through his identification with, and the enjoying of, the gross as well as the enjoyer of the gross, the subtle as well as the enjoyer of the subtle, and through his identification (with the third body) enjoying bliss in the fourth. He has four feet. The one presiding over the waking state is gross; and since he is the enjoyer of Vis'va (the universe), he becomes the sṭhūla-prajñā (gross consciousness). He has nineteen[1] facets and eight parts. He is pervading everywhere and the Lord. He is the enjoyer of the gross and is the chaṭurāṭma called Vis'va. He alone is the Purusha called Vais'vānara. He alone is Vis'vajiṭ (the conqueror of the universe). This is the first foot. When this Lord attains the dreaming condition, he is the sūkshma-prajña (subtle consciousness). O conqueror of all, he is the one having eight limbs, and there is none else. He is the enjoyer of the subtle and is chaṭurāṭma, named Ṭaijasa and the protector of elements. He alone is the Hiraṇyagarbha, presiding over the gross (or subtle matter rather). He is said to form the second foot. Sushupṭi (or the dreamless sleep) is that state where one sleeps without any desire and where one sees not any dreams. The one identified with this dreamless sleep is Prajñāna-ghana, is blissful, of the nature of eternal bliss and the Āṭmā in all creatures; yet he is enjoyer of bliss, has cheṭas (consciousness) as his (one) foot, is all-pervading, indestructible,

[1] The nineteen are the five organs of sense, the five organs of action, the five prāṇas, and the four of the mind.

chaṭurāṭmā and the Lord, and is named Prājña, the third foot. He alone is the Lord of all, the knower of all, the subtle-thoughted, the latent one, and the cause of all creation. He alone is the origin and the destruction. These three (states) are obstacles to all creatures obtaining (the final) peace. As is svapna, so is sushupṭi, it (also) being said to be illusory. The chaṭurāṭmā, the fourth, as he is Saṭ, Chiṭ and Ēkarasa (the one essence), ends as the fourth and follows (upon the heels of each of the above states), is the knower of the means of vikalpa-jñāna and is the anujñāṭā (the one following knower). Having known them, and known as māyā the three vikalpas of sushupṭi, svapna and ānṭara (the inner), even in this state, is he not (to be known as) Saṭ-Chiṭ-Ēkarasa? This shall be expressed as differentiated thus: It is not even the gross prajñā; nor is it the very subtle prajñā; nor is it prajñā itself (of the causal body): O muni neither is it the trifling prajñā; nor is it the non-prajñā; nor is it the dual prajñā; nor is it the internal prajñā, though it is without prajñā; it is Prajñāna-ghana. It can never be known by the organs; nor it can be known by the reason; it cannot be grasped by the organs of action. It cannot be proved. It cannot be reached by thought. It cannot be proved by analogy. It can be realised by Self-realisation alone. It is with the waking state, etc. It is the auspicious, with changes, without a second. Such a one is thought to be Ṭurya. This alone is Brahman, Brahma-praṇava. This should be known. There is no other Ṭurya. To the aspirants after salvation, it is the support, like the sun everywhere; it is the Self-light. As it alone is Brahman, this Brahma-Ākāś is shining always. Thus is the Upanishaḍ."

UPAḌEŚA IX

Nāraḍa asked: "Who is Brahma-swarūpa?" To which Brahmā replied thus: "Brahma-swarūpa is thus: Those who know that 'he (Brahman) is one and I am another' are only paśus (animals). The real paśus (animals) are no animals. The wise man who knows Brahman thus (as himself, and himself as Brahman) escapes out of the mouth of death. There is no other path to salvation.

"Is time the cause (of origination of universes)?[1] or nature? or karma? or accident? or the (great) elements? or Purusha? This should be considered. It is not the union of them. (Then) there is the Āṭmā, but (jīva-) Āṭmā is not the Lord, as it is subject to pleasures and pains. Those (Ṛshis) following ḍhyāna-yoga have beheld, as the cause, the ḍevāṭma-s'akṭi concealed by its own qualities of that One that presides over all the causes associated with time and Āṭmā. Him (the Universal Soul), we consider as the wheel which has one circumference, which is covered by three (layers), which has sixteen end-parts, which has fifty spokes and twenty counter-spokes, which has six times eight (nails), which has one rope of various forms, which has the threefold path, and which has delusion arising from the twofold cause. Him (we worship as a river) which has (water) oozing out of the five currents (of organs), which is terrible and crooked through the five causes (of elements), whose praṇas are the five waves, which has buḍḍhi, etc., as the root cause, which has five whirlpools, which is impelled by the velocity of the five pains, which has fifty differences (or has the five miseries), and which has the five obstacles. In this wheel of Brahman, which is the support of life and the last abiding place of all beings, and which is infinite, is whirling deluded the jīva, thinking that it is different from the one (Lord) Ordainer. Being blessed by Him, he gains salvation through such (a blessing). This is declared as Brahman, as the supreme and the indestructible. In it, are the three (the enjoyer, the enjoyed and enjoyment). Hence it is the firm abode (of all). The knowers of Brahman having known Brahman within (the universe, etc.,) attain samāḍhi in Brahman and are absorbed in Brahman. Īs'vara upholds this universe, closely associated with the destructible and the indestructible, which are manifest and unmanifest; but the not-ruler of (jīva-) Āṭmā is bound through the thought of its being the enjoyer; and having known the Lord is freed from all

[1] The Sveṭāsvaṭara Upanishaḍ begins thus.

fetters. Both Īs'vara and jīva are birthless; one (the former) is jñānī and the other (latter) is ajñānī. (The goddess of) Brahmāṭma-s'akṭi, is birthless, is alone engaged (in this world), on account of the enjoyment of the enjoyers. Āṭmā is endless. The universe is His form. He is not the agent. Whoever knows the Brahman that is threefold (as jīva, Īs'vara and the universe) is released from bondage. It is praḍhāna alone that is destructible. It is Īs'vara that is immortal and indestructible. The one Lord (Īs'vara) ordains Praḍhāna and Purusha.

"The illusion of the universe disappears through meditation on union (or absorption) and saṭṭva-bhāva of Parames'vara always. Through knowing the Lord, aviḍyā and the rest are destroyed. Through the removal of such pains, there is freedom from birth and death. Through the meditation of that Parames'vara, the third body is acquired after this (physical) body, all wealth is enjoyed, and he attains whatever should be attained. He should know with certitude that all the three things (*viz.*,) the enjoyer, the enjoyed, and enjoyment are nothing but Brahman, and are of the nature of his own Self. There is none but It to be known. All Āṭmic knowledge is through ṭapas (only). That, Brahman contains in itself all excellence. Having known thus, whoever meditates upon the (Āṭma-) svarūpa, to him where then is grief? Where then is delusion? Therefore the Virāt is the past, present, and future time, and is of indestructible nature.

"Āṭmā, that is the atom of atoms and the greatest of the greatest, is in the cave of the heart of all creatures. One without the thought of objects and without grief, knows the Āṭmā capable of neither increase nor decrease through the grace of Īs'vara or through the non-attraction to the objects of the senses. He (Āṭmā) walks speedily without legs, lifts objects without hands, sees without eyes and hears without ears. He knows all, but none knows Him. He is said to be the foremost Mahā-Purusha. Having known Āṭmā that is bodiless in this fleeting body, the great, the all-pervading, the support of all, with incomprehensible power, fit to be known through the meaning, etc., of all the Upanishaḍs, the supreme of the supreme, the supreme object fit to be known, the one remaining after all, the all-knowing, the eternal, the foremost of all foremost beings, the ordainer of all, the one fit to be worshipped by all angels, the one without beginning, end, and middle, without limit or destruction, the cause of Brahmā, Vishṇu, and Ruḍra, the one that has all the universe latent in himself, of the nature of the five elements with the expansion of all the quintuplicated creation, without being enveloped by his own limbs of quintuplicated objects, superior to the supreme, greater than the greatest, of the nature of effulgence, the eternal and the auspicious, the undaunted personage never grieves. One who has neither given up vicious actions, nor controlled his organs, nor mastered his mind, nor given up longing after fruits of actions though the mind is undisturbed, nor brought his mind to one state (or point), will not attain this Āṭmā.

"This (Brahman) is neither internal nor external consciousness; is neither gross, nor jñāna, nor ajñāna; nor is it the state between the waking and the dreaming states. It cannot be cognised by the organs; is not subject to proof; is within. He who knows that which is by Itself alone is an emancipated person."

The Lord Brahmā said that he becomes an emancipated person. He who knows Reality is a Parivrāt. Such a Parivrāt roams about alone. Through fear, he is like a terrified deer. He will not be opposed to going anywhere. Having given up all but his body, he will live like a bee, and without considering others as foreign to himself; ever meditating upon Reality, he attains liberation in himself. Such a Parivrāt will be without delusion, without action or causing others to act, being absolved from teacher, disciple, books, etc., and having abandoned all samsāra. Such a Parivrāt roams about thus—without wealth, being happy, able to get wealth (if wanted), having crossed jñāna and ajñāna as well as happiness and grief, being Self-effulgence, being fit to be known by the Veḍas, having known all, able to confer siḍḍhis and remaining himself as Brahman, the Lord. Such a Parivrāt attains the supreme abode of Vishṇu, from which a yogin that has gone to it does not return, and where the sun and the moon do not shine. He does not return. Such is Kaivalya. Such is the Upanishaḍ.

S'AṆDILYA-UPANISHAḌ

OF

AṬHARVAṆAVEḌĀ

Chapter I

Om. S'āṇdilya questioned Āṭharvan thus: "Please tell me about the eight aṅgas (parts) of Yoga which is the means of attaining to Āṭmā."

Āṭharvan replied: "The eight aṅgas of yoga are yama, niyama, āsana, prāṇāyāma, praṭyāhāra, ḍhāraṇā, ḍhyāna, and samāḍhi. Of these, yama is of ten kinds: and so is niyama. There are eight āsanas. Prāṇāyāma is of three kinds; praṭyāhāra is of five kinds: so also is ḍhāraṇā. Ḍhyāna is of two kinds, and samāḍhi is of one kind only.

"Under yama (forbearance) are ten:[1] ahimsā, saṭya, asṭeya brahmacharya, ḍayā, ārjava, kshamā, ḍhṛṭi, miṭāhāra, and s'aucha. Of these, ahimsā is the not causing of any pain to any living being at any time through the actions of one's mind, speech, or body. Saṭya is the speaking of the truth that conduces to the well-being of creatures, through the actions of one's mind, speech, or body. Asṭeya is not coveting of another's property through the actions of one's mind, speech, or body. Brahmacharya is the refraining from sexual intercourse in all places and in all states in mind, speech or body. Ḍayā is kindliness towards all creatures in all places. Ārjava is the preserving of equanimity of mind, speech, or body in the performance or non-performance of the actions ordained or forbidden to be done. Kshamā is the bearing patiently of all pleasant or unpleasant things, such as praise or blow. Ḍhṛṭi is

[1] Under yama and niyama Paṭañjali has five kinds only.

the preserving of firmness of mind during the period of gain or loss of wealth or relatives. Miṭāhāra is the taking of oily and sweet food, leaving one-fourth of the stomach empty. S'aucha is of two kinds, external and internal. Of these, the external is the cleansing of the body by earth and water; the internal is the cleansing of the mind. This (the latter) is to be obtained by means of the aḍhyāṭma-viḍyā (science of Self).

"Under niyama (religious observances), are ten, *viz.*, ṭapas, sanṭosha, āsṭikya, ḍāna, Īs'varapūjana, siḍḍhānṭa-s'ravaṇa, hrīḥ, maṭi, japa, and vraṭa. Of these ṭapas, is the emancipation of the body through the observances of such penances as kṛchchhra, chānḍrāyaṇa, etc., according to rules. Sanṭosha is being satisfied with whatever comes to us of its own accord. Āsṭikya is the belief in the merits or demerits of actions as stated in the Veḍas. Ḍāna is the giving with faith to deserving persons, money, grains, etc., earned lawfully. Īs'varapūjana is the worshipping of Vishṇu, Ruḍra, etc., with pure mind according to one's power. Siḍḍhānṭa-s'ravaṇa is the inquiry into the significance of Veḍānṭa. Hrīḥ is the shame felt in the performance of things contrary to the rules of the Veḍas and of society. Maṭi is the faith in the paths laid down by the Veḍas. Japa is the practising of the manṭras into which one is duly initiated by his spiritual instructor, and which is not against (the rules of) the Veḍas. It is of two kinds—the spoken and the mental. The mental is associated with contemplation by the mind. The spoken is of two kinds—the loud and the low. The loud pronunciation gives the reward as stated (in the Veḍas): (while) the low one (gives) a reward thousand times (that). The mental (gives) a reward a crore (of times that). Vraṭa is the regular observance of or the refraining from the actions enjoined or prohibited by the Veḍas.

"Āsanas (the postures) are (chiefly) eight, *viz.*, svasṭika, gomukha, paḍma, vīra, simha, bhaḍra, mukṭa, and mayūra.

"Svasṭika is the sitting at ease with the body erect, placing each foot between the thighs and knees of the other. Gomukha is (the sitting at ease with the body erect,) placing the hollow of the left foot under the side of the right posteriors and the hollow of the right foot under the side of the left posteriors, resembling Gomukha (cow's face). Paḍma is (the sitting at ease with the body erect) placing the back of each foot in the thigh of the other, the right hand grasping the right toe and the left hand the left toe. This, O S'āṇḍilya, is praised by all. Vīra is the sitting at ease (with the body erect), placing one foot on the thigh of the other and the other foot underneath the corresponding (opposite thigh.) Simha is (the sitting at ease with the body erect,) pressing the right side (of the thigh) with the hollow of left heel and *vice versa*. Rest your hands on the knees, spread out the fingers, open your mouth and carefully fix your gaze on the tip of your nose. This is always praised by the yogins. Siḍḍha[1] is (the sitting at ease with the body erect), pressing the perineum with the left heel and placing the heel of the right foot above the genital organ, concentrating the mind between the two eyebrows. Bhaḍra is (the sitting at ease with the body erect,) pressing the two ankles of the two feet firmly together against the Sīvinī (*viz.*, lower part of the seed) and binding the knees firmly with the hands. This is the bhaḍra which destroys all diseases and poisons. Mukṭa is (the sitting at ease with the body erect,) pressing with the left heel the right side of the tender part of the Sīvinī, and with the right heel the left side of the tender part of the Sīvinī. Mayūra—(lit., peacock). Rest your body upon the ground with both palms and place your elbows on the sides of the navel, lift up the head and feet and remain like a stick in the air, (like the plant balance in gymnastics). This is the mayūra posture which destroys all sins. By these, all the diseases within the body are destroyed; all the poisons are digested. Let the person who is unable to practise all these postures betake himself to any one (of these) which he may find easy and pleasant. He who conquers (or gets mastery over) the postures—he conquers the three worlds. A person who has the practice of yama and niyama should practise prāṇāyāma; by that the nādis become purified."

Then S'āṇḍilya questioned Āṭharvan thus: "By what means are the nādis purified? How many are they in number?

[1] In the explanation one more posture is introduced.

How do they arise? What vāyus (vital airs) are located in them? What are their seats? What are their functions? Whatever is worthy of being known in the body, please tell me." To that Ātharvan replied (thus): "This body is ninety-six digits in length. Prāṇa extends twelve digits beyond the body. He who through the practice of yoga reduces his prāṇa within his body to make it equal to or not less than the fire in it becomes the greatest of the yogins. In men, the region of fire which is triangular in form and brilliant as the molten gold is situated in the middle of the body. In four-footed animals, it (fire) is quadrangular. In birds, it is round. In its (the region of fire's) centre, the purifying, beneficial, and subtle flame is situate. Two digits above the anus and two digits below the sexual organ is the centre of the body for men. For four-footed animals, it is the middle of the heart. For birds, it is the middle of the body. Nine digits from (or above) the centre of the body and four digits in length and breadth is situated an oval form. In its midst is the navel. In it, is situated the chakra (*viz.*, wheel) with twelve spokes. In the middle of the chakra, the jīva (Āṭmā) wanders, driven by its good and bad deeds. As a spider flies to and fro within a web of fine threads, so prāṇa moves about here. In this body, the jīva rides upon prāṇa. Lying in the middle of the navel and above it, is the seat of kuṇḍalinī. The kuṇḍalinī s'akṭi is of the form of eight prakṛṭis (matter) and coils itself eight ways or (times). The movement of vāyus (vital airs) checks duly the food and drink all round by the side of skanḍha.[1] It closes by its head (the opening of) the brahmaranḍhra, and during the time of (the practice of) yoga is awakened by the fire (in the apāna); then it shines with great brilliancy in the ākās' of the heart in the shape of wisdom. Depending upon kuṇḍalinī which is situated in the centre, there are fourteen principal nādis (*viz.*,) Idā, Piṅgalā, Sushumnā, Sarasvaṭī, Vāruṇī, Pūshā, Hasṭijihvā, Yas'asvinī, Vis'voḍharī, Kuhūḥ, S'āṅkhinī, Payasvinī, Alambusā, and Gānḍhārī. Of them, Sushumnā is said to be the

[1] In Varāha Upanishaḍ and later on, this is named "Kanḍha". Herein is described the web of life.

sustainer of the universe and the path of salvation. Situated at the back of the anus, it is attached to the spinal column and extends to the brahmarandhra of the head and is invisible and subtle and is vaishṇavī (or has the s'akṭi force of Vishṇu). On the left of Sushumnā is situated Idā, and on the right is Piṅgalā. The moon moves in Idā and the sun in Piṅgalā. The moon is of the nature of ṭamas and the sun of rajas. The poison share is of the sun and the nectar of the moon. They both direct (or indicate) time and Sushumnā is the enjoyer (or consumer) of time. To the back and on the side of Sushumnā are situate Sarasvaṭī and Kuhūḥ respectively. Between Yas'asvinī and Kuhūḥ stands Vāruṇī. Between Pūshā and Sarasvaṭī lies Payasvinī.[1] Between Gānḍhārī and Sarasvaṭī is situated Yas'asvinī.[2] In the centre of the navel is Alambusā. In front of Sushumnā there is Kuhūḥ, which proceeds as far as the genital organ. Above and below kuṇdalinī is situated Vāruṇī, which proceeds everywhere. Yas'asvinī which is beautiful (or belonging to the moon), proceeds to the great toes. Piṅgalā goes upwards to the right nostril. Payasvinī goes to right ear. Sarasvaṭī goes to the upper part or the tongue and S'āṅkhinī to the left ear, (while) Gānḍhārī goes from the back of Idā to the left eye. Alambusā goes upwards and downwards from the root of the anus. From these fourteen nādis, other (minor) nādis spring; from them springing others, and from them springing others; so it should be known. As the leaf of the as'vaṭṭha tree (*ficus religiosa*) etc., is covered with minute fibres so also is this body permeated with nādis.

"Prāṇa, Āpāna, Samāna, Uḍāna, Vyāna, Nāga, Kūrma, Kṛkara, Ḍevaḍaṭṭa, and Ḍhanañjaya—these ten vāyus (vital airs) move in all the nādis. Prāṇa moves in the nostrils, the throat, the navel, the two great toes and the lower and the upper parts of kuṇdalinī. Vyāna moves in the ear, the eye, the loins, the ankles, the nose, the throat and the buttocks. Apāna moves in the anus, the genitals, the thighs, the knees. the stomach, the seeds, the loins, the calves, the navel, and the

[1] This should be perhaps—between Piṅgalā and Payasvinī is Pūshā.
[2] Yasasvinī should be "Sāṅkhinī."

seat of the anus of fire. Uḍāna lives in all the joints and also in the hands and legs. Samāna lives, permeating in all parts of the body. Along with the fire in the body, it causes the food and drink taken in, to spread in the body. It moves in the seventy-two thousand nādis and pervades all over the body along with the fire. The five vāyus beginning with Nāga go towards the skin, the bones, etc. The Prāṇa which is in the navel separates the food and drink which is there and brings about the rasas (juices) and others.[1] Placing the water above the fire and the food above (or in) the water, it goes to the Āpāna and along with it, fans up the fire in the centre of the body. The fire thus fanned up by the Āpāna gradually increases in brightness in the middle of the body. Then it causes through its flames the water which is brought in the bowels by the Prāṇa to grow hot. The fire with the water causes the food and condiments, which are placed above, to be boiled to a proper degree. Then Prāṇa separates these into sweat, urine, water, blood, semen, the fæces and the like. And along with the Samāna, it takes the juice (or essence) to all the nādis and moves in the body in the shape of breath. The vāyus excrete the urine, the fæces, etc., through the nine openings in the body which are connected with the outside air. The functions of Prāṇa are inspiration, expiration, and cough. Those of Āpāna are the excretion of the fæces and the urine. Those of Vyāna are (such actions as) giving and taking. Those of Uḍāna are keeping the body straight, etc. Those of Samāna are nourishing the body. Those of Nāga are vomiting, etc.; of Kūrma, the movement of the eyelids; of Kṛkara, the causing of hunger, etc., of Ḍevaḍaṭṭa, idleness, etc., and Ḍhanañjaya, phlegm.

"Having thus acquired a thorough knowledge of the seat of the nādis and of the vāyus with their functions, one should begin with the purification of the nādis. A person possessed of yama and niyama, avoiding all company, having finished his course of study, delighting in truth and virtue, having conquered (his) anger, being engaged in the service of his spiritual instructor and having been obedient to his parents

[1] Here the process of digestion of food is described.

and well instructed in all the religious practices and the knowledge of his order of life, should go to a sacred grove abounding in fruits, roots, and water. There he should select a pleasant spot always resounding with the chanting of the Veḍas, frequented by the knowers of Brahman that persevere in the duties of their orders of life and filled with fruits, roots, flowers, and water. (Else) either in a temple or on the banks of a river or in a village or in a town, he should build a beautiful monastery. It should be neither too long nor too high, should have a small door, should be besmeared well with cow-dung and should have every sort of protection.[1] There listening to the exposition of veḍānṭa, he should begin to practise yoga. In the beginning having worshipped Vināyaka[2] (Gaṇes'a), he should salute his Ishta-Ḍevaṭā (tutelary deity) and sitting in any of the above-mentioned postures on a soft seat, facing either the east or the north and having conquered them, the learned man keeping his head and neck erect and fixing his gaze on the tip of his nose, should see the sphere of the moon between his eyebrows and drink the nectar (flowing therefrom through his eyes. Inhaling the air through Idā[3] for the space of twelve māṭrās,[4] he should contemplate on the sphere of fire[5] situated in the belly as surrounded with flames and having as its seed र (ra); then he should exhale it through Piṅgalā. Again inhaling it through Piṅgalā[3] and retaining it (within), he should exhale it through Idā. For the period of twenty-eight months,[6] he should practise six times at every sitting through the three sanḍhyās (morning, noon, and evening)

[1] Both by physical protection and that of manṭras to scare away evil spirits.

[2] He is the son of Siva, having an elephant's face symbolical of wisdom. He is considered as the remover of all obstacles, and as such is he invoked and worshipped in the beginning of every religious rite.

[3] Idā and Piṅgalā are the two nādis upon which our breaths alternate from the left nostril to the right and *vice versa* and between which is Sushumnā. Hence these two terms are applied to and mean the left and right nostrils.

[4] According to Yogaṭaṭṭva-Upanishaḍ, a māṭrā is the time occupied in circling the knee once with the palm of the hand and filliping the fingers.

[5] According to Varāha-Upanishaḍ the seat of fire is the mūlāḍhāra (sacral plexus).

[6] The original is not clear. It says, "For the space of 3, 4, 3, 4, 7, 3 and 4 months" which when added becomes 28.

and during the intervals. By this, the nādis become purified. Then the body becomes light and bright, the (gastric) fire is increased (within) and there is the manifestation of nāḍa (internal sound).

"Prāṇāyāma is said to be the union of Prāṇa and Āpāna. It is of three kinds—expiration, inspiration, and cessation. They are associated with the letters of the (Samskṛṭ) alphabet[1] (for the right performance of prāṇāyāma). Therefore Praṇava (OM) only is said to be Prāṇāyāma. Sitting in the paḍma posture, the person should meditate that there is at the tip of his nose Gāyaṭrī,[2] a girl of red complexion surrounded by the numberless rays of the image of the moon and mounted on a hamsa (swan) and having a mace in her hand. She is the visible symbol of the letter Ā. The letter U has as its visible symbol Sāviṭrī,[2] a young woman of white colour having a disk in her hand and riding on a garuda (eagle). The letter M has as its visible symbol Sarasvaṭī,[2] an aged woman of black colour riding on a bull, having a trident in her hand. He should meditate that the single letter—the supreme light—the praṇava (OM)—is the origin or source of these three letters Ā, U, and M. Drawing up the air through Idā for the space of sixteen māṭrās, he should meditate on the letter Ā during that time; retaining the inspired air for the space of sixty-four māṭrās, he should meditate on the letter U during the time; he should then exhale the inspired air for the space of thirty-two mātrās, meditating on the letter M during that time. He should practise this in the above order over and over again.

"Then having become firm in the posture and preserved perfect self-control, the yogin should, in order to clear away the impurities of the Sushumnā, sit in the paḍmāsana (paḍma posture), and having inhaled the air through the left nostril, should retain it as long as he can and should exhale it through the right. Then drawing it again through the right and having retained it, he should exhale it through the left in the order

[1] According to the Manṭra Sāsṭra, Prāṇayāma is performed through the letters of Samskṛṭ alphabet, the vowels corresponding to inspiration, etc.

[2] These are the Goddesses representing Sakṭi and being the wives of Brahmā, Vishṇu, and Ruḍra.

that he should draw it through the same nostril by which he exhaled it before and retained it. In this context, occur (to memory) the following verses: "In the beginning having inhaled the breath (Prāṇa) through the left nostril, according to the rule, he should exhale it through the other; then having inhaled the air through the right nostril, should retain it and exhale it through the other." To those who practise according to these rules through the right and left nostrils, the nādis become purified within three months. He should practise cessation of breath at sunrise, in the midday, at sunset and at midnight slowly till eighty (times a day) for four weeks. In the early stages, perspiration is produced; in the middle stage the tremor of the body, and in the last stage levitation in the air. These (results) ensue out of the repression of the breath, while sitting in the paḍma posture. When perspiration arises with effort, he should rub his body well. By this, the body becomes firm and light. In the early course of his practice, food with milk and ghee is excellent. One sticking to this rule becomes firm in his practice and gets no ṭāpa (or burning sensation in the body). As lions, elephants and tigers are gradually tamed, so also the breath, when rightly managed (comes under control); else it kills the practitioner.[1]

"He should (as far as is consistent with his health and safety) properly exhale it, properly inhale it or retain it properly. Thus (only) will he attain success. By thus retaining the breath in an approved manner and by the purification of the nādis, the brightening of the (gastric) fire, the hearing distinctly of (spiritual) sounds and (good) health result. When the nervous centres have become purified through the regular practice of Prāṇāyāma, the air easily forces its way up through the mouth of the Sushumnā which is in the middle. By the contraction of the muscles of the neck and by the contraction of the one below (*viz.,*) Āpāna, the Prāṇa (breath) goes into the Sushumnā which is in the middle from the west nādi.[2] Drawing

[1] This passage clearly indicates the dreadful consequences of the performance of Prāṇāyāma rashly and without a guru.

[2] As already pointed out, the Sushumnā nādi is between Idā and Piṅgalā. If Prāṇa which alternates ordinarily between Idā and Piṅgalā is restrained by long

up the Āpāna and forcing down the Prāṇa from the throat, the yogin free from old age becomes a youth of sixteen.

"Seated in a pleasant posture and drawing up the air through the right nostril and retaining it inside from the top of the hair to the toe nails, he should exhale it through the same nostril. Through it, the brain becomes purified and the diseases in the air nādis[1] are destroyed. Drawing up the air through the nostrils with noise (so as to fill the space) from the heart to the neck, and having retained it (within) as long as possible, he should exhale it through the nose. Through this, hunger, thirst, idleness and sleep do not arise.

"Taking in the air through the mouth (wide open) and having retained it as long as possible, he should expel it through the nose. Through this, (such diseases as) gulma, pleeha (both being splenetic diseases), bile and fever as also hunger, etc., are destroyed.

"Now we shall proceed to kumbhaka (restraint of breath). It is of two kinds—sahiṭa and kevala. That which is coupled with expiration and inspiration is called sahiṭa. That which is devoid of these is called kevala (alone). Until you become perfect in kevala, practise sahiṭa. To one who has mastered kevala, there is nothing unattainable in the three worlds. By kevala-restraint of breath, the knowledge of kuṇḍalinī arises. Then he becomes lean in body, serene in face and clear-eyed, hears the (spiritual) sounds distinctly, becomes free from all diseases and conquers his (binḍu) seminal fluid,[1] his gastric fire being increased.

"Centring one's mind on an inward object whilst his eyes are looking outside without the shutting and opening of his eyelids, has been called Vaishṇavīmuḍrā. This is kept hidden in all the

kumbhaka, then it along with the soul, its attendant will enter the Sushumnā (central nādi) at one of the three places where it yields space for entrance through such restraint of breath and in the navel, from the Sarasvaṭi nādi on the west. After such entry it is that the yogin becomes dead to the world, being in the state called trance.

[1] Through such and other methods of Prāṇāyāma prescribed in this passage and the subsequent ones, chronic diseases that defy European doctors will be rooted out.

[2] **He becomes an Ūrḍhva-rēṭas—his vital energy goes up.**

ṭānṭric works. With his mind and breath absorbed in an internal object, the yogin, though he does not really see the objects outside and under him, still (appears to) see them with eyes in which the pupils are motionless. This is called Khecharīmuḍrā. It has as its sphere of extension one object and is very beneficial. (Then) the real seat of Vishṇu, which is void and non-void, dawns on him. With eyes half closed and with a firm mind, fixing his eyes on the tip of his nose and becoming absorbed in the sun and moon, he after remaining thus unshaken (becomes conscious of) the thing which is of the form of light, which is free from all externals, which is resplendent, which is the supreme truth and which is beyond. O S'āṇdilya, know this to be Ṭaṭ (That). Merging the sound in the light and elevating the brows a little, this is of the way of (or is a part of) the former practice. This brings about the state of Unmanī which causes the destruction of the mind. Therefore he should practise the Khecharīmuḍrā. Then he attains to the state of Uumanī and falls into the yoga sleep (trance). To one who obtains this yoga sleep, time does not exist. Placing the mind in the midst of s'akṭi and s'akṭi [1] in the midst of the mind and looking on the mind with the mind, O S'āṇdilya be happy. Place the Āṭmā in the midst of ākās' and ākās' in the midst of Āṭmā, and having reduced everything to ākās', do not think of anything else. You should not (then) entertain thoughts, either external or internal. Abandoning all thoughts, become abstract thought itself. As camphor in fire and salt in water become absorbed, so also the mind becomes absorbed in the Ṭaṭṭva (Truth). What is termed manas (mind) is the knowledge of everything that is known and its clear apprehension. When the knowledge and the object cognised are lost alike, there is no second path (or that is the only path). By its giving up all cognition of objects, it (the mind) is absorbed and when the mind is absorbed, kaivalya (isolation) alone remains.

"For the destruction of the chiṭṭa, there are two ways—yoga and jñāna. O prince of sages! yoga is the (forcible)

[1] There are six centres of energy in the body (mūlāḍhāra, sacral plexus, etc.), which are presided over by six s'akṭis (goddesses of energy).

repression of the modifications of the mind, and jñāna is the thorough inquiry into them. When the modifications of the mind are repressed, it (the mind) verily obtains peace. Just as the actions of the people cease with the stopping of the fluctuations of the sun (*viz.*, with sunset), so when the fluctuations of the mind cease, this cycle of births and deaths comes to an end. (Then) the fluctuations of prāṇa are prevented, when one has no longing for this mundane existence or when he has gratified his desires therein—through the study of religious books, the company of good men, indifference (to enjoyments), practice and yoga or long contemplation with intentness on any desired (higher) object or through practising one truth firmly.

"By the repression of the breath through inhalation, etc., by continual practice therein which does not cause fatigue, and by meditating in a secluded place, the fluctuations of the mind are arrested. Through the right realisation of the true nature of the sound which is at the extreme end of the pronunciation of the syllable Om (*viz.*, Arḍhamāṭrā), and when sushupṭi (dreamless sleeping state) is rightly cognised through consciousness, the fluctuations of prāṇa are repressed. When the passage at the root of the palate which is like the bell, *viz.*, uvula, is closed by the tongue with effort and when the breath goes up through (the upper hole), then the fluctuations of prāṇa are stopped. When the consciousness (samviṭ) is merged in prāṇa, and when through practice the prāṇa goes through the upper hole into the ḍvāḍas'ānṭa[1] (the twelfth centre) above the palate, then the fluctuations of prāṇa are stopped. When the eye of consciousness (*viz.*, the spiritual or third eye) becomes calm and clear so as to be able to distinctly see in the transparent ākās' at a distance of twelve digits from the tip of his nose, then the fluctuations of prāṇa are stopped. When the thoughts arising in the mind are bound up in the calm contemplation of the world of ṭāraka (star or eye) between one's eyebrows and are (thus) destroyed, then the fluctuations cease. When the knowlege which is of the form of the knowable,

[1] This twelfth centre is identified by some with the pituitary body in the head, there being six centres in the brain besides the six below the brain.

which is beneficent and which is untouched by any modifications arises in one and is known as OM only and no other, then the fluctuations of prāṇa cease. By the contemplation for a long time of the ākās' which is in the heart, and by the contemplation of the mind free from vāsānās, then the fluctuations of prāṇa cease. By these methods and various others suggested by (one's) thought and by means of the contact of the many (spiritual) guides, the fluctuations cease.

" Having by contraction opened the door of kuṇḍalinī, one should force open the door of moksha. Closing with her mouth the door through which one ought to go, the kuṇḍalinī sleeps spiral in form and coiled up like a serpent. He who causes this kuṇḍalinī to move—he is an emancipated person. If this kuṇḍalinī were to sleep in the upper part of the neck of any yogin, it goes towards his emancipation. (If it were to sleep) in the lower part (of the body), it is for the bondage of the ignorant. Leaving the two nādis, Idā and the other (Piṅgalā), it (prāṇa) should move in the Sushumnā. That is the supreme seat of Vishṇu. One should practise control of breath with the concentration of the mind. The mind should not be allowed by a clever man to rest on any other thing. One should not worship Vishṇu during the day alone. One should not worship Vishṇu during the night alone; but should always worship Him, and should not worship Him merely during day and night. The wisdom-producing opening (near uvula) has five passages. O S'āṇḍilya this is the khecharīmuḍrā; practise it. With one who sits in the khecharīmuḍrā, the vāyu which was flowing before through the left and right nādis now flows through the middle one (Sushumnà). There is no doubt about it. You should swallow the air through the void (Sushumnā) between Idā and Piṅgalā. In that place is khecharīmuḍrā situated, and that is the seat of Truth. Again that is khecharīmuḍrā which is situated in the ākās'a-chakra (in the head) in the nirālamba (supportless) seat between the sun and moon (*viz.*, Idā and Piṅgalā). When the tongue has been lengthened to the length of a kalā (digit) by the incision (of the frænum lingum) and by rubbing and milking it (*viz.*, the tongue), fix the gaze between the two eyebrows and close the hole in the skull with the tongue reversed. This is khecharīmuḍrā. When the tongue and the chiṭṭa (mind) both move in the ākās' (khecharī), then the person with his tongue raised up becomes immortal. Firmly pressing the yoni (perineum) by the left heel, stretching out the right leg, grasping the feet with both hands and inhaling the air through the nostrils, practise kaṇtha-banḍha,[1] retaining the air upwards. By that, all afflictions are destroyed; then poison is digested as if it were nectar. Asthma, splenetic disease, the turning up of the anus and the numbness of the skin are removed. This is the means of conquering prāṇa and destroying death. Pressing the yoni by the left heel, place the other foot over the left thigh: inhale the air, rest the chin on the chest, contract the yoni and contemplate, (as far as possible), your Āṭmā as situated within your mind. Thus is the direct perception (of truth) attained.

"Inhaling the prāṇa from outside and filling the stomach with it, centre the prāṇa with the mind in the middle of the navel, at the tip of the nose and at the toes during the sanḍhyās (sunset and sunrise) or at all times. (Thus) the yogin is freed from all diseases and fatigue. By centring his prāṇa at the tip of his nose, he obtains mastery over the element of air; by centring it at the middle of his navel, all diseases are destroyed; by centring it at the toes, his body becomes light. He who drinks the air (drawn) through the tongue destroys fatigue, thirst and diseases. He who drinks the air with his mouth during the two sanḍhyās and the last two hours of the night, within three months the auspicious Sarasvaṭī (goddess of speech) is present in his vāk (speech) *viz.*, (he becomes eloquent and learned in his speech). In six months, he is free from all diseases. Drawing the air by the tongue, retain the air at the root of the tongue. The wise man thus drinking nectar enjoys all prosperity. Fixing the Āṭmā in the Āṭmā itself in the middle of the eyebrows, (having inhaled) through Idā and breaking through that (centre) thirty times, even a sick man is freed from disease. He who draws the air through the nādis and retains it for twenty-four minutes in the navel and in

[1] Lit., binding the air up the throat.

the sides of the stomach becomes freed from disease. He who for the space of a month during the three sanḍhyās (sunset, sunrise, and midnight or noon) draws the air through the tongue, pierces thirty times and retains his breath in the middle of his navel, becomes freed from all fevers and poisons. He who retains the prāṇa together with the mind at the tip of his nose even for the space of a muhūrṭa (forty-eight minutes), destroys all sins that were committed by him during one hundred births.

"Through the samyama of ṭāra (OM), he knows all things. By retaining the mind at the tip of his nose, he acquires a knowledge of Inḍra-world;[1] below that, he acquires a knowledge of Āgni-(fire) world.[1] Through the samyama of chiṭṭa in the eye, he gets a knowledge of all worlds: in the ear, a knowledge of Yama-(the god of death) world:[1] in the sides of the ear, a knowledge of Nṛṛṭi-world:[1] in the back of it (the ear), a knowledge of Varuṇa-world:[1] in the left ear, a knowledge of Vāyu-world:[1] in the throat, a knowledge of Soma-(moon) world:[1] in the left eye, a knowledge of S'iva-world:[1] in the head, a knowledge of Brahmā-world:[1] in the soles of the feet, a knowledge of Āṭala world:[2] in the feet, a knowledge of Viṭala world: in the ankles, a knowledge of Niṭala (rather Suṭala) world: in the calves, a knowledge of Suṭala (rather Ṭalāṭāla world): in the knees, a knowledge of Mahāṭala world: in the thighs, a knowledge of Rasāṭala world: in the loins, a knowledge of Ṭalāṭala (rather Pāṭāla) world: in the navel, a knowledge of Bhūrloka (earth-world): in the stomach, a knowledge of Bhuvar (world): in the heart, a knowledge of Suvar (world): in the place above the heart, a knowledge of Mahar world: in the throat, a knowledge of Jana world: in the middle of the brows, a knowledge of Ṭapa world: in the head, a knowledge of Saṭya world.

"By conquering ḍharma and aḍharma, one knows the past and the future. By centring it on the sound of every creature, a knowledge of the cry (or language) of the

[1] These correspond severally to the several directions and the ḍevaṭās presiding over them, corresponding respectively to east, south-east, south, south-west, west, north-west, north, and north-east.

[2] The fourteen worlds, lokas and ṭalas are referred to: the order in ṭalas seems to be wrong, Ṭalāṭala should be in the middle.

animal is produced. By centring it on the sañchiṭa-karma (past karma yet to be enjoyed), a knowledge of one's previous births arises in him. By centring it on the mind of another, a knowledge of the mind (or thoughts) of others is induced. By centring it on the kāya-rūpa (or form of the body), other forms are seen. By fixing it on the bala (strength), the strength of persons like Hanūmān is obtained. By fixing it on the sun, a knowledge of the worlds arises. By fixing it on the moon, a knowledge of the constellation is produced. By fixing it on the Ḍhruva (Polar star) a perception of its motion is induced. By fixing it on his own (Self), one acquires the knowledge of Purusha; on the navel, he attains a knowledge of the kāya-vyūha (mystical arrangement of all the particles of the body so as to enable a person to wear out his whole karma in one life): on the well of the throat, freedom from hunger and thirst arises: on the Kūrma nādi (which is situated in the well of the throat), a firmness (of concentration) takes place. By fixing it on the ṭārā (pupil of the eye), he obtains the sight of the siḍḍhas (spiritual personages). By conquering the ākās' in the body, he is able to soar in the ākās': (in short) by centring the mind in any place, he conquers the siḍḍhis appertaining to that place.

"Then comes praṭyāhāra, which is of five kinds. It is the drawing away of the organs from attaching themselves to the objects of senses. Contemplating upon everything that one sees as Āṭmā is praṭyāhāra. Renouncing the fruits of one's daily actions is praṭyāhāra. Turning away from all objects of sense is praṭyāhāra. Ḍhāraṇā in the eighteen important places (mentioned below) is praṭyāhāra, (*viz.*,) the feet, the toes, the ankles, the calves, the knees, the thighs, the anus, the penis, the navel, the heart, the well of the throat, the palate, the nose, the eyes, the middle of the brows, the forehead, and the head in ascending and descending orders.

"Then (comes) ḍhāraṇā. It is of three kinds, (*viz.*,) fixing the mind in the Āṭmā, bringing the external ākās' into the ākas' of the heart and contemplating the five mūrṭis (forms of ḍevaṭās) in the five elements—earth, āpas, fire, vāyu, and ākās'.

"Then comes ḍhyāna. It is of two kinds, saguṇa (with guṇas or quality) and nirguṇa (without quality). Saguṇa is the meditation of a mūrṭi. Nirguṇa is on the reality of Self.

"Samāḍhi is the union of the Jīvāṭmā (individual self) and the Paramāṭmā (higher self) without the threefold state, (*viz.*, the knower, the known, and the knowledge). It is of the nature of extreme bliss and pure consciousness.

"Thus ends the first chapter of S'āṇdilya Upanishaḍ."

Chapter II

Then the Bṛahmarshi S'āṇdilya not obtaining the knowledge of Brahman in the four Veḍas, approached the Lord Āṭharvan and asked him: "What is it? Teach me the science of Brahman by which I shall obtain that which is most excellent."

Āṭharvan replied: "O S'āṇdilya, Brahman is saṭya, vijñāna and ananṭa in which all this (world) is interwoven, warp-wise and woof-wise, from which all originated and into which all are absorbed, and which being known makes everything else known. It is without hands and feet, without eyes and ears, without tongue or without body, and is unreachable and undefinable. From which, vāk (speech) and mind return, being unable to obtain (or reach) It. It is to be cognised by jñāna and yoga.[1] From which, prajñā of old sprang. That which is one and non-dual, that which pervades everything like ākās', which is extremely subtle, without a blemish, actionless, saṭ (be-ness) only, the essence of the bliss of consciousness, beneficent, calm and immortal and which is beyond. That is Brahman. Thou art That. Know That by wisdom. He who is the one, the shining, the giver of the power of Āṭmā, the omniscient, the lord of all, and the inner soul of all beings, who lives in all beings, who is hidden in all beings and the source of all beings, who is reachable only through yoga and who creates, supports and destroys everything—He is Āṭmā. Know the several worlds in the Āṭmā. Do not grieve, O knower of Āṭmā, thou shalt reach the end of pains."

[1] Some texts leave the words "and yoga".

Chapter III

Then S'āṇdilya questioned Āṭharvan thus: "From the Brahman that is Om, imperishable, actionless, beneficial, saṭ (be-ness) only and supreme, how did this universe arise? How does it exist in It? And how is it absorbed in It? Please solve me this doubt."

Āṭharvan replied: The Supreme Brahman, the Truth, is the imperishable and the actionless. Then from the formless Brahman, three forms (or aspects) arose, (*viz.*,) nishkalā (partless,) sakalā (with parts), and sakalā-nishkalā (with and without parts). That which is saṭya, vijñāna and ānanḍa, That which is actionless, without any impurity, omnipresent, extremely subtle, having faces in every direction, undefinable and immortal—that is His nishkalā aspect. Mahes'vara (the great Lord) who is black and yellow rules, with aviḍyā, mūlaprakṛṭi or māyā that is red, white, and black, and that is co-existent with Him. This is his sakalā-nishkalā aspect. Then the Lord desired (or willed) by his spiritual wisdom (thus): May I become many?; may I bring forth? Then from this Person who was contemplating and whose desires are fulfilled, three letters sprang up. Three vyāhṛṭis,[1] the three-footed Gāyaṭrī,[2] the three Veḍas, the three ḍevas, the three varṇas (colours or castes) and the three fires sprang. That Supreme Lord who is endowed with all kinds of wealth, who is all pervading, who is situated in the hearts of all beings, who is the Lord of māyā and whose form is māyā—He is Brahmā. He is Vishṇu: He is Ruḍra: He is Inḍra: He is all the ḍevas: He is all the bhūṭas (elements or beings): He only is before: He only is behind: He only is on our left: He only is on our right: He only is below: He only is above: He only is the all. That form of him as Ḍaṭṭāṭreya,[3] who sports with his S'akṭi, who is kind to his devotees, who is brilliant as fire, resembling the petals or a red lotus and is of four hands, who is mild and shines sinlessly—this is His sakalā form."

[1]—[2] These relate to the Gāyaṭri mantras depending upon sound.

[3] According to Bhāgavaṭa, he is one of the minor incarnations of Vishṇu.

Then S'āṇdilya questioned Āṭharvan, " O Lord, that which is Saṭ only and the essence of the bliss of consciousness—why is He called Parabrahman ? "

Āṭharvan replied : " Because He increases *bṛhaṭi* and causes to increase everything (*bṛhanṭi*) ; so he is called Parabrahman. Why is He called Ātmā ? Since He obtains (*āpnoṭi*) everything, since He takes back everything and since He is everything, so he is called Āṭmā. Why is He called Mahes'vara (the great Lord) ? Since by the sound of the words Mahaṭ-Īs'a (the great Lord) and by His own power, the great Lord governs everything. Why is He called Ḍaṭṭāṭreya ? Because the Lord being extremely pleased with Āṭri (Ṛshi) who was performing a most difficult penance and who had expressed his desire to see Him who is light itself, offered Himself (ḍaṭṭa) as their son, and because the woman Anasūyā was his mother and Āṭri was his father. Therefore he who knows the (secret) meaning knows everything. He who always contemplates on the supreme that It is himself becomes a knower of Brahman. Here these s'lokas (stanzas) occur (to memory). 'He who contemplates always the Lord of Lords and the ancient thus—as Ḍaṭṭāṭreya, the beneficent, the calm, of the colour of sapphire, one who delights in his own māyā and the Lord who has shaken off everything, as naked and as one whose whole body is besmeared with the holy ashes, who has matted hair, who is the Lord of all, who has four arms, who is bliss in appearance, whose eyes are like full-blown lotus, who is the store of jñāna and yoga, who is the spiritual instructor of all the worlds and who is dear to all the yogins, and one who is merciful towards His devotees, who is the witness of all and who is worshipped by all the siḍḍhas is freed from all sins and will attain (the Spirit).'

" OM Saṭyam (truth). Thus ends the Upanishaḍ."

YOGAṬAṬṬVA-UPANISHAḌ

OF

KṚSHṆĀ-YĀJURVEḌĀ

I SHALL now describe yoga-ṭaṭṭva (yoga-truth) for the benefit of yogins who are freed from all sins through the hearing and the studying of it. The supreme Purusha called Vishṇu, who is the great yogin, the great being and the great ṭapasvin, is seen as a lamp in the path of the truth. The Grandfather (Brahmā) having saluted the Lord of the universe (Vishṇu) and having paid Him due respects, asked Him (thus): " Pray, explain to us the truth of yoga which includes in it the eight subservients." To which Hṛshīkes'a (the Lord of the senses or Vishṇu) replied thus: " Listen. I shall explain its truth. All souls are immersed in happiness and sorrow through the snare of māyā. Kaivalya, the supreme seat, is the path which gives them emancipation, which rends asunder the snare of māyā, which is the destroyer of birth, old age and disease and which enables one to overcome death. There are no other paths to salvation. Those who go round the net of S'āsṭras are deluded by that knowledge. It is impossible even for the Ḍevas to describe that indescribable state. How can that which is self-shining be illuminated by the S'āsṭras? That only which is without parts and stains and which is quiescent beyond all and free from decay becomes the jīva (self) on account of the results of past virtues and sins. How did that which is the seat of Paramāṭmā, is eternal, and above the state of all existing things and is of the form of wisdom and without stains attain the state of jīva? A bubble arose in it as in water and in this (bubble) arose ahaṅkāra. To it arose a ball (of body) made of the five (elements) and bound by ḍhāṭus. Know that to be jīva which is associated with happiness and misery and hence is the term jīva applied to Paramāṭmā which is pure. That jīva is cousidered to be the kevala (alone) which is freed from the stains of passion, anger, fear, delusion, greed, pride, lust, birth, death, miserliness, swoon, giddiness, hunger, thirst, ambition, shame, fright, heart-burning, grief and gladness.

"So I shall tell you the means of destroying (these) sins. How could jñāna capable of giving moksha arise certainly without yoga? And even yoga becomes powerless in (securing) moksha when it is devoid of jñāna. So the aspirant after emancipation should practise (firmly) both yoga and jñāna. The cycle of births and deaths comes only through ajñāna and perishes only through jñāna. Jñāna alone was originally. It should be known as the only means (of salvation). That is jñāna through which one cognises (in himself) the real nature of kaivalya as the supreme seat, the stainless, the partless, and of the nature of Sachchiḍānanḍa without birth, existence and death and without motion and jñāna.

"Now I shall proceed to describe yoga to you. Yoga is divided into many kinds on account of its actions: (*viz.,*) Manṭrayoga, Layayoga, Hathayoga, and Rājayoga. There are four states common to all these: (*viz.,*) Ārambha, Ghata, Parichaya, and Nishpaṭṭi. O Brahmā, I shall describe these to you. Listen attentively. One should practise the Manṭra along with its māṭrikās (proper intonations of the sounds) and others for a period of twelve years; then he gradually obtains wisdom along with the siḍḍhis, (such as) aṇimā, etc. Persons of weak intellect who are the least qualified for yoga practise this. The (second) Laya-yoga tends towards the absorption of the chiṭṭa and is described in myriads of ways; (one of which is)—one should contemplate upon the Lord who is without parts (even) while walking, sitting, sleeping, or eating. This is called Laya-yoga. Now hear (the description of) Hatha-yoga. This yoga is said to possess (the following) eight subservients, yama (forbearance), niyama (religious observance), āsana (posture), prāṇāyāma (suppression of breath), praṭyāhāra (subjugation of the senses), ḍhāraṇā (concentration), ḍhyāna, the contemplation on Hari in the middle of the eyebrows and samāḍhi that is the state of equality. Mahāmuḍrā, Mahābanḍha and Khecharī, Jālanḍhara, Uddiyāṇa, and Mūlabanḍha, uttering without intermission Praṇava (OM) for a long time, and hearing the exposition of the supreme truths, Vajrolī, Amarolī and Sahajolī, which form a triad—all these separately I shall give a true description of. O four-faced one (Brahmā), among (the duties of) yama moderate eating—and not others—forms the principal factor; and non-injury is most important in niyama. (The chief postures are) four (*viz.*,) Siḍḍha, Paḍma, Simha and Bhaḍra. During the early stages of practice, the following obstacles take place, O four-faced one, (*viz.*,) laziness, idle talk, association with bad characters, acquisition of manṭras, etc., playing with metals (alchemy) and woman, etc., and mirage. A wise man having found out these should abandon them by the force of his virtues. Then assuming Paḍma posture, he should practise prāṇāyāma. He should erect a beautiful monastery with a very small opening and with no crevices. It should be well pasted with cow-dung or with white cement. It should be carefully freed from bugs, mosquitoes and lice. It should be swept well every day with a broom. It should be perfumed with good odours; and fragrant resins should burn in it. Having taken his seat neither too high nor too low on a cloth, deerskin and kus'a grass spread, one over the other, the wise man should assume the Paḍma posture and keeping his body erect and his hands folded in respect, should salute his tutelary deity. Then closing the right nostril with his right thumb, he should gradually draw in the air through the left nostril. Having restrained it as long as possible, he should again expel it through the right nostril slowly and not very fast. Then filling the stomach through the right nostril, he should retain it as long as he can and then expel it through the left nostril. Drawing the air through that nostril by which he expels, he should continue this in uninterrupted succession. The time taken in making a round of the knee with the palm of the hand, neither very slowly nor very rapidly, and snapping the fingers once is called a māṭrā. Drawing the air through the left nostril for about sixteen māṭrās and having retained it (within) for about sixty-four māṭrās, one should expel it again through the right nostril for about thirty-two māṭrās. Ȧgain fill the right nostril as before (and continue the rest). Practise cessation of breath four times daily (*viz.*,) at sunrise, noon, sunset and midnight, till eighty (times are reached). By a continual practice for about three months, the purification of the nādis takes place. When the nādis have become purified, certain external signs appear on the body of the yogin. I shall proceed to describe them. (They are) lightness of the body, brilliancy of complexion, increase of the gastric fire, leanness of the body, and along with these, absence of restlessness in the body. The proficient in yoga should abandon the food detrimental to the practice of yoga. He should give up salt, mustard, things sour, hot, pungent, or bitter, vegetables, asafœtida, etc., worship of fire, women, walking, bathing at sunrise, emaciation of the body by fasts, etc. During the early stages of practice, food of milk and ghee is ordained; also food consisting of wheat, green pulse and red rice are said to favour the progress. Then he will be able to retain his breath as long as he likes. By thus retaining the breath as long as he likes, kevala kumbhaka (cessation of breath without inspiration and expiration) is attained. When kevala kumbhaka is attained by one, and thus expiration and inspiration are dispensed with, there is nothing unattainable in the three worlds to him. In the commencement (of his practice), sweat is given out; he should wipe it off. Even after that, owing to the retaining of the breath, the person practising it gets phlegm. Then by an increased practice of ḍhāraṇā, sweat arises. Ȧs a frog moves by leaps, so the yogin sitting in the Padma posture moves on the earth. With a (further) increased practice, he is able to rise from the ground. He, while seated in Paḍma posture, levitates. There arises to him the power to perform extraordinary feats. He does (or should) not disclose to others his feats of great powers (in the path). Ȧny pain small or great, does not affect the yogin. Then excretions and sleep are diminished; tears, rheum in the eye, salivary flow, sweat and bad smell in the mouth do not arise in him. With a still further practice, he acquires great strength by which he attains Bhūchara siḍḍhi, which enables him to bring under his control all the creatures that tread this earth; tigers, s'arabhas,[1] elephants, wild bulls or lions die on being struck by the palm of the yogin. He becomes as beautiful as the god of love himself. All females being taken up with the beauty of his person will desire to have intercourse with him. If he so keeps connection, his virility will be lost; so abandoning all copulation with women, he should continue his practice with great assiduity. By the preservation of the semen, a good odour pervades the body of the yogin. Then sitting in a secluded place, he should repeat Praṇava (OM) with three pluṭa-māṭrās (or prolonged intonation) for the destruction of his former sins. The manṭra, Praṇava (OM) destroys all obstacles and all sins. By practising thus he attains the ārambha (beginning or first) state.

"Then follows the ghata (second state)—one which is acquired by constantly practising suppression of breath. When a perfect union takes place between prāṇa and apāna, manas and buḍḍhi, or jīvāṭmā and Paramāṭmā without opposition, it is called the ghata state. I shall describe its signs. He may now practise only for about one-fourth of the period prescribed for practice before. By day and evening, let him practise only for a yāma (3 hours). Let him practise kevala kumbhaka once a day. Drawing away completely the organs from the objects of sense during cessation of breath is called praṭyāhāra. Whatever he sees with his eyes, let him consider as Āṭmā. Whatever he hears with his ears let him consider as Āṭmā. Whatever he smells with his nose let him consider as Āṭmā. Whatever he tastes with his tongue let him consider as Āṭmā. Whatever the yogin touches with his skin let him consider as Āṭmā. The yogin should thus unwearied gratify his organs of sense for a period of one yāma every day with great effort. Then various wonderful powers are attained by the yogin, such as clairvoyance,

[1] An animal said to have eight legs and to be stronger than lion.

clairaudience, ability to transport himself to great distances within a moment, great power of speech, ability to take any form, ability to become invisible, and the transmutation of iron into gold when the former is smeared over with his excretion.

"That yogin who is constantly practising yoga attains the power to levitate. Then should the wise yogin think that these powers are great obstacles to the attainment of yoga, and so he should never take delight in them. The king of yogins should not exercise his powers before any person whatsoever. He should live in the world as a fool, an idiot, or a deaf man, in order to keep his powers concealed. His disciples would, without doubt, request him to show his powers for the gratification of their own desires. One who is actively engaged in one's duties forgets to practise (yoga); so he should practise day and night yoga without forgetting the words of the guru. Thus passes the ghata state to one who is constantly engaged in yoga practice. To one nothing is gained by useless company, since thereby he does not practise yoga. So one should with great effort practise yoga. Then by this constant practice is gained the parichaya state (the third state). Vāyu (or breath) through arduous practice pierces along with agni the Kuṇḍalinī through thought and enters the Sushumnā uninterrupted. When one's chiṭṭa enters Sushumnā along with prāṇa, it reaches the high seat (of the head probably) along with prāṇa.

"There are the five elements (*viz.*,) pṛṭhivī, āpas, agni, vāyu and ākās'. To the body of the five elements, there is the fivefold ḍhāraṇā. From the feet to the knees is said to be the region of pṛṭhivī, is four-sided in shape, is yellow in colour and has the varṇa (or letter) *La*. Carrying the breath with the letter *La* along the region of earth (*viz.*, from the foot to the knees) and contemplating upon Brahmā with four faces and four mouths and of a golden colour, one should perform ḍhāraṇā there for a period of two hours. He then attains mastery over the earth. Death does not trouble him, since he has obtained mastery over the earth element. The region of āpas is said to extend from the knees to the anus. Āpas is semi-lunar in shape and white in colour and has *Va* for its bīja (seed) letter. Carrying up the breath with the letter *Va* along the region of āpas, he should contemplate on the God Nārāyaṇa having four arms and a crowned head, as being of the colour of pure crystal, as dressed in orange clothes and as decayless; and practising ḍhāraṇā there for a period of two hours, he is freed from all sins. Then there is no fear for him from water, and he does not meet his death in water. From the anus to the heart is said to be the region of agni. Agni is triangular in shape, of red colour, and has the letter *Ra* for its (bīja) seed. Raising the breath made resplendent through the letter *Ra* along the region of fire, he should contemplate on Ruḍra, who has three eyes, who grants all wishes, who is of the colour of the midday sun, who is daubed all over with holy ashes and who is of a pleased countenance. Practising ḍhāraṇā there for a period of two hours, he is not burnt by fire even though his body enters the fire-pit. From the heart to the middle of the eyebrows is said to be the region of vāyu. Vāyu is hexangular in shape, black in colour and shines with the letter *Ya*. Carrying the breath along the region of vāyu, he should contemplate on Īs'vara, the Omniscient, as possessing faces on all sides; and practising ḍhāraṇā there for two hours, he enters vāyu and then ākās'. The yogin does not meet his death through the fear of vāyu. From the centre of the eyebrows to the top of the head is said to be the region of ākās', is circular in shape, smoky in colour and shining with the letter *Ha*. Raising the breath along the region of ākās', he should contemplate on Saḍās'iva in the following manner, as producing happiness, as of the shape of binḍu, as the great ḍeva, as having the shape of ākās', as shining like pure crystal, as wearing the rising crescent of moon on his head, as having five faces, ten heads and three eyes, as being of a pleased countenance, as armed with all weapons, as adorned with all ornaments, as having Umā (the goddess) in one-half of his body, as ready to grant favours, and as the cause of all the causes. By practising ḍhāraṇā in the region of ākās', he obtains certainly the power of levitating in the ākās' (ether). Wherever he stays, he enjoys supreme bliss. The proficient in yoga should practise these five ḍhāraṇās. Then his body becomes strong and he does not know death. That great-minded man does not die even during the deluge of Brahmā.

" Then he should practise ḍhāraṇā for a period of six ghaṭikās (2 hours, 24 minutes). Restraining the breath in (the region of) ākās' and contemplating on the deity who grants his wishes—this is said to be saguṇa[1] ḍhyāna capable of giving (the siḍḍhis) aṇimā, etc. One who is engaged in nirguṇa[1] ḍhyāna attains the stage of samāḍhi. Within twelve days at least, he attains the stage of samāḍhi. Restraining his breath, the wise one becomes an emancipated person. Samāḍhi is that state in which the jīvāṭmā (lower self) and the Paramāṭmā (higher self) are differenceless (or of equal state). If he desires to lay aside his body, he can do so. He will become absorbed in Parabrahman and does not require uṭkrānṭi (going out or up). But if he does not so desire, and if his body is dear to him, he lives in all the worlds possessing the siḍḍhis of aṇimā, etc. Sometimes he becomes a ḍeva and lives honoured in svarga; or he becomes a man or an yaksha through his will. He can also take the form of a lion, tiger, elephant, or horse through his own will. The yogin becoming the great Lord can live as long as he likes. There is difference only in the modes of procedure but the result is the same.

" Place the left heel pressed on the anus, stretch the right leg and hold it firmly with both hands. Place the head on the breast and inhale the air slowly. Restrain the breath as long as you can and then slowly breathe out. After practising it with the left foot, practise it with the right. Place the foot that was stretched before on the thigh. This is mahābanḍha and should be practised on both sides. The yogin sitting in mahābanḍha and having inhaled the air with intent mind, should stop the course of vāyu (inside) by means of the throat-muḍrā, and occupying the two sides (of the throat) with speed. This is called mahāveḍha and is frequently practised by the siḍḍhas. With the tongue thrust

[1] Lit., "with guṇas" and "without guṇas".

into the interior cavity of the head (or throat) and with the eyes intent on the spot between the eyebrows, this is called khecharīmuḍrā. Contracting the muscles of the neck and placing the head with a firm will on the breast, this is called the jālanḍhara (banḍha) and is a lion to the elephant of death. That banḍha by which prāṇa flies through Sushumnā is called uddiyāṇabanḍha by the yogins. Pressing the heel firmly against the anus, contracting the anus and drawing up the apāna, this is said to be yonibanḍha. Through mūlabanḍha, prāṇa and apāna as well as nāḍa and binḍu are united and gives success in yoga: there is no doubt about this. To one practising in a reversed manner (or on both sides) which destroys all diseases, the gastric fire is increased. Therefore a practitioner should collect a large quantity of provisions, (for) if he takes a small quantity of food, the fire (within) will consume his body in a moment.

"On the first day, he should stand on his head with the feet raised up for a moment. He should increase this period gradually every day. Wrinkles and greyness of hair will disappear within three months. He who practises only for a period of a yāma (twenty-four minutes) every day conquers time. He who practises vajrolī becomes a yogin and the repository of all siḍḍhis. If the yoga siḍḍhis are ever to be attained, he only has them within his reach. He knows the past and the future and certainly moves in the air. He who drinks of the nectar thus is rendered immortal day by day. He should daily practise vajrolī. Then it is called amarolī. Then he obtains the rājayoga and certainly he does not meet with obstacles. When a yogin fulfils his action by rājayoga, then he certainly obtains discrimination and indifference to objects. Vishṇu, the great yogin, the grand one of great austerities and the most excellent Purusha is seen as a lamp in the path of truth.

"That breast from which one suckled before (in his previous birth) he now presses (in love) and obtains pleasure. He enjoys the same genital organ from which he was born before. She who was once his mother will now be wife and she who is now wife is (or will be) verily mother. He who is now father will be again son, and he who is now son will be again father. Thus are the egos of this world wandering in the womb of birth and death like a bucket in the wheel of a well and enjoying the worlds. There are the three worlds, three veḍas, three sanḍhyās, (morning, noon and evening), three svaras (sounds), three agnis, and guṇas, and all these are placed in the three letters (Oм). He who understands that which is indestructible and is the meaning of the three (Oм)—by him are all these worlds strung. This is the Truth, the supreme seat. Ås the smell in the flower, as the ghee in the milk, as the oil in the gingelly seed and as the gold in the quartz, so is the lotus situated in the heart. Its face is downwards and its stem upwards. Its binḍu is downwards and in its centre is situated manas. By the letter Å, the lotus becomes expanded ; by the letter U, it becomes split (or opened), by the letter M, it obtains nāḍa ; and the arḍhamāṭrā (half-metre) is silence. The person engaged in yoga obtains the the supreme seat, which is like a pure crystal, which is without parts and which destroys all sins. Ås a tortoise draws its hands and head within itself, so drawing in air thus and ex-pelling it through the nine holes of the body, he breathes upwards and forwards. Like a lamp in an air-tight jar which is motionless, so that which is seen motionless through the process of yoga in the heart and which is free from turmoil, after having been drawn from the nine holes, is said to be Åṭmā alone."

ḌHYĀNABINḌU-UPANISHAḌ[1]

OF

SĀMAVEḌĀ

Even if sin should accumulate to a mountain extending over many yojanas (distance), it is destroyed by ḍhyānayoga. At no time has been found a destroyer of sins like this. Bījākshara (seed-letter) is the supreme binḍu. Nāḍa (spiritual sound) is above it. When that nāḍa ceases along with letter, than the nāḍa-less is supreme state. That yogin who considers as the highest that which is above nāḍa, which is anāhaṭa,[2] has all his doubts destroyed. If the point of a hair be divided into one-hundred thousand parts, this (nāḍa) is one-half of that still further divided; and when (even) this is absorbed, the yogin attains to the stainless Brahman. One who is of a firm mind and without the delusion (of sensual pleasures) and ever resting in Brahman, should see like the string (in a rosary of beads) all creatures (as existing) in Āṭmā like odour in flowers, ghee in milk, oil in gingelly seeds and gold in quartz. Again just as the oil depends for its manifestation upon gingelly seeds and odour upon flowers, so does the Purusha depend for its existence upon the body, both external and internal. The tree is with parts and its shadow is without parts but with and without parts, Āṭmā exists everywhere.

The one akshara (letter Om) should be contemplated upon as Brahman by all who aspire for emancipation. Pṛṭhivī, agni, ṛgveḍa, bhūḥ and Brahmā—all these (are absorbed) when Akāra

[1] The Upanishaḍ of the seed of meditation.

[2] Of the heart.

(Ā), the first ams'a (part) of praṇava (OM) becomes absorbed. Anṭariksha, yajurveḍa, vāyu, bhuvaḥ and Vishṇu, the Janārḍana—all these (are absorbed) when Ukāra (U), the second ams'a of praṇava becomes absorbed. Ḍyur, sun, sāmaveḍa, suvaḥ and Mahes'vara—all these (are absorbed) when Makāra (M), the third ams'a of praṇava becomes absorbed. Ākāra is of (pīṭa) yellow colour and is said to be of rajoguṇa; Ukāra is of white colour and of saṭṭvaguṇa; Makāra is of dark colour and of ṭamoguṇa. He who does not know Omkāra as having eight aṅgas (parts), four pāḍas (feet), three sṭhānas (seats) and five ḍevaṭās (presiding deities) is not a Brāhmaṇa. Praṇava is the bow. Āṭmā is the arrow and Brahman is said to be the aim. One should aim at it with great care and then he, like the arrow, becomes one with It. When that Highest is cognised, all karmas return (from him, *viz.*, do not affect him). The Veḍas have Omkāra as their cause. The swaras (sounds) have Omkara as their cause. The three worlds with (all) the locomotive and the fixed (ones in them) have Omkāra as their cause. The short (accent of OM) burns all sins, the long one is decayless and the bestower of prosperity. United with arḍhamāṭrā (half-metre of OM), the praṇava becomes the bestower of salvation. That man is the knower of the Veḍas who knows that the end (*viz.*, arḍhamāṭrā) of praṇava should be worshipped (or recited) as uninterrupted as the flow of oil and (resounding) as long as the sound of a bell. One should contemplate upon Omkāra as Īs'vara resembling an unshaken light, as of the size of a thumb and as motionless in the middle of the pericarp of the lotus of the heart. Taking in vāyu through the left nostril and filling the stomach with it, one should contemplate upon Omkāra as being in the middle of the body and as surrounded by circling flames. Brahmā is said to be inspiration; Vishṇu is said to be cessation (of breath), and Ruḍra is said to be expiration. These are the ḍevaṭās of prāṇāyāma. Having made Āṭmā as the (lower) araṇi (sacrificial wood) and praṇava as the upper araṇi, one should see the God in secret through the practice of churning which is ḍhyāna. One should practise restraint of breath as much as it lies in his power along with (the uttering of)

Omkāra sound, until it ceases completely. Those who look upon OM as of the form of Hamsa staying in all, shining like crores of suns, being alone, staying in gamāgama (ever going and coming) and being devoid of motion—at last such persons are freed from sin. That manas which is the author of the actions (*viz.*), creation, preservation and destruction of the three worlds, is (then) absorbed (in the supreme One). That is the highest state of Vishṇu.

The lotus of the heart has eight petals and thirty-two filaments. The sun is in its midst: the moon is in the middle of the sun. Āgni is in the middle of the moon: the prabhā (spiritual light) is in the middle of agni. Pītha (seat or centre) is in the midst of prabhā, being set in diverse gems. One should meditate upon the stainless Lord Vāsuḍeva as being (seated) upon the centre of Pītha, as having S'rīvaṭsa[1] (black mark) and Kausṭubha (garland of gems) on his chest and as adorned with gems and pearls resembling pure crystal in lustre and as resembling crores of moons in brightness. He should meditate upon Mahā-Vishṇu as above or in the following manner. (That is) he should meditate with inspiration (of breath) upon Mahā-Vishṇu as resembling the aṭasī flower and as staying in the seat of navel with four hands; then with restraint of breath, he should meditate in the heart upon Brahmā, the Grandfather as being on the lotus with the gaura (pale-red) colour of gems and having four faces: then through expiration, he should meditate upon the three-eyed S'iva between the two eyebrows shining like the pure crystal, being stainless, destroying all sins, being in that which is like the lotus facing down with its flower (or face) below and the stalk above or like the flower of a plantain tree, being of the form of all Veḍas, containing one hundred petals and one hundred leaves and having the pericarp full-expanded. There he should meditate upon the sun, the moon and the agni, one above another. Passing above through the lotus which has the brightness of the sun, moon and agni, and taking its Hrīm bīja (letter), one leads his Āṭmā firmly. He is the knower of Veḍas

[1] The black mark on the breast standing for mūlaprakṛṭi and the garland for the five elements.

who knows the three seats, the three māṭrās, the three Brahmās, the three aksharas (letters) and the three mātrās associated with the arḍhamāṭrā. He who knows that which is above binḍu, nāḍa and kalā as uninterrupted as the flow of oil and (resounding) as long as the sound of a bell—that man is a knower of the Veḍas. Just as a man would draw up (with his mouth) the water through the (pores of the) lotus-stalk, so the yogin treading the path of yoga should draw up the breath. Having made the lotus-sheath of the form of arḍhamāṭrā, one should draw up the breath through the stalk (of the nādis Sushumnā, Idā and Piṅgalā) and absorb it in the middle of the eyebrows. He should know that the middle of the eyebrows in the forehead which is also the root of the nose is the seat of nectar. That is the great place of Brahman.

Postures, restraint of breath, subjugation of the senses ḍhāraṇā, ḍhyāna and samāḍhi are the six parts of yoga. There are as many postures as there are living creatures; and Mahes'vara (the great Lord) knows their distinguishing features. Siḍḍha, bhaḍra, simha and paḍma are the four (chief) postures. Mūlāḍhāra is the first chakra. Svāḍhishthāna is the second. Between these two is said to be the seat of yoni (perineum), having the form of Kāma (God of love). In the Ādhāra of the anus, there is the lotus of four petals. In its midst is said to be the yoni called Kāma and worshipped by the siḍḍhas. In the midst of the yoni is the Liṅga facing the west and split at its head like the gem. He who knows this, is a knower of the Veḍas. A four-sided figure is situated above agni and below the genital organ, of the form of molten gold and shining like streaks of lightning. Prāṇa is with its sva (own) sound, having Svāḍhishthāna as its aḍhishthāna (seat), (or since sva or prāṇa arises from it). The chakra Svāḍhishthāna is spoken of as the genital organ itself. The chakra in the sphere of the navel is called Maṇipūraka, since the body is pierced through by vāyu like maṇis (gems) by string. The jīva (ego) urged to actions by its past virtuous and sinful karmas whirls about in this great chakra of twelve[1] spokes, so long as it

[1] In other places, it is ten.

does not grasp the truth. Above the genital organ and below the navel is kanda of the shape of a bird's egg. There arise (from it) nādis seventy-two thousand in number. Of these seventy-two are generally known. Of these, the chief ones are ten and carry the prāṇas. Idā, Piṅgalā, Sushumnā, Gānḍhārī, Hasṭijihvā, Pūshā, Yas'asvinī, Alambusā, Kuhūh and S'āṅkhinī are said to be the ten. This chakra of the nādis should ever be known by the yogins. The three nādis Ida, Piṅgalā and Sushumnā are said to carry prāṇa always and have as their ḍevaṭās, moon, sun and agni. Idā is on the left side and Piṅgalā on the right side, while the Sushumnā is in the middle. These three are known to be the paths of prāṇa. Prāṇa, Apāna, Samāna, Udāna, and Vyāna; Nāga, Kūrma, Kṛkara, Ḍevaḍaṭṭa and Ḍhanañjaya; of these, the first five are called prāṇas, etc., and last five Nāga, etc. are called vāyus (or sub-prāṇas). All these are situated (or run along) the one thousand nādis, (being) in the form of (or producing) life. Jīva which is under the influence of prāṇa and apāna goes up and down. Jīva on account of its ever moving by the left and right paths is not visible. Just as a ball struck down (on the earth) with the bat of the hand springs up, so jīva ever tossed by prāṇa and apāna is never at rest. He is knower of yoga who knows that prāṇa always draws itself from apāna and apāna draws itself from prāṇa, like a bird (drawing itself from and yet not freeing itself) from the string (to which it is tied).

The jīva comes out with the letter *Ha* and gets in again with the letter *Sa*. Thus jīva always utters the manṭra 'Hamsa,' 'Hamsa'. The jīva always utters the manṭra twenty-one thousand and six hundred times in one day and night. This is called Ajapā Gāyaṭrī and is ever the bestower of nirvāṇa to the yogins. Through its very thought, man is freed from sins. Neither in the past nor in the future is there a science equal to this, a japa equal to this or a meritorious action equal to this. Parames'varī (*viz.*, kuṇdalinī s'akṭi) sleeps shutting with her mouth that door which leads to the decayless Brahma-hole. Being aroused by the contact of agni with manas and prāṇa, she takes the form of a needle and pierces up through Sushumnā. The yogin should open with great effort this door which is shut. Then he will pierce the door to salvation by means of kuṇḍalinī. Folding firmly the fingers of the hands, assuming firmly the Paḍma posture, placing the chin firmly on the breast and fixing the mind in ḍhyāna, one should frequently raise up the apāna, fill up with air and then leave the prāṇa. Then the wise man gets matchless wisdom through (this) s'akṭi. That yogin who assuming Paḍma posture worships (*i.e.*, controls) vāyu at the door of the nādis and then performs restraint of breath is released without doubt. Rubbing off the limbs the sweat arising from fatigue, abandoning all acid, bitter and saltish (food), taking delight in the drinking of milk and rasa, practising celibacy, being moderate in eating and ever bent on yoga, the yogin becomes a siḍḍha in little more than a year. No inquiry need be made concerning the result. Kuṇḍalinī s'akṭi, when it is up in the throat, makes the yogi get siḍḍhi. The union of prāṇa and apāna has the extinction of urine and fæces.

One becomes young even when old through performing mūlabanḍha always. Pressing the yoni by means of the heels and contracting the anus and drawing up the apāna—this is called mūlabanḍha. Uddiyāṇa banḍha is so called because it is (like) a great bird that flies up always without rest. One should bring the western part of the stomach above the navel. This Uddiyāṇa banḍha is a lion to the elephant of death, since it binds the water (or nectar) of the ākās' which arises in the head and flows down. The Jālanḍhara banḍha is the destroyer of all the pains of the throat. When this Jālanḍhara banḍha which is destroyer of the pains of the throat is performed, then nectar does not fall on agni nor does the vāyu move. When the tongue enters backwards into the hole of the skull, then there is the mudrā of vision latent in the eyebrow called khecharī. He who knows the muḍrā, khecharī has not disease, death, sleep, hunger, thirst, or swoon. He who practises this muḍrā is not affected by illness or karma; nor is he bound by the limitations of time. Since chiṭṭa moves in the kha (ākās') and since the tongue has entered (in the muḍrā) kha (*viz.*, the hole in the mouth), therefore the muḍrā is called khecharī and worshipped by the siḍḍhas. He whose hole (or passage) above the uvula is closed (with the tongue backwards) by means of khecharīmuḍrā never loses his virility, even when embraced by a lovely woman. Where is the fear of death, so long as the binḍu (virility) stays in the body. Binḍu does not go out of the body, so long as the khecharīmuḍra is practised. (Even) when binḍu comes down to the sphere of the perineum, it goes up, being prevented and forced up by violent effort through yonimuḍrā. This binḍu is twofold, white and red. The white one is called s'ukla and the red one is said to contain much rajas. The rajas which stays in yoni is like the colour of a coral. The binḍu stays in the seat of the genital organs. The union of these two is very rare. Binḍu is s'iva and rajas is s'akṭi. Binḍu is the moon and rajas is the sun. Through the union of these two is attained the highest body; when rajas is roused up by agitating the s'akṭi through vāyu which unites with the sun, thence is produced the divine form. S'ukla being united with the moon and rajas with the sun, he is a knower of yoga who knows the proper mixture of these two. The cleansing of the accumulated refuse, the unification of the sun and the moon and the complete drying of the rasas (essences), this is called mahāmuḍrā. Placing the chin on the breast, pressing the anus by means of the left heel, and seizing (the toe of) the extended right leg by the two hands, one should fill his belly (with air) and should slowly exhale. This is called mahāmuḍrā, the destroyer of the sins of men.

Now I shall give a description of Āṭmā. In the seat of the heart is a lotus of eight petals. In its centre is jīvāṭmā of the form of jyoṭis and atomic in size, moving in a circular line. In it is located everything. It knows everything. It does everything. It does all these actions attributing everything to its own power, (thinking) I do, I enjoy, I am happy, I am miserable, I am blind, I am lame, I am deaf, I am mute, I am lean, I am stout, etc. When it rests on the eastern petal which is of s'veta (white) colour, then it has a mind (or is inclined) to ḍharma with bhakṭi (devotion). When it rests on the south-eastern petal, which is of rakṭa (blood colour), then it is inclined to sleep and laziness. When it rests on the southern petal, which is of kṛshṇa (black) colour, then it is inclined to hate and anger. When it rests on the south-western petal which is of nīla (blue) colour, then it gets desire for sinful or harmful actions. When it rests on the western petal which is of crystal colour, then it is inclined to flirt and amuse. When it rests on the north-western petal which is of ruby colour, then it has a mind to walk, rove and have vairāgya (or be indifferent). When it rests on the northern petal which is pīṭa (yellow) colour, then it is inclined to be happy and to be loving. When it rests on the north-eastern petal which is of vaidūrya (lapis lazuli) colour, then it is inclined to amassing money, charity and passion. When it stays in the interspace between any two petals, then it gets the wrath arising from diseases generated through (the disturbance of the equilibrium of) vāyu, bile and phlegm (in the body). When it stays in the middle, then it knows everything, sings, dances, speaks and is blissful. When the eye is pained (after a day's work), then in order to remove (its) pain, it makes first a circular line and sinks in the middle. The first line is of the colour of banḍhūka flower (Bassia). Then is the state of sleep. In the middle of the state of sleep is the state of dream. In the middle of the state of dream, it experiences the ideas of perception, Veḍas, inference, possibility, (sacred) words, etc. Then there arises much fatigue. In order to remove this fatigue, it circles the second line and sinks in the middle. The second is of the colour of (the insect) Inḍragopa (of red or white colour). Then comes the state of dreamless sleep.

During the dreamless sleep, it has only the thought connected with Parames'vara (the highest Lord) alone. This state is of the nature of eternal wisdom. Afterwards it attains the nature of the highest Lord (Parames'vara). Then it makes a round of the third circle and sinks in the middle. The third circle is of the colour of paḍmarāga (ruby). Then comes the state of ṭurya (the fourth). In ṭurya, there is only the connection of Paramāṭmā. It attains the nature of eternal wisdom. Then one should gradually attain the quiescence of buḍḍhi with self-control. Placing the manas in Āṭmā, one should think of nothing else. Then causing the union of prāṇa and apāna, he concentrates his aim upon the whole universe being of the nature of Āṭmā. Then comes the state of ṭuryāṭīṭa (*viz.*, that state beyond the fourth). Then everything appears as bliss. He is beyond the pairs (of happiness and pains, etc.). He stays here as long as he should wear his body. Then he attains the nature of Paramāṭmā and attains emancipation through this means. This alone is the means of knowing Āṭmā.

When vāyu (breath) which enters the great hole associated with a hall where four roads meet gets into the half of the well-placed triangle,[1] then is Açhyuṭa (the indestructible) seen. Above the aforesaid triangle, one should meditate on the five bīja (seed) letters of (the elements) pṛṭhivi, etc., as also on the five prāṇas, the colour of the bījas and their position. The letter य[2] is the bīja of prāṇa and resembles the blue cloud. The letter र is the bīja of agni, is of apāna and resembles the sun. The letter ल is the bīja of pṛṭhivī, is of vyāna and resembles bandhūka flower. The letter व is the bīja of jīva (or vayu), is of uḍāna and is of the colour of the conch. The letter ह is the bīja of ākās', is of samāna, and is of the colour of crystal. Prāṇa stays in the heart, navel, nose, ear, foot, finger, and other places, travels through the seventy-two thousand nādis, stays in the twenty-eight crores of hair-pores and is yet the same everywhere. It is that which is called jīva. One should perform the three, expiration, etc., with a firm will and great control: and drawing in everything (with the breath) in slow degrees, he should bind prāṇa and apāna in the cave of the lotus of the heart and utter praṇava, having contracted his throat and the genital organ. From the Mūlāḍhāra (to the head) is the Sushumnā resembling the shining thread of the lotus. The nāḍa is located in the Vīṇāḍaṇda (spinal column); that sound from its middle resembles (that of) the conch, etc. When it goes to the hole of the ākās', it resembles that of the peacock. In the middle of the cave of the

[1] Probably it refers to the triangle of the initiates.

[2] There seems to be some mistake in the original.

skull between the four doors shines Āṭmā, like the sun in the sky. Between the two bows in the Brahma-hole, one should see Purusha with s'akṭi as his own Āṭmā. Then his manas is absorbed there. That man attains kaivalya who understands the gems, moonlight, nāḍa, binḍu, and the seat of Mahes'vara (the great Lord).

Thus is the Upanishaḍ.

HAMSA[1]-UPANISHAḌ

OF

S'UKLA-YAJURVEḌA

Gauṭama addressed Sanaṭkumāra thus: "O Lord, thou art the knower of all ḍharmas and art well versed in all S'āsṭras, pray tell me the means by which I may obtain a knowledge of Brahmavidyā. Sanaṭkumāra replied thus:

"Hear, O Gauṭama, that Ṭaṭṭva as expounded by Pārvaṭī after inquiring into all ḍharmas and ascertaining S'iva's opinion. This treatise on the nature of Hamsa which gives the fruit of bliss and salvation and which is like a treasure to the yogin, is (a) very mystic (science) and should not be revealed (to the public).

"Now we shall explain the true nature of Hamsa and Paramahamsa for the benefit of a brahmachārin (a seeker after Brahman or celibate), who has his desires under control, is devoted to his guru and always contemplates (as) Hamsa, and realises thus: It (Hamsa) is permeating all bodies like fire (or heat) in all kinds of wood or oil in all kinds of gingelly seeds. Having known (It) thus, one does not meet with death.

"Having contracted the anus (with the heels pressed against it), having raised the vāyu (breath) from (Mūla)[2] Āḍhāra

[1] This word "Hamsa" is very mysterious and has manifold meanings according to different standpoints. It is composed of Ham (or Aham) and Sa (ha), which mean "I" (am) "that". In its highest sense, it is Kālahamsa (or Parabrahman). It is also Brahmā when he has Hamsa (or swan) as the vehicle or Hamsa-vāhana. When Hamsa which is the manifestation of Prāṇa is applied to the human breath, we are said to exhale with Ha and to inhale with Sa. It is also called Ajapā-Gāyaṭri.

[2] The different chakras of those that are above the anus, in the genitals, navel, heart, and throat, between the eyebrows and in the head.

(chakra), having made circuit thrice round Svāḍhishṭhāna, having gone to Maṇipūraka, having crossed Ānāhaṭa, having controlled Prāṇa in Vis'uḍḍhi and then having reached Ājñā, one contemplates in Brahmaranḍhra (in the head), and having meditated there always 'I am of three māṭrās,' cognises (his Self) and becomes formless. The S'isna [1] (penis) has two sides (left and right from head to foot). This is that Paramahamsa (Supreme Hamsa or Higher Self) having the resplendence of crores of suns and by whom all this world is pervaded.

"It (this Hamsa which has buḍḍhi as vehicle) [2] has eightfold vṛṭṭi. (When it is) in the eastern [3] petal, there is the inclination (in a person) to virtuous actions; in the south-eastern petal, there arise sleep, laziness, etc.; in the southern, there is the inclination to cruelty; in the south-western, there is the inclination to sins; in the western, there is the inclination to sensual sport; in the north-western, there arise the desire of walking, and others; in the northern, there arises the desire of lust; in the north-eastern, there arises the desire of amassing money; in the middle (or the interspaces between the petals), there is the indifference to material pleasures. In the filament (of the lotus), there arises the waking state; in the pericarp, there arises the svapna (dreaming state); in the bīja (seed of pericarp), there arises the sushupṭi (dreamless sleeping state); when leaving the lotus, there is the ṭurya (fourth state). When Hamsa is absorbed in Nāḍa (spiritual sound), the state beyond the fourth is reached. Nāḍa (which is at the end of sound and beyond speech and mind) is like a pure crystal extending from (Mūla) Ādhāra to Brahmaranḍhra.. It is that which is spoken of as Brahmā and Paramāṭmā.

" (Here the performance of Ajapā Gāyaṭrī is given).

"Now Hamsa is the ṛshi; the metre is Avyakṭā Gāyaṭrī; Paramahamsa is the ḍevaṭā (or presiding deity) 'Ham' is the bīja; 'Sa' is the s'akṭī; So'ham is the kīlaka.[4] Thus there are

[1] This is omitted in the Calcutta edition and seemingly makes no sense here.
[2] This is how a commentator explains.
[3] This refers to the different petals in the heart. *Vide* the same in Nāraḍa-Parivrājaka and Ḍhyānabinḍu Upanishaḍs.
[4] Kīlaka means wedge. In the Ajapā manṭra 'Hamsa-so'ham', So'ham is the wedge to which the whole manṭra is fastened.

six. There are 21, 600 Hamsas (or breaths)[1] in a day and night. (Salutation[2] to) Surya, Soma, Nirañjana (the stainless) and Nirābhāsa (the universeless). Ājapā mānṭra. (May) the bodiless and subtle one guide[3] (or illuminate my understanding). Vaushat to Āgni-Soma. Then Aṅganyāsas and Karanyāsas occur (or should be performed after the manṭras as they are performed before the manṭras) in the heart and other (seats). Having done so, one should contemplate upon Hamsa as the Āṭmā in his heart. Āgni and Soma are its wings (right and left sides); Omkāra is its head; Ukāra and binḍu are the three eyes[4] and face respectively; Ruḍra and Ruḍrāṇī (or Ruḍra's wife) are the feet kanthaṭa (or the realisation of the oneness of jīvāṭmā or Hamsa, the lower self with Paramāṭmā or Paramahamsa, the Higher Self) is done in two ways, (samprajñāṭa[5] and asamprajñāṭa).

"Āfter that, Unmanī[6] is the end of the Ājapā (manṭra). Having thus reflected upon manas by means of this (Hamsa), one hears Nāḍa after the uttering of this japa (manṭra) a crore of times. It (Nāḍa) is (begun to be heard as) of ten kinds. The first is chini (like the sound of that word); the second is chini-chini; the third is the sound of bell; the fourth is that of conch; the fifth is that of ṭanṭri (lute); the sixth is that sound of ṭāla (cymbals); the seventh is that of flute; the eighth is that of bheri (drum); the ninth is that of mṛḍaṅga (double drum); and the tenth is that of clouds (*viz.*, thunder). He may experience the tenth without the first nine sounds (through the initiation of

[1] One commentator gives the table for 21,600 thus: 60 breaths make one Prāṇa; 6 Prāṇas, one nādi; and 60 nādis, one day and night.

[2] The words are: Sūryāya, Somāya, Nirañjanāya, Nirabhāsāya. It is with the pronunciation of these words that the different places in the body are touched, *viz.*, Aṅganyāsas and Karanyāsas are performed. The first word is pointed to the heart with the thumb; the second, to the head, and the third, to the hair of the head. With the last, a kavacha (armour) is made by circling the fingers round the head and then circling one hand over another. This process is carried on again after the pronunciation of Ajapā mantra which follows. Here Soma (moon) is that which is united with Umā or the emblem of the union of the lower and higher Selves. Sūrya or Sun is the causer of the state of one-ness.

[3] As it stands, it means "the bodiless, the subtle and the guide. The original is Aṭanu Sukshmam Prachoḍayāṭ.

[4] The three eyes are the two eyes commonly now in use with the Divine eye.

[5] Contemplation with an object as seed and the seedless one.

[6] A state above manas or when manas is transcended.

a guru). In the first stage, his body becomes chini-chini; in the second, there is the (bhañjana) breaking (or affecting) in the body; in the third, there is the (bheḍana) piercing; in the fourth, the head shakes; in the fifth, the palate produces saliva; in the sixth, nectar is attained; in the seventh, the knowledge of the hidden (things in the world) arises; in the eighth, Parāvāk is heard; in the ninth, the body becomes invisible and the pure divine eye is developed; in the tenth, he attains Parabrahman in the presence of (or with) Āṭmā which is Brahman. After that, when manas is destroyed, when it which is the source of saṅkalpa and vikalpa disappears, owing to the destruction of these two, and when virtues and sins are burnt away, then he shines as Saḍāśiva of the nature of Śakṭi pervading everywhere, being effulgence in its very essence, the immaculate, the eternal, the stainless and the most quiescent Om. Thus is the teaching of the Veḍas; and thus is the Upanishaḍ."

AMṚṬANĀḌA-UPANISHAD[1]

OF

KṚSHṆA-YAJURVEḌA

The wise, having studied the S'āsṭras and reflected on them again and again and having come to know Brahman, should abandon them all like a firebrand. Having ascended the car of Om with Vishṇu (the Higher Self) as the charioteer, one wishing to go to the seat of Brahmaloka intent on the worship of Ruḍra, should go in the chariot so long as he can go. Then abandoning the car, he reaches the place of the Lord of the car. Having given up māṭrā, liṅga,[2] and paḍa,[3] he attains the subtle paḍa (seat or word) without vowels or consonants by means of the letter M without the svara (accent). That is called praṭyāhāra when one merely thinks of the five objects of sense, such as sound, etc., as also the very unsteady mind as the reins of Āṭmā. Praṭyāhāra (subjugation of the senses), ḍhyāna (contemplation), prāṇāyāma (control of breath), ḍhāraṇā (concentration), tārka[4] and samāḍhi are said to be the six parts of yoga. Just as the impurities of mountain-minerals are burnt by the blower, so the stains committed by the organs are burned by checking prāṇa. Through prāṇāyāmas should be burnt the stains; through dhāraṇā, the sins; through praṭyāhāra,

[1] The Upanishaḍ treating of Nāda (spiritual sound) which is Amṛṭa (nectar). Here Prāṇas are spoken of, as they produce Nāḍa within and without.

[2] It is said to be the subtle, gross and other microcosmic bodies. It also means sign.

[3] It is said to be the macrocosmic bodies of Virāt, etc. It means a word or letter.

[4] In this classification, tārka is introduced newly. It means; the examination of the mind being attracted to objects and knowing that siḍḍhis are impediments to progress.

the (bad) associations; and through ḍhyāna, the godless qualities. Having destroyed the sins, one should think of Ruchira (the shining). Ruchira (cessation), expiration and inspiration—these three are prāṇāyāma of (rechaka, pūraka and kumbhaka) expiration, inspiration and cessation of breath. That is called (one) prāṇāyāma when one repeats with a prolonged (or elongated) breath three times the Gāyaṭrī with its vyāhṛṭis and Praṇava (before it) along with the s'iras[1] (the head) joining after it. Raising up the vāyu from the ākās' (region, *viz.*, the heart) and making the body void (of vāyu) and empty and uniting (the soul) to the state of void, is called rechaka (expiration). That is called pūraka (inspiration) when one takes in vāyu, as a man would take water into his mouth through the lotus-stalk. That is called kumbhaka (cessation of breath) when there is no expiration or inspiration and the body is motionless, remaining still in one state. Then he sees forms like the blind, hears sounds like the deaf and sees the body like wood. This is the characteristic of one that has attained much quiescence. That is called ḍhāraṇā when the wise man regards the mind as saṅkalpa and merging saṅkalpa into Āṭmā, contemplates upon his Āṭmā (alone). That is called ṭārka when one makes inference which does not conflict with the Veḍas. That is called samāḍhi in which one, on attaining it, thinks (all) equal.

Seating himself on the ground on a seat of kus'a grass which is pleasant and devoid of all evils, having protected himself mentally (from all evil influences), uttering raṭha-maṇdala,[2] assuming either paḍma, svasṭika, or bhaḍra posture or any other which can be practised easily, facing the north and closing the nostril with the thumb, one should inspire through the other nostril and retain breath inside and preserve the Āgni (fire). Then he should think of the sound (Om) alone. Om, the one letter is Brahman; Om should not be breathed out. Through this divine manṭra (Om), it should be done many times to rid himself of

[1] The vyāhṛtis are Bhūh, Bhuvah, etc., and the head is Om, Āpo, etc.

[2] Lit., car-circle which is a mystical chakra or diagram for invoking the ḍevaṭā; but some commentators make raṭha mean Om: and maṇdala, the circle of Siva.

impurity. Then as said before, the manṭra-knowing wise should regularly meditate, beginning with the navel upwards in the gross, the primary (or less) gross and subtle (states). The greatly wise should give up all (sight) seeing across, up or down, and should practise yoga always being motionless and without tremor. The union as stated (done) by remaining without tremor in the hollow stalk (*viz.*, Sushumnā) alone is ḍhāraṇā. The yoga with the ordained duration of twelve māṭrās is called (ḍhāraṇā). That which never decays is Akshara (Om) which is without ghosha (third, fourth, and fifth letters from K), consonant, vowel, palatal, guttural, nasal, letter R and sibilants. Prāṇa travels through (or goes by) that path through which this Akshara (Om) goes. Therefore it should be practised daily, in order to pass along that (course). It is through the opening (or hole) of the heart, through the opening of vāyu (probably navel), through the opening of the head and through the opening of moksha. They call it bila (cave), sushira (hole), or maṇḍala (wheel).[1]

(Then about the obstacles of yoga). A yogin should always avoid fear, anger, laziness, too much sleep or waking and too much food or fasting. If the above rule be well and strictly practised each day, spiritual wisdom will arise of itself in three months without doubt. In four months, he sees the ḍevas; in five months, he knows (or becomes) Brahmanishtha; and truly in six months he attains Kaivalya at will. There is no doubt.

That which is of the earth is of five māṭrās (or it takes five māṭrās to pronounce Pārṭhiva-Praṇava). That which is of water is of four māṭrās; of agni, three māṭrās; of vāyu, two; and of ākās', one. But he should think of that which is with no māṭrās. Having united Āṭmā with manas, one should contemplate upon Āṭmā by means of āṭmā. Prāṇā is thirty [2] digits long. Such is the position (or range) of prāṇas. That is called Prāṇa which is the seat of the external prāṇas. The breaths by

[1] There are four openings in the body; three from which the astral, the lower mental and the higher mental bodies escape: the last being of ṭurya.

[2] As measured by the width of the middle finger: Yājñavalkya says, Prāṇa is 12 digits beyond the body.

day and night are numbered as 1,13,180.[1] (Of the prāṇas) the first (*viz.,*) Prāṇa is pervading the heart; Āpāna, the anus; Samāna, the navel; Uḍāna, the throat; and Vyāna, all parts of the body. Then come the colours of the five prāṇas in order. Prāṇa is said to be of the colour of a blood-red gem (or coral); Āpâna which is in the middle is of the colour of Inḍragopa (an insect of white or red colour); Samāna is between the colour of pure milk and crystal (or oily and shining), between both (Prāṇa and Āpāna): Uḍāna is apāṇdara (pale white); and Vyāna resembles the colour of archis (or ray of light). That man is never reborn wherever he may die, whose breath goes out of the head after piercing through this maṇdala (of the pineal gland). That man is never reborn.

---

[1] One commentator makes it thus: Taking 21,600 for each of the five Prāṇas, we get 1,08,000: for the five sub-prāṇas, 5 × 1036 is 5,180. Hence the total is 1,13,180. Another commentator makes it 21,600 alone.

VARĀHA[1]-UPANISHAḌ

OF

KṚSHṆA-YĀJURVEḌA

CHAPTER I

THE great sage Ṛbhu performed penance for twelve ḍeva (divine) years. At the end of the time, the Lord appeared before him in the form of a boar. He said: "Rise, rise and choose your boon." The sage got up and having prostrated himself before him said: "O Lord, I will not, in my dream, wish of thee those things that are desired by the worldy. All the Veḍas, S'āsṭras, Iṭihāsas[2] and all the hosts of other sciences, as well as Brahmā and all the other Ḍevas, speak of emancipation as resulting from a knowledge of thy nature. So impart to me that science of Brahman which treats of thy nature."

Then the boar-shaped Bhagavān (Lord) said: "Some disputants hold that there are twenty-four ṭaṭṭvas (principles) and some thirty-six, whilst others maintain that there are ninety-six. I shall relate them in their order. Listen with an attentive mind. The organs of sense are five, *viz.*: ear, skin, eye and others. The organs of action are five, *viz.*: mouth, hand, leg and others. Prāṇas (vital airs) are five;[3] sound and others (*viz.*, rudimentary principles) are five.[4] Manas, buḍḍhi, chiṭṭa and ahaṅkāra are four;[5] thus

[1] This means boar and refers to the incarnation of Vishṇu as a boar.

[2] Books such as *Mahābhāraṭa* and *Rāmāyaṇa.*

[3] Prāṇa, Apāna, Uḍāna, Vyāna and Samāna, having their respective places and functions in the body.

[4] Sound, touch, form, taste and odour.

[5] Producing respectively uncertainty, certain knowledge, fluctuation of thought, and egoism and having certain centres in the body.

those that know Brahman know these to be the twenty-four ṭaṭtvas. Besides these, the wise hold the quintuplicated elements to be five, *viz.*: earth, water, fire, vāyu and ākās'; the bodies to be three, *viz.*: the gross, the subtle and the kāraṇa or causal; the states of consciousness to be three, *viz.*: the waking, the dreaming and the dreamless sleeping. The munis know the total collection of ṭaṭṭvas to be thirty-six (coupled with jīva).

"With these ṭaṭṭvas, there are six changes, *viz.*: existence, birth, growth, transformation, decay and destruction. Hunger, thirst, grief, delusion, old age and death are said to be the six infirmities. Skin, blood, flesh, fat, marrow and bones are said to be the six sheaths. Passion, anger, avarice, delusion, pride and malice are the six kinds of foes. Vis'va, Ṭaijasa and Prājña [1] are the three aspects of the jīva. Saṭṭva, rajas and ṭamas are the three guṇas (qualities). Prārabḍha,[2] sañchiṭa and āgāmin are the three karmas. Talking, lifting, walking, excreting and enjoying are the five actions (of the organs of action); and there are also thought, certainty, egoism, compassion, memory (functions of manas, etc.,), complacency, sympathy and indifference: ḍik (the quarters), Vāyu, Sun, Varuṇa,[3] As'vini ḍevas,[4] Āgni, Inḍra, Upenḍra,[5] and Mṛṭyu (death): and then the moon, the four-faced Brahmā, Ruḍra, Ksheṭrajña,[6] and Īs'vara. Thus these are the ninety-six ṭaṭṭvas. Those that worship, with devotion, me of the form of boar, who am other than the aggregate of these ṭaṭṭvas and am without decay are released from ajñāna and its effects and become jīvanmukṭas. Those that know these ninety-six ṭaṭṭvas will attain salvation in whatever order of life they may be, whether they have matted hair or are of shaven head or have (only) their tuft of hair on.[7] There is no doubt of this. Thus ends the first chapter."

[1] In the states of waking, dreaming and dreamless sleeping.

[2] Being past karmas now being enjoyed, past karmas being in store to be enjoyed hereafter and the karmas now produced to be enjoyed hereafter.

[3] Presiding over water or tongue.

[4] Presiding over odour or nose.

[5] Presiding over leg or nether world.

[6] *Vide* the translation of Sarvasāra-Upanishaḍ.

[7] This refers to the several class of persons in different modes of life who wear their hair in different ways as yogins, ascetics and so on.

CHAPTER II

The great Ṛbhu (again) addressed the Lord of Lakshmī of the form of boar thus: "O Lord, please initiate me into the supreme Brahmaviḍyā (or science)." Then the Lord who removes the miseries of his devotees being thus questioned, answered thus: "Through (the right observance of) the duties of one's own caste and orders of life, through religious austerities and through the pleasing of the guru (by serving him rightly), arise to persons the four, vairāgya, etc. They are the discrimination of the eternal from the non-eternal; indifference to the enjoyments of this and the other worlds; the acquisition of the six virtues, s'ama,[1] etc., and the longing after liberation. These should be practised. Having subdued the sensual organs and having given up the conception of 'mine' in all objects, you should place your consciousness of 'I' in (or identify yourself with) me, who am the witness Chaiṭanya (consciousness). To be born as a human being is difficult—more difficult it is to be born as a male being—and more so is it to be born as a Brāhman. Even then, if the fool does not cognise through the hearing,[2] etc., of veḍānṭa, the true nature of the Sachchiḍānanḍa (of Brahman) that is all-pervading, and that is beyond all caste and orders of life, when will he obtain moksha? I alone am happiness. There is none other. If there is said to be another, then it is not happiness. There is no such thing as love, except on my account. The love that is on account of me is not natural to me. As I am the seat of supreme love, that 'I am not' is not. He who is sought after by all, saying "I should become such," is myself, the all-pervading. How can non-light affect Āṭmā, the self-shining which is no other than the light whence originates the words 'I am not light'. My firm conviction is, whoever knows for certain that (Āṭmā) which is self-shining and has itself no basis (to rest upon), is one of vijñāna.

[1] Meaning respectively mental restraint, bodily restraint, the renunciation or practising of works without reference to their fruits, endurance of heart and soul, etc., faith and settled peace of mind.

[2] Meaning meditation and reflection thereon.

"The universe, jīva, Īsvara, māya and others do not really exist, except my full Āṭmā. I have not their characteristics. Karma which has ḍhāraṇā and other attributes and is of the form of darkness and ajñāna is not fit to touch (or affect) me, who am Āṭmā, the self-resplendent. That man who sees (his) Āṭmā which is all-witness and is beyond all caste and orders of life as of the nature of Brahman, becomes himself Brahman. Whoever sees, through the evidence of veḍānṭa, this visible universe as the Supreme Seat which is of the form of light, attains moksha at once. When that knowledge which dispels the idea that this body (alone) is Āṭmā, arises firmly in one's mind as was before the knowledge that this body (alone) is Āṭmā, then that person, even though he does not desire moksha, gets it. Therefore how will a person be bound by karma, who always enjoys the bliss of Brahman which has the characteristics of Sachchiḍānanḍa, and which is other than ajñāna? Persons with spiritual eyes see Brahman, that is the witness of the three states that has the characteristics of be-ness, wisdom and bliss, that is the underlying meaning of the words 'Thou' (Ṭvam) and 'I' (Aham), and that is untouched by all the stains. As a blind man does not see the sun that is shining, so an ignorant person does not see (Brahman). Prajñāna alone is Brahman. It has truth and prajñāna as its characteristics. By thus cognising Brahman well, a person becomes immortal. One who knows his own Āṭmā as Brahman, that is bliss, and without duality and guṇas (qualities), and that is truth and absolute consciousness is not afraid of anything. That which is consciousness alone which is all-pervading, which is eternal, which is all-full, which is of the form of bliss, and which is indestructible, is the only true Brahman. It is the settled determination of Brahmajñānīs that there *is* naught else but that. As the world appears dark to the blind and bright to those having good eyes, so this world full of manifold miseries to the ignorant is full of happiness to the wise. In me, of the form of boar, who am infinite and the Bliss of absolute Consciousness, if there is the conception of non-dualism, where then is bondage? And who is the one to be emancipated? The real nature of all embodied objects is ever the absolute Consciousness. Like the pot seen by the eyes, the body and its aggregates are not (*viz.*, do not really exist). Knowing, as Āṭmā, all the locomotive and fixed worlds that appear as other than Āṭmā, meditate upon them as 'It I am'. Such a person then enjoys his real nature. There is no other to be enjoyed than one-Self. If there is anything that is, then Brahman alone has that attribute. One who is perfect in Brahmajñāna, though he always sees this established universe, does not see it other than his Āṭmā. By cognising clearly my form, one is not trammelled by karma. He is an undaunted person who by his own experience cognises as his own real nature all (the universe and Brahman) that is without the body and the organs of sense—that is the all-witness—that is the one noumenal vijñāna, that is the blissful Āṭmā (as contrasted with jīvāṭmā or the lower self) and that is the self-resplendent. He is one that should be known as 'I' (myself). O Ṛbhu, may you become He. After this, there will be never any experience of the world. Thereafter there will always be the experience of the wisdom of one's own true nature. One who has thus known fully Āṭmā has neither emancipatiou nor bondage. Whoever meditates, even for one muhūrṭa (48 minutes) through the cognition of one's own real form, upon Him who is dancing as the all-witness, is released from all bondage. Prostrations—prostrations to me who am in all the elements, who am the Chiḍāṭmā (*viz*, Āṭmā of the nature of wisdom) that is eternal and free and who am the Praṭyagāṭmā. O Ḍevaṭā, you are I. I am you. Prostrations on account of myself and yourself who are infinite and who are Chiḍāṭmā, myself being the supreme Īs'a (Lord) and yourself being S'iva (of a beneficent nature). What should I do? Where should I go? What should I reject? (Nothing, because) the universe is filled by me as with the waters of the universal deluge. Whoever gives up (fond) love of the external, love of the internal and love of the body and thus gives up all associations, is merged in me. There is no doubt about it. That Paramahamsa (ascetic) who, though living in the world, keeps aloof from human congregation as from serpent, who regards a beautiful woman as a (living) corpse and the endless sensual objects as poison, and who has abandoned all passion and is indifferent towards all objects is no other than Vāsuḍeva,[1] (*viz.*,) myself. This is saṭya (truth). This is nothing but truth. It is truth alone that is now said. I am Brahman, the truth. There is naught else but I.

"(The word) 'upavāsa' (lit., dwelling near) signifies the dwelling near (or union) of jīvāṭmā and Paramāṭmā and not (the religious observance as accepted by the worldy of) emaciating the body through fasts. To the ignorant, what is the use of the mere drying up of the body? By beating about the hole of a snake, can we be said to have killed the big snake within. A man is said to attain paroksha (indirect) wisdom when he knows (theoretically) that there is Brahman; but he is said to attain sākshāṭkāra (direct cognition) when he knows (or realises) that he is himself Brahman. When a yogin knows his Āṭmā to be the Absolute, then he becomes a jīvanmukṭa. To mahāṭmās, to be always in the state 'I am Brahman' conduces to their salvation. There are two words for bondage and moksha. They are 'mine' and 'not mine'. Man is bound by 'mine', but he is released by 'not mine'. He should abandon all the thoughts relating to externals and so also with reference to internals. O Ṛbhu having given up all thoughts, you should rest content (in your Āṭmā) ever.

"The whole of the universe is caused through saṅkalpa alone. It is only through saṅkalpa that the universe manifests. Having abandoned the universe, which is of the form of saṅkalpa and having fixed your mind upon the nirvikalpa (one which is changeless), meditate upon my abode in your heart. O most intelligent being, pass your time in meditating upon me, glorifying me in songs, talking about me to one another and thus devoting yourself entirely to me as the Supreme. Whatever is chiṭ (consciousness) in the universe is only Chinmāṭra. This universe is Chinmaya only. You are Chiṭ. I am Chiṭ: contemplate upon the worlds also as Chiṭ. Make the desires *nil*. Always be without any stain. How then can the bright lamp of Āṭmic vijñāna

[1] *Viz.*, Vishṇu, the Lord of all persons.

arising through the Vedas be affected by the karma arising from the ignorance of the actor and the agent? Having given up not-Ātmā and being in the world unaffected by it, delight only in the Chinmātra within, ever intent on the One. As the ākās' of the pot and that of the house are both located in the all-pervading ākās', so the jīvas and Īs'vara are only evolved out of me, the Chidākās' (the one ākās' of universal consciousness). So that which did not exist before the evolution of Ātmās (jīvas and Īs'vara) and that which is rejected at the end (*viz.*, universal deluge) is called māyā by Brahmajñānīs through their discrimination. Should māyā and its effects (the universe) be annihilated, there is no state of Īs'vara, there is no state of jīva. Therefore like the ākās' without its vehicle, I am the immaculate and Chit.

"The creation, sentient as well as non-sentient from īkshaṇā (thinking) to praves'a (entry) (as stated in Chhāndogya-Upanishad, Prapāthaka VI, Khaṇdas II and III) of those having the forms of jīvas and Īs'vara is due to the creation (or illusion) of Īs'vara; while the samsāra (worldly existence) from the waking state to salvation is due to the creation of jīva. So the karmas ordained in the sacrifice (called) Triṇāchaka (so called after Nachiketas of Katha-Upanishad) to yoga are dependent upon the illusion of Īs'vara; while (the systems from) Lokāyata (atheistical system) to sāṅkhya rest on the illusion of jīva. Therefore aspirants after salvation should never make their heads enter into the field of controversy regarding jīva and Īs'vara. But with an undisturbed mind, the tattvas of Brahman should be investigated. Those who do not cognise the tattva of the secondless Brahman are all deluded persons only. Whence (then) is salvation to them? Whence then is happiness (to them) in this universe? What if they have the thoughts of the superiority and inferiority (of Īs'vara and jīva)? Will sovereignty and mendicancy (experienced by a person) in the dreaming state affect him in his waking state? When buddhi is absorbed in ajñāna, then it is termed, by the wise, sleep. Whence then is sleep to me who have not ajñāna and its effects? When buddhi is in full bloom, then it is said to be the jāgrat (waking state).

Ås I have no changes, etc., there is no waking state to me. The moving about of buḍḍhi in the subtle nādis constitutes the dreaming state. In me without the act of moving about, there is no dreaming. Then at the time of sushupṭi when all things are absorbed, enveloped by ṭamas, he then enjoys the highest bliss of his own nature in an invisible state. If he sees everything as Chiṭ without any difference, he alone is an actual vijñānī. He alone is S'iva. He alone is Hari. He alone is Brahmā. This mundane existence which is an ocean of sorrow, is nothing but a long-lived dream, or an illusion of the mind or a long-lived reign of the mind. From rising from sleep till going to bed, the one Brahman alone should be contemplated upon. By causing to be absorbed this universe which is but a superimposition, the chiṭṭa partakes of my nature. Having annihilated all the six powerful enemies, through their destruction become the non-dual One like the scent-elephant. Whether the body perishes now or lasts the age of moon and stars, what matters it to me having Chiṭ alone as my body? What matters it to the ākās' in the pot, whether it (the pot) is destroyed now or exists for a long time. While the slough of a serpent lies cast off lifeless in its hole, it (the serpent) does not evince any affection towards it. Likewise the wise do not identify themselves with their gross and subtle bodies. If the delusive knowledge (that the universe is real) with its cause should be destroyed by the fire of āṭmajñāna, the wise man becomes bodiless, through the idea 'It (Brahman) is not this; It is not this.' Through the study of S'āsṭras, the knowledge of reality (of the universe) perishes. Through direct perception of truth, one's fitness for action (in this universe) ceases. With the cessation of prārabḍha (the portion of the past karma which is being enjoyed in this life), the destruction of the manifestation (of the universe) takes place. Māyā is thus destroyed in a threefold manner. If within himself no identification (of jīva) with Brahman takes place, the state (of the separateness) of jiva does not perish. If the non-dual one is truly discerned, then all affinities (for objects) cease. With the cessation of prārabḍha (arising from the cessation of affinities), there is that of the body. Therefore it is certain that māyā perishes thus entirely.

"If it is said that all the universe is, that Brahman alone is that is of the nature of Saṭ. If it is said that the universe shines, then it is Brahman alone that shines. (The mirage of) all the water in an oasis is really no other than the oasis itself. Through inquiry of one's Self, the three worlds (above, below and middle) are only of the nature of Chiṭ. In Brahman, which is one and alone, the essence of whose nature is absolute Consciousness and which is remote from the differences of jīva, Īs'vara and guru, there is no ajñāna. Such being the case, where then is the occasion for the universe there? I am that Brahman which is all full. While the full moon of wisdom is robbed of its lustre by the rāhu (one of the two nodes of the moon) of delusion, all actions [1] such as the rites of bathing, alms-giving and sacrifice performed during the time of eclipse are all fruitless. As salt dissolved in water becomes one, so if Āṭmā and manas become identified, it is termed samāḍhi. Without the grace of a good (perfect) guru, the abandonment of sensual objects is very difficult of attainment; so also the perception of (divine) truth and the attainment of one's true state. Then the state of being in one's own self shines of its own accord in a yogin in whom jñāna-s'akṭi [2] has dawned and who has abandoned all karmas. The (property of) fluctuation is natural to mercury and mind. If either mercury is bound (or consolidated) or mind is bound (or controlled), what then on this earth cannot be accomplished? He who obtains mūrchchhā [3] cures all diseases. The dead are brought to life again. He who has bound (his mind or mercury) is able to move in the air. Therefore mercury and mind confer upon one the state of Brahman. The master of inḍriyas (the organs) is manas (mind). The master of manas is prāṇa. The master of prāṇa is laya (absorption yoga). Therefore laya-yoga should be practised. To the yogins, laya (-yoga) is said to be

[1] During the solar and lunar eclipses, these rites are done by the Hinḍūs.

[2] Of the six sakṭis, she is one that gives wisdom.

[3] Either controlling the breath through prāṇāyāma or the consolidation of mercury through some means, leading in both cases to siḍḍhis, etc.

without actions and changes. This laya (absorption) of mind which is above speech and in which one has to abandon all saṅkalpas and to give up completely all actions, should be known through one's own (experience). As an actress, though subject (or dancing in harmony) to music, cymbals and other musical instruments of time, has her mind intent upon the protection of the pot on her head, so the yogin, though intent for the time being upon the hosts of objects, never leaves off the mind contemplating on Brahman. The person who desires all the wealth of yoga should, after having given up all thoughts, practise with a subdued mind concentration on nāḍa (spiritual sound) alone."

CHAPTER III

"The One Principle cannot at any time become of manifold forms. As I am the partless, there is none else but myself. Whatever is seen and whatever is heard is no other than Brahman. I am that Parabrahman, which is the eternal, the immaculate, the free, the one, the undivided bliss, the non-dual, the truth, the wisdom, and the endless. I am of the nature of bliss; I am of undivided wisdom; I am the supreme of the supreme; I am the resplendent absolute Consciousness. As the clouds do not touch the ākās', so the miseries attendant on mundane existence do not affect me. Know all to be happiness through the annihilation of sorrow and all to be of the nature of saṭ (be-ness) through the annihilation of asaṭ (not-be-ness). It is only the nature of Chiṭ (Consciousness) that is associated with this visible universe. Therefore my form is partless. To an exalted yogin, there is neither birth nor death, nor going (to other spheres), nor returning (to earth); there is no stain or purity or knowledge but (the universe) shines to him as absolute Consciousness. Practise always silence 'I am (*viz.*, that you yourself are) Parabrahman' which is truth and absolute Consciousness, which is undivided and non-dual, which is invisible, which is stainless, which is pure, which is secondless, and which is beneficent. It (Brahman) is not subject to birth and death, happiness and misery. It is not subject to caste, law, family and goṭra (clan). Practise silence—I am Chiṭ which is the vivarṭa-upāḍāna[1] (*viz.*, the illusory cause) of the universe. Always practise silence—I am (*viz.*, you are) the Brahman, that is the full, the secondless, the undivided consciousness which has neither the relationship nor the differences existing in the universe and which partakes of the essence of the non-dual and the supreme Saṭ and Chiṭ.

"That which always is and that which preserves the same nature during the three periods of time, unaffected by anything, is my eternal form of Saṭ. Even the state of happiness which is eternal without upāḍhis (vehicles) and which is superior to all the happiness derivable from sushupṭi is of my bliss only. As by the rays of the sun, thick gloom is soon destroyed, so darkness, the cause of rebirth is destroyed by Hari (Vishṇu) *viz.*, the sun's lustre. Through the contemplation and worship of my (Hari's) feet, every person is delivered from his ignorance. The means of destroying deaths and births is only through the contemplation of my feet. As a lover of wealth praises a wealthy man, so if with earnestness a person praises the Cause of the universe, who will not be delivered from bondage?

"As in presence of the sun the world of its own accord begins to perform its actions, so in my presence all the worlds are animated to action. As to the mother-of-pearl, the illusory conception of silver is falsely attributed, so to me is falsely attributed through māyā this universe which is composed of mahaṭ, etc. I am not with those differences that are (observable) in the body of low caste men, the body of cow, etc., the fixed ones, the bodies of brāhmaṇas and others. As to a person, even after being relieved from the misconception of the directions, the (same misconception of) direction continues (as before),

[1] Of the two causes of the universe, Spirit is the nimiṭṭa (instrumental) cause while matter is the upāḍāna (material) cause. This material cause is again subdivided into three: *viz.*, ārambha (initial), pariṇāma (changed) and vivarṭa (illusory). The first or material cause may be exemplified by the cotton or woollen thread being the initial material cause of cloth or dresses which are woven out of these threads without changing the threads; the second by milk being the changed cause of curd, since a change takes place in the milk which becomes curd; the third by a serpent being the illusory cause of a rope, for here through illusion we mistake the rope for the serpent.

just so is to me the universe though destroyed by vijñāna. Therefore the universe is not. I am neither the body nor the organs of sense and action, nor prāṇas, nor manas, nor buḍḍhi, nor ahankāra, nor chiṭṭa, nor māyā, nor the universe including ākās' and others. Neither am I the actor, the enjoyer, nor he who causes the enjoyment. I am Brahman that is Chiṭ, Saṭ and Ānanḍa alone and that is Janārḍana (Vishṇu).

" Ās, through the fluctuation of water, the sun (reflected therein) is moved, so Āṭmā arises in this mundane existence through its mere connection with ahankāra. This mundane existence has chiṭṭa as its root. This (chiṭṭa) should be cleansed by repeated effort. How is it you have your confidence in the greatness of chiṭṭa ? Ālas, where is all the wealth of the kings ! Where are the Brahmāṣ ? Where are all the worlds ? Āll old ones are gone. Many fresh evolutions have occurred. Many crores of Brahmās have passed away. Many kings have flitted away like particles of dust. Even to a jñānī, the love of the body may arise through the asura (demoniacal) nature. If the asura nature should arise in a wise man, his knowledge of truth becomes fruitless. Should rajas and others generated in us be burnt by the fire of discriminative (divine) wisdom, how can they germinate again ? Just as a very intelligent person delights in the shortcomings of another, so if one finds out his own faults (and corrects them) who will not be relieved from bondage ? O Lord of munis, only he who has not āṭmajñāna and who is not an emancipated person, longs after siḍḍhis. He attains such siḍḍhis through medicine, [1] (or wealth), manṭras, religious works, time and skill. In the eyes of an āṭmajñānī, these siḍḍhis are of no importance. One who has become an āṭmajñānī, one who has his sight solely on āṭmā, and one who is content with Āṭmā (the higher self) through (his) āṭmā (or the lower self), never follows (the dictates of) aviḍyā. Whatever exists in this world, he knows to be of the nature of aviḍyā. How then will an āṭmajñānī who has relinquished aviḍyā be immersed in (or affected by) it. Though medicine, manṭras, religious work, time and skill (or mystical

[1] The mystic Hinḍū Tamil books teem with works on medicine through which the higher siḍḍhis can be developed.

expressions) lead to the development of siddhis, yet they cannot in any way help one to attain the seat of Pàramāṭmā. How then can one who is an āṭmajñānī and who is without his mind be said to long after siddhis, while all the actions of his desires are controlled?"

CHAPTER IV

On another occasion Niḍāgha asked Lord Ṛbhu to enlighten him as to the characteristics of jīvanmukti.[1] To which Ṛbhu replied in the affirmative and said the following:

"In the seven bhūmikās or (stages of development of wisdom) there are four kinds of jīvanmukṭas.[1] Of these the first stage[2] is s'ubhechchhā (good desire); the second is vichāraṇā (inquiry); the third is ṭanumānasī (or pertaining to the thinned mind); the fourth is saṭṭvāpaṭṭi (the attainment of saṭṭva); the fifth is asamsakṭi (non-attachment); the sixth is the paḍārṭhabhāvanā (analysis of objects) and the seventh is the ṭurya (fourth or final stage). The bhūmikā which is of the form of praṇava (OM) is formed of (or is divided into) akāra—A, ukāra—U, makāra—M, and arḍhamāṭrā. Ākāra and others are of four kinds on account of the difference of sṭhūla (gross), sūkshma (subtle), bīja (seed or causal), and sākshī (witness). Their avasṭhās are four: waking, dreaming, dreamless sleeping and ṭurya (fourth). He who is in (or the entity that identifies itself with) the waking state in the gross ams'a (essence or part) of akāra is named Vis'va; in the subtle essence, he is termed Ṭaijasa; in the bīja essence, he is termed Prājña; and in the sāksbī essence, he is termed Ṭurya.

"He who is in the dreaming state (or the entity which identifies itself with the dreaming state) in the gross essence of ukāra is Vis'va; in the subtle essence, he is termed Ṭaijasa; in the bīja essence, is termed Prājña; and in the sākshī essence, he is termed Ṭurya.

"He who is in the sushupṭi state in the gross essence of makāra is termed Vis'va; in the subtle essence, Ṭaijasa; in the

[1] Jīvanmukti is emancipation. Jīvanmukṭas are those that have attained emancipation.

[2] This word and others are explained in full later on in the text.

bīja essence, he is termed Prājña; and in the sākshī essence, he is termed Ṭurya.

"He who is in ṭurya state in the gross essence of arḍhamāṭrā is termed Ṭurya-vis'va. In the subtle, he is termed Ṭaijasa; in the bīja essence, he is termed Prājña; and in the sākshī essence, he is termed Ṭurya-ṭurya.

"The ṭurya essence of akāra is (or embraces) the first, second and third (bhūmikās or stages of the seven). The ṭurya essence of ukāra embraces the fourth bhūmikā. The ṭurya essence of makāra embraces the fifth bhūmikā. The ṭurya essence of arḍhamāṭrā is the sixth stage. Beyond this, is the seventh stage.

"One who functions in the (first) three bhūmikās is called mumukshu; one who functions in the fourth bhūmikā is called a brahmaviṭ; one who functions in the fifth bhūmikā is called a brahmaviḍvara; one who functions in the sixth bhūmikā is called a brahmaviḍvarīya; and one in the seventh bhūmikā is called a brahmaviḍvarishtha. With reference to this, there are s'lokas. They are:

"'S'ubhechchhā is said to be the first jñānabhūmi (or stage of wisdom); vichāraṇā, the second; ṭanumānasī, the third; saṭṭvāpaṭṭi, the fourth; then come asamsakṭi as the fifth, paḍārṭhabhāvanā as the sixth and ṭurya as the seventh.'

"The desire that arises in one through sheer vairāgya (after resolving) 'Shall I be ignorant? I will be seen by the S'āsṭras and the wise (or I will study the books and be with the wise)' is termed by the wise as S'ubhechchhā. The association with the wise and S'āsṭras and the following of the right path preceding the practice of indifference is termed vichāraṇā. That stage wherein the hankering after sensual objects is thinned through the first and second stages is said to be ṭanumānasī. That stage wherein having become indifferent to all sensual objects through the exercise in the (above) three stages, the purified chiṭṭa rests on Āṭmā which is of the nature of saṭ is called saṭṭvāpaṭṭi. The light (or manifestation) of saṭṭvaguṇa that is firmly rooted (in one) without any desire for the fruits of actions through the practice in the above four stages is termed asamsakṭi. That stage wherein through the practice in the (above) five stages one, having found delight in Āṭmā, has no conception of the internals or externals (though before him) and engages in actions only when impelled to do so by others is termed paḍārṭhabhāvanā, the sixth stage. The stage wherein after exceedingly long practice in the (above) six stages one is (immovably) fixed in the contemplation of Āṭmā alone without the difference (of the universe) is the seventh stage called ṭurya. The three stages beginning with S'ubhechchā are said to be attained with (or amidst) differences and non-differences. (Because) the universe one sees in the waking state he thinks to be really existent. When the mind is firmly fixed on the non-dual One and the conception of duality is put down, then he sees this universe as a dream through his union with the fourth stage. As the autumnal cloud being dispersed vanishes, so this universe perishes. O Niḍāgha, be convinced that such a person has only saṭṭva remaining. Then having ascended the fifth stage called sushupṭipaḍa (dreamless sleeping seat), he remains simply in the non-dual state, being freed from all the various differences. Having always introvision though ever participating in external actions, those that are engaged in the practice of this (sixth stage) are seen like one sleeping when fatigued (*viz.*, being freed from all affinities). (Lastly) the seventh stage which is the ancient and which is called gūḍhasupṭi[1] is generally attained. Then one remains in that secondless state without fear and with his consciousness almost annihilated where there is neither saṭ nor asaṭ, neither self nor not-self. Like an empty pot in the ākās', there is void both within and without; like a filled vessel in the midst of an ocean, he is full both within and without. Do not become either the knower or the known. May you become the Reality which remains after all thoughts are given up. Having discarded (all the distinctions of) the seer, the sight and the seen with their affinities, meditate solely upon Āṭmā which shines as the supreme Light.

"He is said to be a jīvanmukṭa (emancipated person) in whom, though participating in the material concerns of the

[1] Lit., secret sleep.

world, the universe is not seen to exist like the invisible ākās'. He is said to be a jīvanmukṭa, the light of whose mind never sets or rises in misery or happiness, and who does not seek to change what happens to him (*viz.*, either to diminish his misery or increase his happiness). He is said to be a jīvanmukṭa who though in his sushupṭi is awake and to whom the waking state is unknown and whose wisdom is free from the affinities (of objects).

"He is said to be a jīvanmukṭa whose heart is pure like ākās', though acting (as if) in consonance to love, hatred, fear and others. He is said to be a jīvanmukṭa who has not the conception of his being the actor and whose buḍḍhi is not attached to material objects, whether he performs actions or not. He is said to be a jīvanmukṭa, of whom people are not afraid, who is not afraid of people and who has given up joy, anger and fear. He is said to be a jīvanmukṭa who, though participating in all the illusory objects, is cool amidst them and is a full Āṭmā, (being) as if they belonged to others. O muni, he is called a jīvanmukṭa who, having eradicated all the desires of his chiṭṭa, is (fully) content with me who am the Āṭmā of all. He is said to be a jīvanmukṭa who rests with an unshaken mind in that all pure abode which is Chinmāṭrā and free from all the modifications of chiṭṭa. He is said to be a jīvanmukṭa in whose chiṭṭa do not dawn (the distinctions of) the universe, I, he, thou and others that are visible and unreal. Through the path of the guru and S'āsṭras, enter soon Saṭ—the Brahman that is immutable, great, full and without objects—and be firmly seated there. S'iva alone is Guru; S'iva alone is Veḍas; S'iva alone is Lord; S'iva alone is I; Siva alone is all. There is none other than S'iva. The undaunted Brāhmaṇa having known Him (S'iva) should attain wisdom. One need not utter many words as they but injure the organ of speech.

"(The Ṛshi) S'uka[1] is a mukṭa (emancipated person). (The Ṛshi) Vāmaḍeva is a mukṭa. There are no others (who have attained emancipation) than through these (*viz.*, the two

[1] Suka is a Ṛshi, the son of the present Vyāsa and the narrator of *Bhāgavaṭa Purāṇa*. Vāmaḍeva is also a Ṛshi.

paths of these two Ṛshis). Those brave men who follow the path of S'uka in this world become saḍyomukṭas (*viz.*, emancipated) immediately after (the body wers away); while those who always follow the path of veḍānṭa in this world are subject again and again to rebirths and attain krama (gradual) emancipation, through yoga, sāṅkhya and karmas associated with saṭṭva (guṇa). Thus there are two paths laid down by the Lord of Ḍevas (*viz.*,) the S'uka and Vāmaḍeva paths. The S'uka path is called the bird's path: while the Vāmaḍevā path is called the ant's path.[1] Those persons that have cognised the true nature of their Āṭmā through the mandatory and prohibitory injunctions (of the Veḍas), the inquiry into (the true meaning of) mahāvākyas (the sacred sentences of the Veḍas), the samāḍhi of sāṅkhya yoga or asamprajñāṭa samāḍhi[2] and that have thereby purified themselves, attain the supreme seat through the S'uka path. Having, through hathayoga[3] practice with the pain caused by yama, postures, etc., become liable to the ever recurring obstacles caused by aṇimā and other (siḍḍhis) and having not obtained good results, one is born again in a great family and practises yoga through his previous (kārmic) affinities. Then through the practice of yoga during many lives, he attains salvation (*viz.*,) the supreme seat of Vishṇu through the Vāmaḍeva path. Thus there are two paths that lead to the attainment of Brahman and that are beneficent. The one confers instantaneous salvation and the other confers gradual salvation.

"To one that sees (all) as the one (Brahman), where is delusion? Where is sorrow? Those that are under the eyes of those whose buḍḍhi is solely occupied with the truth (of Brahman) that is the end of all experience are released from all heinous sins. All beings inhabiting heaven and earth that fall under the vision of Brahmaviṭs are at once emancipated from the sins committed during many crores of births."

[1] Bird's path, like birds which fly at once to the place they intend to go; Ant's path, like ants which move slowly.

[2] It is that of intense self-absorption when one loses his consciousness of individuality.

[3] Hathayoga, as stated in Paṭañjali's Yoga Philosophy.

Chapter V

Then Niḍāgha asked Lord Ṛbhu to enlighten him as to the rules (to be observed) in the practice of Yoga. Accordingly He (the Lord) said thus:

"The body is composed of the five elements. It is filled with five maṇdalas (spheres).[1] That which is hard is Pṛṭhivī (earth), one of them; that which is liquid is Āpas; that which is bright is Ṭejas (fire); motion is the property of Vāyu; that which pervades everywhere is Ākās'. All these should be known by an aspirant after Yoga. Through the blowing of Vāyu-maṇdala in this body, (there are caused) 21,600 breaths every day and night. If there is a diminution in the Pṛṭhivīmaṇdala, there arise folds in the body; if there is diminution in the essence of Āpas, there arises gradually greyness of hair; if there is diminution in the essence of Ṭejas, there is loss of hunger and lustre; if there is diminution in the essence of Vāyu, there is incessant tremor; if there is diminution in the essence of Ākās', one dies. The jīviṭa (*viz.*, Prāṇa) which possesses these elements having no place to rest (in the body) owing to the diminution of the elements, rises up like birds flying up in the air. It is for this reason that it is called Uḍyāna (lit., flying up). With reference to this, there is said to be a banḍha (binding, also meaning a posture called Uddiyāṇabanḍha, by which this flight can be arrested). This Uddiyāṇabanḍha[2] is to (or does away with) death, as a lion to an elephant. Its experience is in the body, as also the banḍha. Its binding (in the body) is hurtful. If there is agitation of Āgni (fire) within the belly, then there will be caused much of pain. Therefore this (Uddiyāṇa-banḍha) should not be practised by one who is hungry or who has urgency to make water or void excrement. He should take

[1] There are either the five elements or Mūlāḍhāra (sacral plexus), Svāḍhishṭhāna (epigastric or prostatic plexus), Maṇipūraka (solar plexus), Anābata (cardiac plexus) and Visuḍḍhi (laryngeal or pharyngeal plexus). These are situated respectively in the anus, the genital organs, navel, heart and throat. The last or the sixth plexus is omitted here, as the five plexuses mentioned above correspond to the five elements. This chapter treating of yoga is very mystical.

[2] This is one of the postures treated of in *Siva Samhiṭa* and other books.

many times in small quantities proper and moderate food. He should practise Manṭrayoga,[1] Layayoga and Hathayoga, through mild, middling and transcendental methods (or periods) respectively. Laya, Manṭra, and Hathayogas have each (the same) eight subservients. They are yama, niyama, āsana, prāṇāyāma, praṭyāhāra, ḍhāraṇā, ḍhyāna, and samāḍhi.[2] (Of these), yama is of ten kinds. They are non-injury, truth, non-coveting, continence, compassion, straightforwardness, patience, courage, moderate eating, and purity (bodily and mental). Niyama is of ten kinds. They are ṭapas (religious austerities), contentment, belief in the existence of God or Veḍas, charity, worship of Īśvara (or God), listening to the exposition of religious doctrines, modesty, a (good) intellect, japa (muttering of prayers), and vraṭa (religious observances). There are eleven postures beginning with chakra. Chakra, paḍma, kūrma, mayūra, kukkuta, vīra, svasṭika, bhaḍra, simha, mukṭa, and gomukha, are the postures enumerated by the knowers of yoga. Placing the left ankle on the right thigh and the right ankle on the left thigh, and keeping the body erect (while sitting) is the posture "Chakra". Prāṇāyāma should be practised again and again in the following order, *viz.*, inspiration, restraint of breath and expiration. The prāṇāyāma is done through the nādis (nerves). Hence it is called the nādis themselves.

"The body of every sentient being is ninety-six digits long. In the middle of the body, two digits above the anus and two digits below the sexual organ, is the centre of the body (called Mūlāḍhāra or sacral plexus). Nine digits above the genitals, there is kanḍa of nādis which revolves oval-shaped, four digits high and four digits broad. It is surrounded by fat, flesh, bone, and blood. In it, is situate a nādī-chakra (wheel of nerves) having twelve spokes. Kuṇdalī by which this body is supported is there. It is covering by its face the Brahmaranḍhra (*viz.*, Brahmā's hole) of Sushumnā. (By the side) of Sushumnā dwell the nādis

[1] There are four kinds of yoga—the fourth being Rājayoga. Manṭrayoga is that in which perfection is obtained through the pronunciation of mantras. Layayoga is that in which perfection is obtained through laya (absorption).

[2] They mean respectively forbearance, religious restraint, posture, restraint of breath, subjugation of the senses, contemplation, meditation, and intense self-absorption.

Alambusā and Kuhūḥ. In the next two (spokes) are Vāruṇā and Yas'asvinī. On the spoke south of Sushumnā is, in regular course, Piṅgalā. On the next two spokes, are Pūsha and Payasvinī. On the spoke west of Sushumnā is the nādi called Sarasvaṭī. On the next two spokes are S'āṅkhinī and Gānḍhārī. To the north of Sushumnā dwells Idā; in the next is Hasṭijihvā; in the next is Vis'voḍarā. In these spokes of the wheel, the twelve nādis carry the twelve vāyus from left to right (to the different parts of the body). The nādis are like (*i.e.*, woven like the warp and woof of) cloth. They are said to have different colours. The central portion of the cloth (here the collection of the nādis) is called the Nābhichakra (navel plexus). Jvalanṭī, Nāḍarūpiṇī, Pararanḍhrā, and Sushumnā are called the (basic) supports of nāḍa (spiritual sound). These four nādis are of ruby colour. The central portion of Brahmarandhra is again and again covered by Kuṇdalī. Thus ten vāyus move in these nādis. A wise man who has understood the course of nādis and vāyus should, after keeping his neck and body erect with his mouth closed, contemplate immovably upon Ṭuryaka (Āṭmā) at the tip of his nose, in the centre of his heart and in the middle of binḍu,[1] and should see, with a tranquil mind through the (mental) eyes, the nectar flowing from there. Having closed the anus and drawn up the vāyu and caused it to rise through (the repetition of) praṇava (Om), he should complete with S'rī bīja. He should contemplate upon his Āṭmā as S'rī (or Parās'akṭi) and as being bathed by nectar. This is kālavañchana (lit., time illusion). It is said to be the most important of all. Whatever is thought of by the mind is accomplished by the mind itself. (Then) agni (fire) will flame in jala (water) and in the flame (of agni) will arise the branches and blossoms. Then the words uttered and the actions done regarding the universe, are not in vain. By checking the binḍu in the path, by making the fire flame up in the water and by causing the water to dry up, the body is made firm. Having contracted simultaneously the anus and yoni (the womb) united together, he should draw up Āpāna and unite with it Samāna. He

[1] Lit., germ.

should contemplate upon his Āṭmā as S'iva and then as being bathed by nectar. In the central part of each spoke, the yogin should commence to concentrate bala (will or strength). He should try to go up by the union of Prāṇa and Āpāna. This most important yoga brightens up in the body the path of siḍḍhis. As a dam across the water serves as an obstacle to the floods, so it should ever be known by the yogins that the chhāyā of the body is (to jīva). This banḍha is said of all nādis. Through the grace of this banḍha, the Ḍevaṭā (goddess) becomes visible. This banḍha of four feet serves as a check to the three paths. This brightens up the path through which the siḍḍhas obtained (their siḍḍhis). If with Prāṇa is made to rise up soon Uḍāna, this banḍha checking all nādis goes up. This is called Samputayoga or Mūlabanḍha. Through the practising of this yoga, the three banḍhas are mastered. By practising day and night intermittingly or at any convenient time, the vāyu will come under his control. With the control of vāyu, agni (the gastric fire) in the body will increase daily. With the increase of agni, food, etc., will be easily digested. Should food be properly digested, there is increase of rasa (essence of food). With the daily increase of rasa, there is the increase of ḍhāṭus (spiritual substances). With the increase of ḍhāṭus, there is the increase of wisdom in the body. Thus all the sins collected together during many crores of births are burnt up.

"In the centre of the anus and the genitals, there is the triangular Mūlāḍhāra. It illumines the seat of S'iva of the form of binḍu. There is located the Parās'akṭi named kuṇdalinī. From that seat, vāyu arises. From that seat, agni becomes increased. From that seat, binḍu originates and nāḍa becomes increased. From that seat, Hamsa is born. From that seat, manas is born. The six chakras beginning with Mūlāḍhāra are said to be the seat of S'akṭi (Goddess). From the neck to the top of the head is said to the seat of S'ambhu (S'iva). To the nādis, the body is the support (or vehicle); to Prāṇa, the nādis are the support; to jīva, Prāṇa is the dwelling place; to Hamsa, jīva is the support; to S'akṭi, Hamsa is the seat and the locomotive and fixed universe.

"Being without distraction and of a calm mind, one should practise prāṇāyāma. Even a person who is well-skilled in the practice of the three banḍhas should try always to cognise with a true heart that Principle which should be known and is the cause of all objects and their attributes. Both expiration and inspiration should (be stopped and made to) rest in restraint of breath (alone). He should depend solely on Brahman which is the highest aim of all visibles. (The giving out of) all external objects is said to be rechaka (expiration). The (taking in of the) spiritual knowledge of the S'āsṭras is said to be pūraka (inspiration) and (the keeping to oneself of) such knowledge is said to be kumbhaka (or restraint of breath). He is an emancipated person who practises thus such a chiṭṭa. There is no doubt about it. Through kumbhaka, it (the mind) should be always taken up, and through kumbhaka alone it should be filled up within. It is only through kumbhaka that kumbhaka should be firmly mastered. Within it is Paramas'iva. That (vāyu) which is non-motionless should be shaken again through kaṇtha-muḍrā (throat-posture). Having checked the course of vāyu, having become perfect in the practice of expiration and restraint of breath and having planted evenly on the ground the two hands and the two feet, one should pierce the four seats through vāyu through the three yogas. He should shake Mahāmeru with the (aid of) prakotis (forces)[1] at the mouth of vāyu. The two putas (cavities) being drawn, vāyu throbs quickly. The union of moon, sun and agni should be known on account of nectar. Through the motion of Meru, the ḍevaṭās who stay in the centre of Meru move. At first in his Brahma-granṭhi, there is produced soon a hole (or passage). Then having pierced Brahma-granṭhi, he pierces Vishṇu-granṭhi: then he pierces Ruḍra-granṭhi. Then to the yogin comes veḍha[2] (piercing) through his liberation from the impurities of delusion, through the religious ceremonies (performed) in various births, through the grace of gurus and ḍevaṭās and through the practice of yoga.

[1] It is mystic here and later on.

[2] He has pierced all the granṭhis and hence becomes a master of veḍha.

"In the maṇḍala (sphere or region) of Sushumnā (situated between Iḍā and Piṅgalā, vāyu should be made to rise up through the feature known as Muḍrā-banḍha. The short pronunciation (of Praṇava) frees (one) from sins: its long pronunciation confers (on one) moksha. So also its pronunciation in āpyāyana or pluṭa svara (tone). He is a knower of Veḍa, who through the above-mentioned three ways of pronunciation knows the end of Praṇava which is beyond the power of speech, like the never-ceasing flow of oil or the long-drawn bell-sound. The short svara goes to binḍu. The long svara goes to brahmaranḍhra: the pluṭa to ḍvāḍas'ānṭa (twelfth centre). The manṭras should be uttered on account of getting manṭra siḍḍhis. This Praṇava (Om) will remove all obstacles. It will remove all sins. Of this, are four bhūmikās (states) predicated, *viz.*, ārambha, ghata, parichaya, and nishpaṭṭi. Ārambha is that state in which one having abandoued external karmas performed by the three organs (mind, speech and body), is always engaged in mental karma only. It is said by the wise that the ghata state is that in which vāyu having forced an opening on the western side and being full, is firmly fixed there. Parichaya state is that in which vāyu is firmly fixed to ākās', neither associated with jīva nor not, while the body is immovable. It is said that nishpaṭṭi state is that in which there take place creation and dissolution through Āṭmā or that state in which a yogin having become a jīvanmukṭa performs yoga without effort.

"Whoever recites this Upanishaḍ becomes immaculate like agni. Like vāyu, he becomes pure. He becomes freed from the sin of drinking alcohol. He becomes freed from the sins of the theft of gold. He becomes a jīvanmukṭa. This is what is said by the Ṛgveḍa. Like the eye pervading the ākās' (seeing without effort everything above), a wise man sees (always) the supreme seat of Vishṇu. The brāhmaṇas who have always their spiritual eyes wide open praise and illuminate in diverse ways the spiritual seat of Vishṇu.

"Om, thus is the Upanishaḍ."

[1] There are the three kinds of pronunciation with 1 māṭrā, 2 māṭrās and 3 māṭrās. They are respectively hrasva, ḍīrgha and pluṭa which may be translated as short, long and very long.

MAṆḌALABRĀHMAṆA-UPANISHAḌ[1]

OF

S'UKLA-YAJURVEḌA

BRĀHMAṆA I

OM. The great muni Yājñavalkya went to Āḍiṭyaloka (the sun's world) and saluting him (the Purusha of the sun) said: "O reverend sir, describe to me the Āṭma-ṭaṭṭva (the ṭaṭṭva or truth of Āṭmā)."

(To which,) Nārāyaṇa (*viz.*, the Purusha of the sun) replied: "I shall describe the eightfold yoga together with Jñāna. The conquering of cold and heat as well as hunger and sleep, the preserving of (sweet) patience and unruffledness ever and the restraining of the organs (from sensual objects)—all these come under (or are) yama. Devotion to one's guru, love of the true path, enjoyment of objects producing happiness, internal satisfaction, freedom from association, living in a retired place, the controlling of the manas and the not longing after the fruits of actions and a state of vairāgya—all these consitute niyama. The sitting in any posture pleasant to one and clothed in tatters (or bark) is presćribed for āsana (posture). Inspiration, restraint of breath and expiration, which have respectively 16, 64 and 32 (māṭrās) constitute prāṇāyāma (restraint of breath). The restraining of the mind from the objects of

[1] Maṇḍala means sphere. As the Purusha in the maṇḍala or sphere of the sun gives out this Upanishad to Yājñavalkya, hence it is called Maṇḍala-Brāhmaṇa. It is very mystic. There is a book called *Rājayoga Bhāshya* which is a commentary thereon; in the light of it which is by some attributed to Srī Sankarāchārya, notes are given herein.

senses is praṭyāhāra (subjugation of the senses). The contemplation of the oneness of consciousness in all objects is ḍhyāna. The mind having been drawn away from the objects of the senses, the fixing of the chaiṭanya (consciousness) (on one alone) is ḍhāraṇā. The forgetting of oneself in ḍhyāna is samāḍhi. He who thus knows the eight subtle parts of yoga attains salvation.

"The body has five stains (*viz.,*) passion, anger, out-breathing, fear, and sleep. The removal of these can be effected respectively by absence of saṅkalpa, forgiveness, moderate food, carefulness, and a spiritual sight of ṭaṭṭvas. In order to cross the ocean of samsāra where sleep and fear are the serpents, injury, etc., are the waves, ṭṛshṇā (thirst) is the whirlpool, and wife is the mire, one should adhere to the subtle path and overstepping ṭaṭṭva [1] and other guṇas should look out for Ṭāraka.[2] Ṭāraka is Brahman which being in the middle of the two eyebrows, is of the nature of the spiritual effiulgence of Sachchiḍānanḍa. The (spiritual) seeing through the three lakshyas (or the three kinds of introvision) is the means to It (Brahman). Sushumnā which is from the mūlāḍhāra to brahmaranḍhra has the radiance of the sun. In the centre of it, is kuṇḍalinī shining like crores of lightning and subtle as the thread in the lotus-stalk. Ṭamas is destroyed there. Through seeing it, all sins are destroyed. When the two ears are closed by the tips of the forefingers, a phūṭkāra (or booming) sound is heard. When the mind is fixed on it, it sees a blue light between the eyes as also in the heart. (This is anṭarlakshya or internal introvison). In the bahirlakshya (or external introvision) one sees in order before his nose at distance of 4, 6, 8, 10, and 12 digits, the space of blue colour, then a colour resembling s'yāma (indigo-black) and then shining as rakṭa (red) wave and then with the two pīṭa (yellow and orange red) colours. Then he is a yogin. When one looks at the external space, moving

[1] Comm.: Rising above the seven Prāṇas, one should with introvision cognise in the region of Ākās, Ṭamas and should then make Ṭamas get into Rajas, Rajas into Saṭṭva, Saṭṭva into Nārāyaṇa and Nārāyaṇa, into the Supreme One.

[2] Ṭaraka is from *ṭṛ.*, to cross, as it enables one to cross samsāra. The higher vision is here said to take place in a centre between the eyebrows—probably in the brain.

the eyes and sees streaks of light at the corners of his eyes, then his vision can be made steady. When one sees jyoṭis (spiritual light) above his head 12 digits in length, then he attains the state of nectar. In the maḍhyalakshya (or the middle one), one sees the variegated colours of the morning as if the sun, the moon and the fire had joined together in the ākās' that is without them. Then he comes to have their nature (of light). Through practice, he becomes one with ākās', devoid of all guṇas and peculiarities. At first ākās' with its shining stars becomes to him Para-ākās' as dark as ṭamas itself, and he becomes one with Para-ākās' shining with stars and deep as ṭamas. (Then) he becomes one with Mahā-ākās' resplendent (as) with the fire of the deluge. Then he becomes one with Ṭaṭṭva-ākās', lighted with the brightness which is the highest and the best of all. Then he becomes one with Sūrya-ākās' (sun-ākās') brightened by a crore of suns. By practising thus, he becomes one with them. He who knows them becomes thus.

"Know that yoga is twofold through its division into the pūrva (earlier) and the uṭṭara (later). The earlier is ṭāraka and the later is amanaska (the mindless). Ṭāraka is divided into mūrṭi (with limitation) and amūrṭi (without limitation). That is mūrṭi ṭāraka which goes to the end of the senses (or exists till the senses are conquered). That is amūrṭi tāraka which goes beyond the two eyebrows (above the senses). Both these should be performed through manas. Anṭarḍṛshti (internal vision) associated with manas comes to aid ṭāraka. Ṭejas (spiritual light) appears in the hole between the two eyebrows. This ṭāraka is the earlier one. The later is amanaska. The great jyoṭis (light)[1] is above the root of the palate. By seeing it, one gets the siḍḍhis aṇimā, etc. S'āmbhavīmuḍrā occurs when the lakshya (spiritual vision) is internal while the (physical) eyes are seeing externally without winking. This is the great science which is concealed in all the ṭanṭras. When this is known, one does not stay in samsāra. Its worship (or practice) gives salvation. Anṭarlakshya is of

[1] The commentator puts it as 12 digits above the root of the palate—perhaps the Ḍvāḍasānṭa or twelfth centre corresponding to the pituitary body.

the nature of Jalajyoṭis (or waterjyoṭis). It is known by the great Ṛshis and is invisible both to the internal and external senses.

"Sahasrāra (*viz.*, the thousand-petalled lotus of the pineal gland) Jalajyoṭis[1] is the anṭarlakshya. Some say the form of Purusha in the cave of buḍḍhi beautiful in all its parts is anṭarlakshya. Some again say that the all-quiescent Nīlakaṇtha accompanied by Umā (his wife) and having five mouths and latent in the midst of the sphere in the brain is anṭarlakshya. Whilst others say that the Purusha of the dimension of a thumb is anṭarlakshya. A few again say anṭarlakshya is the One Self made supreme through introvision in the state of a jīvanmukṭa. All the different statements above made pertain to Āṭmā alone. He alone is a Brahmanishtha who sees that the above lakshya is the pure Āṭmā. The jīva which is the twenty-fifth ṭaṭṭva, having abandoned the twenty-four ṭaṭtvas, becomes a jīvanmukṭa through the conviction that the twenty-sixth ṭaṭṭva (*viz.*,) Paramāṭmā is 'I' alone. Becoming one with anṭarlakshya (Brahman) in the emancipated state by means of anṭarlakshya (introvision), jīva becomes one with the partless sphere of Paramākās'.

"Thus ends the first Brāhmaṇa."

Brāhmaṇa II

Then Yājñavalkya asked the Purusha in the sphere of the sun: "O Lord, anṭarlakshya has been described many times, but it has never been understood by me (clearly). Pray describe it to me." He replied: "It is the source of the five elements, has the lustre of many (streaks of) lightning, and has four seats having (or rising from) 'That' (Brahman). In its midst, there arises the manifestation of ṭaṭtva. It is very hidden and unmanifested. It can be known (only) by one who has got into the boat of jñāna. It is the object of both bahir and anṭar (external and internal) lakshyas. In its midst is absorbed

[1] The commentator to support the above that anṭarlakshya, *viz.*, Brahman is jala- or water-jyoṭis quotes the Prāṇāyāma-Gāyaṭrī which says: "Om Āpo-jyoṭi-raso'amṛṭam-Brahma, etc."—Āpo-jyoṭis or water-jyoṭis is Brahman.

the whole world. It is the vast partless universe beyond Nāḍa, Binḍu and Kalā. Above it (*viz.*, the sphere of agni) is the sphere of the sun; in its midst is the sphere of the nectary moon; in its midst is the sphere of the partless Brahma-ṭejas (or the spiritual effulgence of Brahman). It has the brightness of S'ukla (white light)[1] like the ray of lightning. It alone has the characteristic of S'āmbhavī. In seeing this, there are three kinds of ḍṛshti (sight), *viz.*, amā (the new moon), praṭipaṭ (the first day of lunar fortnight), and pūrṇimā (the full moon). The sight of amā is the one (seen) with closed eyes. That with half opened eyes is praṭipaṭ; while that with fully opened eyes is pūrṇimā. Of these, the practice of pūrṇimā should be resorted to. Its lakshya (or aim) is the tip of the nose. Then is seen a deep darkness at the root of the palate. By practising thus, a jyoṭis (light) of the form of an endless sphere is seen. This alone is Brahman, the Sachchiḍānanḍa. When the mind is absorbed in bliss thus naturally produced, then does S'āmbhavī take place. She (S'āmbhavī) alone is called Khecharī. By practising it (*viz.*, the muḍrā), a man obtains firmness of mind. Through it, he obtains firmness of vāyu. The following are the signs: first it is seen like a star; then a reflecting (or dazzling) diamond;[2] then the sphere of full moon; then the sphere of the brightness of nine gems; then the sphere of the midday sun; then the sphere of the flame of agni (fire); all these are seen in order.

" (Thus much for the light in pūrva or first stage.) Then there is the light in the western direction (in the uṭṭara or second stage). Then the lustres of crystal, smoke, binḍu, nāḍa, kalā, star, firefly, lamp, eye, gold, and nine gems, etc. are seen. This alone is the form of Praṇava. Having united Prāṇa and Apāna and holding the breath in kumbhaka, one should fix his concentration at the tip of his nose and making shaṇmukhi[3] with the fingers of both his hands, one hears

[1] Comm.: Sukla is Brahman.

[2] The original is, 'Vajra-Ḍarpaṇam.'

[3] Shaṇmukhi is said to be the process of hearing the internal sound by closing the two ears with the two thumbs, the two eyes with the two forefingers, the two nostrils with the two middle fingers, and the mouth with the remaining two fingers of both hands.

the sound of Praṇava (Om) in which manas becomes absorbed. Such a man has not even the touch of karma. The karma of (Sanḍhyāvanḍana or the daily prayers) is verily performed at the rising or setting of the sun. As there is no rising or setting (but only the ever shining) of the sun of Chiṭ (the higher consciousness) in the heart of a man who knows thus, he has no karma to perform. Rising above (the conception of) day and night through the annihilation of sound and time, he becomes one with Brahman through the all-full jñāna and the attaining of the state of unmanī (the state above manas). Through the state of nnmanī, he becomes amanaska (or without manas).

"Not being troubled by any thoughts (of the world) then constitutes the ḍhyāna.[1] The abandoning of all karmas constitutes āvāhana (invocation of god). Being firm in the unshaken (spiritual) wisdom constitutes āsana (posture). Being in the state of unmanī constitutes the pāḍya (offering of water for washing the feet of god). Preserving the state of amanaska (when manas is offered as sacrifice) constitutes the arghya (offering of water as oblation generally). Being in state of eternal brightness and shoreless nectar constitutes snāna (bathing). The contemplation of Āṭmā as present in all constitutes (the application to the idol of) sandal. The remaining in the real state of the ḍṛk (spiritual eye) is (the worshipping with) akshaṭa (non-broken rice). The attaining of Chiṭ (consciousness) is (the worshipping with) flower. The real state of agni (fire) of Chiṭ is the ḍhūpa (burning of incense). The state of the sun of Chiṭ is the ḍīpa (light waved before the image). The union of oneself with the nectar of full moon is the naivēḍya (offering of food, etc.).[2] The immobility in that state (of the ego being one with all) is praḍakshiṇa (going round the image). The conception of 'I am He' is namaskāra (prostration). The silence (then) is the sṭuṭi (praise). The all-contentment (or serenity then) is the visarjana (giving leave to god or finishing worship). (This is

[1] In this paragraph, the higher or secret meaning is given of all actions done in the pūjā or worship of God in the Hinḍū houses as well as temples. Regarding the clothing of the idol which is left out here, the commentator explains it as āvaraṇa or screen.

[2] Here also the commentator brings in nīrājana or the waving of the light before the image. That is according to him, the idea, "I am the self-shining."

the worship of Āṭmā by all Rāja-yogins). He who knows this knows all.

"When the ṭriputi[1] are thus dispelled, he becomes the kaivalya jyoṭis without bhāva (existence) or abhāva (non-existence), full and motionless, like the ocean without the tides or like the lamp without the wind. He becomes a brahmaviṭ (knower of Brahman) by cognising the end of the sleeping state, even while in the waking state. Though the (same) mind is absorbed in sushupṭi as also in samāḍhi, there is much difference between them. (In the former case) as the mind is absorbed in ṭamas, it does not become the means of salvation, (but) in samāḍhi as the modifications of ṭamas in him are rooted away, the mind raises itself to the nature of the Partless. All that is no other than Sāksbi-Chaiṭanya (witness-consciousness or the Higher Self) into which the absorption of the whole universe takes place, inasmuch as the universe is but a delusion (or creation) of the mind and is therefore not different from it. Though the universe appears perhaps as outside of the mind, still it is unreal. He who knows Brahman and who is the sole enjoyer of brāhmic bliss which is eternal and has dawned once (for all in him)—that man becomes one with Brahman. He in whom saṅkalpa perishes has got mukṭi in his hand. Therefore one becomes an emancipated person through the contemplation of Paramāṭmā. Having given up both bhāva and abhāva, one becomes a jīvanmukṭa by leaving off again and again in all states jñāna (wisdom) and jñeya (object of wisdom), ḍhyāna (meditation) and ḍhyeya (object of meditation), lakshya (the aim) and alakshya (non-aim), ḍṛs'ya (the visible) and aḍṛs'ya (the non-visible and ūha (reasoning) and apoha (negative reasoning).[2] He who knows this knows all.

"There are five avasṭhās (states), *viz.*: jāgraṭ (waking), svapna (dreaming), sushupṭi (dreamless sleeping), the ṭurya (fourth) and ṭuryāṭīṭa (that beyond the fourth). The jīva (ego) that is engaged in the waking state becomes attached to the pravṛṭṭi (worldly) path and is the participator of naraka (hell) as the

[1] The Ṭriputi are the three, the knower, the known and the knowledge. Comm.: Ḍhyāna and others stated before wherein the three distinctions are made.

[2] Ūha and apoha—the consideration of the pros and cons.

fruit of sins. He desires svarga (heaven) as the fruit of his virtuous actions. This very same person becomes (afterwards) indifferent to all these saying, "Enough of the births tending to actions, the fruits of which tend to bondage till the end of this mundane existence." Then he pursues the nivṛṭṭi (return) path with a view to attain emancipation. And this person then takes refuge in a spiritual instructor in order to cross this mundane existence. Giving up passion and others, he does only those he is asked to do. Then having acquired the four sāḍhanas (means to salvation), he attains, in the middle of the lotus of his heart, the Reality of anṭarlakshya that is but the Saṭ of Lord and begins to recognise (or recollect) the bliss of Brahman which he had left (or enjoyed) in his sushupṭi state. At last he attains this state of discrimination (thus): 'I think I am the non-dual One only. I was in ajñāna for some time (in the waking state and called therefore Vis'va). I became somehow (or involuntarily) a Ṭaijasa (in the dreaming state) through the reflection (in that state) of the affinities of the forgotten waking state; and now I am a Prājña through the disappearance of those two states. Therefore I am one only. I (appear) as more than one through the differences of state and place. And there is nothing of differentiation of class besides me.' Having expelled even the smack of the difference (of conception) between 'I' and 'That' through the thought 'I am the pure and the secondless Brahman', and having attained the path of salvation which is of the nature of Parabrahman, after having become one with It through the ḍhyāna of the sun's sphere as shining with himself, he becomes fully ripened for getting salvation. Saṅkalpa and others are the causes of the bondage of the mind; and the mind devoid of these becomes fit for salvation. Possessing such a mind free from all (saṅkalpa, etc.,) and withdrawing himself from the outer world of sight and others and so keeping himself out of the odour of the universe, he looks upon all the world as Āṭmā, abandons the conception of 'I', thinks 'I am Brahman' and considers all these as Āṭmā. Through these, he becomes one who has done his duty.

"The yogin is one that has realised Brahman that is all-full beyond ṭurya. They (the people) extol him as Brahman; and becoming the object of the praise of the whole world, he wanders over different countries. Placing the binḍu in the ākās' of Paramāṭmā and pursuing the path of the partless bliss produced by the pure, secondless, stainless, and innate yoga sleep of amanaska, he becomes an emancipated person. Then the yogin becomes immersed in the ocean of bliss. When compared to it, the bliss of Inḍra and others is very little. He who gets this bliss is the supreme yogin.

"Thus ends the second Brāhmaṇa."

Brāhmaṇa III

The great sage Yājñavalkya then asked the Purusha in the sphere (of the sun): "O Lord, though the nature of amanaska has been defined (by you), yet I forget it (or do not understand it clearly). Therefore pray explain it again to me." Accordingly the Purusha said: "This amanaska is a great secret. By knowing this, one becomes a person who has done his duty. One should look upon it as Paramāṭmā, associated with S'āmbhavī-muḍrā and should know also all those that can be known through a (thorough) cognition of them. Then seeing Parabrahman in his own Āṭmā as the Lord of all, the immeasurable, the birthless, the auspicious, the supreme ākās', the supportless, the secondless the only goal of Brahmā, Vishṇu and Ruḍra and the cause of all and assuring himself that he who plays in the cave (of the heart) is such a one, he should raise himself above the dualities of existence and non-existence; and knowing the experience of the numanī of his manas, he then attains the state of Parabrahman which is motionless as a lamp in a windless place, having reached the ocean of brāhmic bliss by means of the river of amanaska-yoga through the destruction of all his senses. Then he resembles a dry tree. Having lost all (idea of) the universe through the disappearance of growth, sleep, disease, expiration and inspiration, his body being always steady, he comes to have a supreme quiescence, being devoid of the movements of his manas and becomes absorbed in Paramāṭmā. The destruction of manas takēs place after the destruction of the collective senses, like the cow's udder (that shrivels up) after the milk has been drawn. It is this that is amanaska. By following this, one becomes always pure and becomes one that has done his duty, having been filled with the partless bliss by means of the path of ṭāraka-yoga through the initiation into the sacred sentences 'I am Paramāṭmā,' 'That art thou,' 'I am thou alone,' 'Thou art I alone,' etc.

"When his manas is immersed in the ākās' and he becomes all-full, and when he attains the nnmanī state, having abandoned all his collective senses, he conquers all sorrows and impurities through the partless bliss, having attained the fruits of kaivalya, ripened through the collective merits gathered in all his previous lives and thinking always 'I am Brahman,' becomes one that has done his duty. 'I am thou alone. There is no difference between thee and me owing to the fullness of Paramāṭmā.' Saying thus, he (the Purusha of the sun) embraced his pupil [1] and made him understand it.

"Thus ends the third Brāhmaṇa."

Brāhmaṇa IV

Then Yājñavalkya addressed the Purusha in the sphere (of the sun) thus: "Pray explain to me in detail the nature of the fivefold division of ākās'." He replied: "There are five (*viz*): ākās', parākās', mahākās', sūryākās', and paramākās'. That which is of the nature of darkness, both in and out is the first ākās'. That which has the fire of the deluge, both in and out is truly mahākās'. That which has the brightness of the sun, both in and out is sūryākās'. That brightness which is indescribable, all-pervading and of the nature of unrivalled bliss is paramākās'. By cognising these according to this description, one becomes of their nature. He is a yogin only in name, who does not cognise well the nine chakras, the six āḍhāras, the three lakshyas and the five ākās'. Thus ends the fourth Brāhmaṇa."

[1] This is a reference to the secret way of imparting higher truth.

Brāhmaṇa V

"The manas influenced by worldly objects is liable to bondage; and that (manas) which is not so influenced by these is fit for salvation. Hence all the world becomes an object of chiṭṭa; whereas the same chiṭṭa when it is supportless and well-ripe in the state of unmanī, becomes worthy of laya (absorption in Brahman). This absorption you should learn from me who am the all-full. I alone am the cause of the absorption of manas. The manas is within the jyoṭis (spiritual light) which again is latent in the spiritual sound which pertains to the anāhaṭa (heart) sound. That manas which is the agent of creation, preservation, and destruction of the three worlds—that same manas becomes absorbed in that which is the highest seat of Vishṇu; through such an absorption, one gets the pure and secondless state, owing to the absence of difference then. This alone is the highest truth. He who knows this, will wander in the world like a lad or an idiot or a demon or a simpleton. By practising this amanaska, one is ever contented, his urine and fæces become diminished, his food becomes lessened: he becomes strong in body and his limbs are free from disease and sleep. Then his breath and eyes being motionless, he realises Brahman and attains the nature of bliss.

"That ascetic who is intent on drinking the nectar of Brahman produced by the long practice of this kind of samāḍhi, becomes a paramahamsa (ascetic) or an avaḍhūṭa (naked ascetic). By seeing him, all the world becomes pure, and even an illiterate person who serves him is freed from bondage. He (the ascetic) enables the members of his family for one hundred and one generations to cross the ocean of samsāra; and his mother, father, wife, and children—all these are similarly freed. Thus is the Upanishaḍ. Thus ends the fifth Brāhmaṇa."

NĀḌABINḌU [1]-UPANISHAḌ

OF

ṚGVEḌA

The syllable Ȧ is considered to be its (the bird Om's) right wing, U, its left: M [2], its tail; and the arḍhamāṭrā (half-metre) is said to be its head.

The (rājasic and ṭāmasic) qualities, its feet upwards (to the loins); saṭṭva, its (main) body; [3] ḍharma is considererd to be its right eye, and aḍharma, its left.

The Bhūrloka is situated in its feet; the Bhuvarloka, in its knees; the Suvarloka, in its loins; and the Maharloka, in its navel.

In its heart is situate the Janoloka; the ṭapoloka in its throat, and the Saṭyaloka in the centre of the forehead between the eyebrows.

Then the māṭrā (or manṭra) beyond the Sahasrāra (thousand-rayed) is explained (*viz.*,) should be explained.

Ȧn adept in yoga who bestrides the Hamsa (bird) thus (*viz.*, contemplates on Om) is not affected by kārṃic influences or by tens of crores of sins.[4]

[1] Lit., Sound-seed.

[2] The commentator says that M is the last letter and hence tail and arḍhamātrā is the head, as it enables one to attain to higher worlds.

[3] Another reading is: The qualities are its feet, etc., and Ṭaṭtva is its body.

[4] Comm.: Since this manṭra has already occurred in the preceding khaṇḍa of the same sākhā, it is simply referred in the text. The manṭra is:

"सहस्राण्यंवियतां वस्यपक्षोंर्हरैहस्यपतत: स्वर्गंसदेवानुस्यपदध्यसाक्षी संपश्यन् भवनानिविश्वा"

The meaning seems to be—the letters A and U are the two wings of the Hamsa (Om) of the form of Vishṇu which goes to svarga, the abode of Sūrya, the thousand-rayed God; that syllable, 'Om' bearing in its heart all the ḍevas (of saṭṭvaguṇa). He goes up to Sahasrānha seeing the worlds personally: Sahasrānha being the seat of the spiritual sun.

The first māṭrā has agni as its ḍevaṭā (presiding deity); the second, vāyu as its ḍevaṭā; the next māṭrā is resplendent like the sphere of the sun and the last, the Arḍhamāṭrā the wise know as belonging to Varuṇa (the presiding deity of water).

Each of these māṭrās has indeed three kalās (parts). This is called Omkāra. Know it by means of the ḍhāraṇās, *viz.*, concentration on each of the twelve kalās, or the variations of the māṭrās produced by the difference of svaras or intonation). The first māṭrā is called ghoshiṇī; the second, viḍyunmālī (or viḍyunmāṭrā); the third, paṭaṅginī; the fourth, vāyuveginī; the fifth, nāmaḍheya; the sixth, ainḍrī; the seventh, vaishṇavī; the eighth, s'āṅkarī; the ninth, mabaṭī; the tenth, ḍhṛṭi (ḍhruva, Calcutta ed.); the eleventh, nārī (mauni, Calcutta ed.); and the twelfth, brāhmī.[1]

If a person happens to die in the first māṭrā (while contemplating on it), he is born again as a great emperor in Bhāraṭavarsha.

If in the second māṭrā, he becomes an illustrious yaksha; if in the third māṭrā, a viḍyāḍhara; if in the fourth, a ganḍharva (these three being the celestial hosts).

If he happens to die in the fifth, *viz.*, ardhamāṭrā, he lives in the world of the moon, with the rank of a ḍeva greatly glorified there.

If in the sixth, he merges into Inḍra; if in the seventh, he reaches the seat of Vishṇu; if in the eighth, Ruḍra, the Lord of all creatures.

If in the ninth, in Maharloka; if in the tenth, in Janoloka (Ḍhruvaloka, Calcutta ed.); if in the eleventh, Ṭapoloka, and if in the twelfth, he attains the eternal[2] state of Brahmā.

[1] Comm.. The four māṭrās are subdivided into twelve by their having each three svaras, Udāṭta, Anudāṭta, and Svarīta. Here the author goes on to give the names of the twelve kalās and shows the method of practising Dhāraṇā on each. Ghoshiṇī is that which gives Prajña: Viḍyunmālī is that which secures entrance into the loka of Viḍyunmālī, the king of the yakshas: Paṭaṅginī is that which confers the power of movement through air like the bird Paṭanginī; Vāyuveginī is that which gives the power of moving very rapidly: Nāmadheya means that which confers existence in Piṭṛloka: Ainḍrī in Inḍraloka: Vaishṇavī and Sāṅkarī in Vishṇu and Siva-lokas respectively Maunī to the loka of Munis or Janoloka and Brāhmi to Brahmaloka.

[2] Eternal here means the lifetime of Brahmā.

That which is beyond these, (*viz.*,) Parabrahman which is beyond (the above māṭrās), the pure, the all-pervading, beyond kalās, the ever resplendent and the source of all jyoṭis (light) should be known.

[1] When the mind goes beyond the organs and the guṇās and is absorbed, having no separate existence and no mental action, then (the guru) should instruct him (as to his further course of development).

That person always engaged in its contemplation and always absorbed in it should gradually leave off his body (or family) following the course of yoga and avoiding all intercourse with society.

Then he, being freed from the bonds of karma and the existence as a jīva and being pure, enjoys the supreme bliss by his attaining of the state of Brahmā.[2]

O intelligent man, spend your life always in the knowing of the supreme bliss, enjoying the whole of your prārabḍha (that portion of past karma now being enjoyed) without making any complaint (of it).

Even after āṭmajñāna (knowledge of Āṭmā or Self) has awakened (in one), prārabḍha does not leave (him); but he does not feel prārabḍha after the dawning of ṭaṭṭvajñāna[3] (knowledge of ṭaṭṭva or truth) because the body and other things are asaṭ (unreal), like the things seen in a dream to one on awaking from it.

That (portion of the) karma which is done in former births, and called prārabḍha does not at all affect the person (ṭaṭṭvajñānī), as there is no rebirth to him.

As the body that exists in the dreaming state is untrue, so is this body. Where then is rebirth to a thing that is illusory? How can a thing have any existence, when there is no birth (to it)?

As the clay is the material cause of the pot, so one learns from Veḍānṭa that ajñāna is the material cause of the

[1] Another edition says: he should enter through yoga the incomparable and quiescent Siva.

[2] Here the Calcutta edition stops.

[3] Taṭṭvajñāna is the discrimination of the taṭṭvas of this universe and man. Āṭmajñāna—the discrimination of Āṭmā or the Self in man.

universe: and when ajñāna ceases to exist, where then is the cosmos?

As a person through illusion mistakes a rope for a serpent, so the fool not knowing Saṭya (the eternal truth) sees the world (to be true.)

When he knows it to be a piece of rope, the illusory idea of a serpent vanishes.

So when he knows the eternal substratum of everything and all the universe becomes (therefore) void (to him), where then is prārabḍha to him, the body being a part of the world? Therefore the word prārabḍha is accepted to enlighten the ignorant (only).

Then as prārabḍha has, in course of time, worn out, he who is the sound resulting from the union of Praṇava with Brahman who is the absolute effulgence itself, and who is the bestower of all good, shines himself like the sun at the dispersion of the clouds.

The yogin being in the siḍḍhāsana (posture) and practising the vaishṇavīmuḍrā, should always hear the internal sound through the right ear.

The sound which he thus practises makes him deaf to all external sounds. Having overcome all obstacles, he enters the ṭurya state within fifteen days.

In the beginning of his practice, he hears many loud sounds. They gradually increase in pitch and are heard more and more subtly.

At first, the sounds are like those proceeding from the ocean, clouds, kettle-drum, and cataracts: in the middle (stage) those proceeding from mardala (a musical instrument), bell, and horn.

At the last stage, those proceeding from tinkling bells, flute, vīṇā (a musical instrument), and bees. Thus he hears many such sounds more and more subtle.

When he comes to that stage when the sound of the great kettle-drum is being heard, he should try to distinguish only sounds more and more subtle.

He may change his concentration from the gross sound to the subtle, or from the subtle to the gross, but he should not allow his mind to be diverted from them towards others.

The mind having at first concentrated itself on any one sound fixes firmly to that and is absorbed in it.

It (the mind) becoming insensible to the external impressions, becomes one with the sound as milk with water, and then becomes rapidly absorbed in chiḍākās' (the ākās' where Chiṭ prevails).

Being indifferent towards all objects, the yogin having controlled his passions, should by continual practice concentrate his attention upon the sound which destroys the mind.

Having abandoned all thoughts and being freed from all actions, he should always concentrate his attention on the sound, and (then) his chiṭṭa becomes absorbed in it.

Just as the bee drinking the honey (alone) does not care for the odour, so the chiṭṭa which is always absorbed in sound, does not long for sensual objects, as it is bound by the sweet smell of nāḍa and has abandoned its flitting nature.

The serpent chiṭṭa through listening to the nāḍa is entirely absorbed in it, and becoming unconscious of everything concentrates itself on the sound.

The sound serves the purpose of a sharp goad to control the maddened elephant—chiṭṭa which roves in the pleasure-garden of the sensual objects.

It serves the purpose of a snare for binding the deer—chiṭṭa. It also serves the purpose of a shore to the ocean waves of chiṭṭa.

The sound proceeding from Praṇava which is Brahman is of the nature of effulgence; the mind becomes absorbed in it; that is the supreme seat of Vishṇu.

The sound exists till there is the ākās'ic conception (ākās'a-saṅkalpa). Beyond this, is the (as'abḍa) soundless Para-brahman which is Paramāṭmā.

The mind exists so long as there is sound, but with its (sound's) cessation, there is the state called unmanī of manas (*viz.*, the state of being above the mind).

This sound is absorbed in the Akshara (indestructible) and the soundless state is the supreme seat.

The mind which along with Prāṇa (Vāyu) has (its) kārmic affinities destroyed by the constant concentration upon nāḍa is absorbed in the unstained One. There is no doubt of it.

Many myriads of nāḍas and many more of binḍus—(all) become absorbed in the Brahma-Praṇava sound.

Being freed from all states and all thoughts whatever, the yogin remains like one dead. He is a mukṭa. There is no doubt about this.

After that, he does not at any time hear the sounds of conch or ḍunḍubhi (large kettle-drum).

The body in the state of unmanī is certainly like a log and does not feel heat or cold, joy or sorrow.

The yogin's chiṭṭa having given up fame or disgrace is in samāḍhi above the three states.

Being freed from the waking and the sleeping states, he attains to his true state.

When the (spiritual) sight becomes fixed without any object to be seen, when the vāyu (prāṇa) becomes still without any effort, and when the chiṭṭa becomes firm without any support, he becomes of the form of the internal sound of Brahma-Praṇava.

Such is the Upanishaḍ.

YOGAKUṆḌALĪ[1]-UPANISHAD

OF

KṚSHṆA-YĀJURVEḌA

CHAPTER I

CHIṬṬA[2] has two causes, vāsanās and (prāṇa) vāyu. If one of them is controlled, then both are controlled. Of these two, a person should control (prāṇa) vāyu always through moderate food, postures, and thirdly s'akṭi-chāla.[3] I shall explain the nature of these. Listen to it, O Gauṭama. One should take a sweet and nutritious food,[4] leaving a fourth (of his stomach) unfilled) in order to please S'iva (the patron of yogins). This is called moderate food. Posture herein required is of two kinds, paḍma and vajra. Placing the two heels over the two opposite thighs (respectively) is the paḍma (posture) which is the destroyer of all sins. Placing one heel below the mūlakanḍa[5] and the other over it and sitting with the neck, body and head erect is the vajra posture. The s'akti (mentioned above) is only kuṇdalinī. A wise man should take it up from its place (*viz.*, the navel, upwards) to the middle of the eyebrows. This is called s'akṭi-chāla. In practising it, two things are necessary,

[1] In this Upanishaḍ are stated the ways by which the Kuṇdalini power is roused from the navel upwards to the middle of the eyebrows and then up to sahasrāra in the head: this being one of the important works of an adept to master the forces of nature.

[2] Chiṭṭa is the flitting aspect of Anṭaḥkaraṇa.

[3] Lit., the moving of sakṭi which is Kuṇdalini.

[4] Regarding the quantity to be taken, one should take of solid food half of his stomach: of liquid food, one quarter, leaving the remaining quarter empty for the air to percolate.

[5] Mūlakanḍa is the root of kanḍa, the genital organ.

Sarasvatīchālana [1] and the restraint of prāṇa (breath). Then through practice, kuṇḍalinī (which is spiral) becomes straightened. Of these two, I shall explain to you first Sarasvaṭī-chālana. It is said by the wise of old that Sarasvaṭī is no other than Arunḍhaṭī.[2] It is only by rousing her up that kuṇḍalinī is roused. When prāṇa (breath) is passing through (one's) Idā (left nostril), he should assume firmly paḍma-posture and should lengthen (inwards) 4 digits the ākās of 12 digits.[3] Then the wise man should bind the (sarasvaṭī) nādi by means of this lengthened (breath) and holding firmly together (both his ribs near the navel) by means of the forefingers and thumbs of both hands, (one hand on each side) should stir up kuṇḍalinī with all his might from right to left often and often; for a period of two muhūrṭas (48 minutes), he should be stirring it up fearlessly. Then he should draw up a little when kuṇḍalinī enters sushumnā. By this means, kuṇḍalinī enters the mouth of sushumnā. Prāṇa (also) having left (that place) enters of itself the sushumnā (along with kuṇḍalinī). By compressing the neck, one should also expand the navel. Then by shaking sarasvaṭī, prāṇa goes above (to) the chest. Through the contraction of the neck, prāṇa goes above from the chest. Sarasvaṭī who has sound in her womb should be shaken (or thrown into vibration) each day. Therefore by merely shaking it, one is cured of diseases. Gulma (a splenetic disease), jaloḍara (dropsy), plīha (a splenetic disease) and all other diseases arising within the belly, are undoubtedly destroyed by shaking this S'akṭi.

I shall now briefly describe to you prāṇāyāma. Prāṇa is the vāyu that moves in the body and its restraint within is known as kumbhaka. It is of two kinds, sahiṭa and kevala.[4] One should practise sahiṭa till he gets kevala. There are four bheḍas (lit., piercings or divisions) *viz.*, sūrya, ujjāyī, s'īṭalī, and bhasṭrī.

[1] The moving of sarasvatī nādi situated on the west of the navel among the 14 nādis (*Vide* Vāraba and other Upanishaḍs).

[2] Sarasvati is called also Arunḍhaṭī who is literally one that helps good actions being done and the wife of Ṛshi Vasishtha—also the star that is shown to the bride on marriage occasions.

[3] In exhalation, prāṇa goes out 16 digits and in inhalation, goes in only for 12, thus losing 4. But if inhaled for 16, then the power is aroused.

[4] Lit., associated with and alone. *Vide* Sāṇdilya-Upanishaḍ.

The kumbhaka associated with these four is called sahiṭa kumbhaka.

Being seated in the paḍma posture upon a pure and pleasant seat which gives ease and is neither too high nor too low, and in a place which is pure, lovely and free from pebbles, etc., and which for the length of a bow is free from cold, fire, and water, one should shake (or throw into vibration) Sarasvaṭī; slowly inhaling the breath from outside, as long as he desires, through the right nostril, he should exhale it through the left nostril. He should exhale it after purifying his skull (by forcing the breath up). This destroys the four kinds of evils caused by vāyu as also by intestinal worms. This should be done often and it is this which is spoken of as sūryabheḍa.

Closing the mouth and drawing up slowly the breath as before with the nose through both the nādis (or nostrils) and retaining it in the space between the heart and the neck, one should exhale it through the left nostril. This destroys the heat caused in the head as well as the phlegm in the throat. It removes all diseases, purifies his body and increases the (gastric) fire within. It removes also the evils arising in the nādis, jaloḍara (water-belly or dropsy) and ḍhāṭus. This kumbhaka is called ujjāyī and may be practised (even) when walking or standing.

Drawing up the breath as before through the tongue with (the hissing sound of) स and retaining it as before, the wise man should slowly exhale it through (both) the nostrils. This is called śīṭalī kumbhaka and destroys diseases, such as gulma, plīha, consumption, bile, fever, thirst, and poison.

Seated in the paḍma posture with belly and neck erect, the wise man should close the mouth and exhale with care through the nostrils. Then he should inhale a little with speed up to the heart, so that the breath may fill the space with noise between the neck and skull. Then he should exhale in the same way and inhale often and often. Just as the bellows of a smith are moved (*viz.*, stuffed with air within and then the air is let out), so he should move the air within his body. If the body gets tired, then he should inhale through the right nostril. If his belly is full of vāyu, then he should press well his nostrils with all his fingers except his forefinger, and performing kumbhaka as before, should exhale through the left nostril. This frees one from diseases of fire in (or inflammation of) the throat, increases the gastric fire within, enables one to know the kuṇḍalinī, produces purity removing sins, gives happiness and pleasure and destroys phlegm which is the bolt (or obstacle) to the door at the mouth of brahmanādi (*viz.*, sushumnā). It pierces also the three granṭhis [1] (or knots) differentiated through the three guṇas. This kumbhaka is known as bhasṭrī and should especially be performed.

Through these four ways when kumbhaka is near (or is about to be performed), the sinless yogin should practise the three banḍhas.[2] The first is called mūlabanḍha. The second is called uddiyāṇa, and the third is jālanḍhara. Their nature will be thus described. Āpāna (breath) which has a downward tendency is forced up by one bending down. This process is called mūlabanḍha. When apāna is raised up and reaches the sphere of agni (fire), then the flame of agni grows long, being blown about by vāyu. Then agni and apāna come to (or commingle with) prāṇa in a heated state. Through this agni which is very fiery, there arises in the body the flaming (or the fire) which rouses the sleeping kuṇḍalinī through its heat. Then this kuṇḍalinī makes a hissing noise, becomes erect like a serpent beaten with stick and enters the hole of brahmanādi (sushumnā). Therefore yogins should daily practise mūlabanḍha often. Uddiyāṇa should be performed at the end of kumbhaka and at the beginning of expiration. Because prāṇa uddīyaṭē (*viz.*, goes up) the sushumnā in this banḍha, therefore it called uddiyāṇa by the yogins. Being seated in the vajra posture and holding firmly the two toes by the two hands, he should press at the kanḍa and at the place near the two ankles. Then he should gradnally upbear the ṭāna [3] (thread or nādi) which is on the western side first to uḍara (the upper part of the abdomen above the navel), then to the heart and then to the neck. When prāṇa reaches the sanḍhi (junction) of navel, slowly it removes

[1] They are Brahmagranṭhi, Vishṇugranthi, and Ruḍragranṭhi.
[2] Banḍhas are certain kinds of position of the body.
[3] This probably refers to Sarasvaṭi Nādi.

the impurities (or diseases) in the navel. Therefore this should be frequently practised. The banḍha called jālanḍhara should be practised at the end of kumbhaka. This jālanḍhara is of the form of the contraction of the neck and is an impediment to the passage of vāyu (upwards). When the neck is contracted at once by bending downwards (so that the chin may touch the breast), prāṇa goes through brahmanādi on the western ṭāna in the middle. Assuming the seat as mentioned before, one should stir up saraswaṭī and control prāṇa. On the first day kumbhaka should be done four times; on the second day it should be done ten times, and then five times separately; on the third day, twenty times will do, and afterwards kumbhaka should be performed with the three banḍhas and with an increase of five times each day.

Diseases are generated in one's body through the following causes, *viz.*, sleeping in daytime, late vigils over night, excess of sexual intercourse, moving in crowd, the checking of the discharge of urine and fæces, the evil of unwholesome food and laborious mental operation with prāṇa. If a yogin is afraid of such diseases (when attacked by them), he says, "my diseases have arisen from my practice of yoga." Then he will discontinue this practice. This is said to be the first obstacle to yoga. The second (obstacle) is doubt; the third is carelessness; the fourth, laziness; the fifth, sleep; the sixth, the not leaving of objects (of sense); the seventh, erroneous perception; the eighth, sensual objects; the ninth, want of faith;[1] and the tenth, the failure to attain the truth of yoga. A wise man should abandon these ten obstacles after great deliberation. The practice of prāṇāyāma should be performed daily with the mind firmly fixed on Truth. Then chiṭṭa is absorbed in sushumnā, and prāṇa (therefore) never moves. When the impurities (of chiṭṭa) are thus removed and prāṇa is absorbed in sushumnā, he becomes a (true) yogin. Āpāna, which has a downward tendency should be raised up with effort by the contraction (of the anus), and this is spoken of as mūlabanḍhā. Āpāna thus raised up mixes with agni and

[1] The text is Anākhiam which has no sense. It has been translated as Anāstha.

then they go up quickly to the seat of prāṇa. Then prāṇa and apāna uniting with one another go to kuṇdalinī, which is coiled up and asleep. Kuṇdalinī being heated by agni and stirred up by vāyu, extends her body in the mouth of sushumnā, pierces the brahmagranṭhi formed of rajas, and flashes at once like lightning at the mouth of sushumnā. Then it goes up at once through vishṇūgranṭhi to the heart. Then it goes up through ruḍragranṭhi and above it to the middle of the eyebrows; having pierced this place, it goes up to the maṇdala (sphere) of the moon. It dries up the moisture produced by the moon in the anāhaṭachakra having sixteen petals.[1] When the blood is agitated through the speed of prāṇa, it becomes bile from its contact with the sun, after which it goes to the sphere of the moon where it becomes of the nature of the flow of pure phlegm. How does it (blood) which is very cold become hot when it flows there? (Since) at the same time the intense white form of moon is speedily heated.[2] Then being agitated, it goes up. Through taking in this, chiṭṭa which was moving amidst sensual objects externally, is restrained there. The novice enjoying this high state attains peace and becomes devoted to Āṭmā. Kuṇdalinī assumes the eight[3] forms of prakṛṭi (matter) and attains S'iva by encircling him and dissolves itself in S'iva. Thus rajas-s'ukla[4] (seminal fluid) which rises up goes to S'iva along with maruṭ (vāyu); prāṇa and apāna which are always produced become equal. Prāṇas flow in all things, great and small, describable or indescribable, as fire in gold. Then this body which is āḍhibhauṭika (composed of elements) becomes āḍhiḍaivaṭa (relating to a tutelar deity) and is thus purified. Then it attains the stage of aṭivāhika.[5] Then the body being freed from the inert state

[1] Twelve seems to be the right number of petals in the anābata-chakra of the heart; but the moon is probably meant having sixteen rays.

[2] The passages here are obscure.

[3] They are Mūlaprakṛṭi, Mahat, Ahaṅkāra and the five elements.

[4] Here it is the astral seminal fluid which, in the case of a neophyte, not having descended to a gross fluid through the absence of sexual desire, rises up being conserved as a spiritual energy.

[5] A stage of being able to convey to other bodies the deity appointed by God to help in the conveying of sūkshma (subtle) body to other bodies at the expiry of good actions which contribute to the enjoyment of material pleasures (*vide* Apte's Dictionary).

becomes stainless and of the nature of Chiṭ. In it, the aṭivāhika becomes the chief of all, being of the nature of That. Like the conception of the snake in a rope, so the idea of the release from wife and samsāra is the delusion of time. Whatever appears is unreal. Whatever is absorbed is unreal. Like the illusory conception of silver in the mother-of-pearl, so is the idea of man and woman. The microcosm and the macrocosm are one and the same; so also the liṅga and sūṭrāṭma, svabhāva (substance) and form and the self-resplendent light and Chiḍāṭmā.

The S'akṭi named kuṇdalinī, which is like a thread in the lotus and is resplendent, is biting with the upper end of its hood (namely, mouth) at the root of the lotus the mūlakanḍa. Taking hold of its tail with its mouth, it is in contact with the hole of brahmaranḍhra (of sushumnā). If a person seated in the paḍma posture and having accustomed himself to the contraction of his anus makes his vāyu go upward with the mind intent on kumbhaka, then agni comes to svāḍhishthāna flaming, owing to the blowing of vāyu. From the blowing of vāyu and agni, the chief (kuṇdalinī) pierces open the brahmagranṭhi and then vishṇugranṭhi. Then it pierces ruḍragranṭhi, after that, (all) the six lotuses (or plexuses). Then S'akṭi is happy with S'iva in sahasrāra kamala (1,000 lotuses' seat or pineal gland). This should be known as the highest avasṭhā (state) and it alone is the giver of final beatitude. Thus ends the first chapter.

Chapter II

I shall hereafter describe the science called khecharī which is such that one who knows it is freed from old age and death in this world. One who is subject to the pains of death, disease and old age should, O sage, on knowing this science make his mind firm and practise khecharī. One should regard that person as his guru on earth who knows khecharī, the destroyer of old age and death, both from knowing the meaning of books and practice, and should perform it with all his heart. The science of khecharī is not easily attainable, as also its practice.

Its practice and melana[1] are not accomplished simultaneously. Those that are bent upon practice alone do not get melana. Only some get the practice, O Brāhman, after several births, but melana is not obtained even after a hundred births. Having undergone the practice after several births, some (solitary) yogin gets the melana in some future birth as the result of his practice. When a yogin gets this melana from the mouth of his guru, then he obtains the siḍḍhis mentioned in the several books. When a man gets this melana through books and the significance, then he attains the state of S'iva freed from all rebirth. Even gurus may not be able to know this without books. Therefore this science is very difficult to master. An ascetic should wander over the earth so long as he fails to get this science, and when this science is obtained, then he has got the siḍḍhi in his hand (*viz.*, mastered the psychical powers). Therefore one should regard as Achyuṭa (Vishṇu) the person who imparts the melana, as also him who gives out the science. He should regard as S'iva him who teaches the practice. Having got this science from me, you should not reveal it to others. Therefore one who knows this should protect it with all his efforts (*viz.*, should never give it out except to persons who deserve it). O Brāhman, one should go to the place where lives the guru, who is able to teach the divine yoga and there learn from him the science khecharī, and being then taught well by him, should at first practise it carefully. By means of this science, a person will attain the siḍḍhi of khecharī. Joining with khecharī s'akṭi (*viz.*, kuṇḍalinī s'akṭi) by means of the (science) of khecharī which contains the bīja (seed of letter) of khecharī, one becomes the lord of khecharas (Ḍevas) and lives always amongst them. Khecharī bīja (seed-letter) is spoken of as agni encircled with water and as the abode of khecharas (Ḍevas). Through this yoga, siḍḍhi is mastered. The ninth (bīja) letter of somāms'a (soma or moon part) should also be pronounced in the reverse order. Then a letter composed of three ams'as of the form of moon has been described; and after that, the eighth letter should be pronounced in

[1] Melana is lit., joining. This is the key to this science which seems to be kept profoundly secret and revealed by adepts only at initiation, as will appear from the subsequent passages in this Upanishaḍ.

the reverse order; then consider it as the supreme and its beginning as the fifth, and this is said to the kūta (horns) of the several bhinnas (or parts) of the moon.[1] This which tends to the accomplishment of all yogas, should be learnt through the initiation of a guru. He who recites this twelve times every day, will not get even in sleep that māyā (illusion) which is born in his body and which is the source of all vicious deeds. He who recites this five lakhs of times with very great care—to him the science of khecharī will reveal itself. Āll obstacles vanish and the ḍevas are pleased. The destruction of valīpaliṭa (*viz.*, wrinkle and greyness of hair) will take place without doubt. Having acquired this great science, one should practise it afterwards. If not, O Brāhman, he will suffer without getting any siḍḍhi in the path of khecharī. If one does not get this nectarlike science in this practice, he should get it in the beginning of melana and recite it always; (else) one who is without it never gets siḍḍhi. Ās soon as he gets this science, he should practise it; and then the sage will soon get the siḍḍhi. Having drawn out the tongue from the root of the palate, a knower of Āṭmā should clear the impurity (of the tongue) for seven days according to the advice of his guru. He should take a sharp knife which is oiled and cleaned and which resembles the leaf of the plant snuhī ("Euphorbia antiquorum") and should cut for the space of a hair (the frænum Lingui). Having powdered sainḍhava (rock-salt) and paṭhya (sea-salt), he should apply it to the place. On the seventh day, he should again cut for the space of a hair. Thus for the space of six months, he should continue it always gradually with great care. In six months, S'iro-banḍha (banḍha at the head),[1] which is at the root of the tongue is destroyed. Then the yogin who knows timely action should encircle with S'īro-vasṭra (lit., the cloth of the head) the Vāk-Īs'varī (the deity presiding over speech) and should draw (it) up. Āgain by daily drawing it up for six months, it comes, O sage, as far as the middle of the eyebrows and obliquely up to the opening of the ears; having gradually practised, it goes to the root of the chin. Then in

[1] All these are very mystic.

three years, it goes up easily to the end of the hair (of the head) It goes up obliquely to S'ākha[1] and downwards to the well of the throat. In another three years, it occupies brahmarandhra and stops there without doubt. Crosswise it goes up to the top of the head and downwards to the well of the throat. Gradually it opens the great adamantine door in the head. The rare science (of khecharī) bīja has been explained before. One should perform the six aṅgas (parts) of this manṭra by pronouncing it in six different intonations. One should do this in order to attain all the siḍḍhis; and this karanyāsam[2] should be done gradually and not all at a time, since the body of one who does it all at once will soon decay. Therefore it should be practised, O best of sages, little by little. When the tongue goes to the brahmaranḍhra through the outer path, then one should place the tongue after moving the bolt of Brahmā which cannot be mastered by the ḍevas. On doing this for three years with the point of the finger, he should make the tongue enter within: then it enters brahmaḍvāra (or hole). On entering the brahmaḍvāra, one should practise maṭhana (churning) well. Some intelligent men attain siḍḍhi even without maṭhana. One who is versed in khecharī manṭra accomplishes it without maṭhana. By doing the japa and maṭhana, one reaps the fruits soon. By connecting a wire made of gold, silver or iron with the nostrils by means of a thread soaked in milk, one should restrain his breath in his heart and seated in a convenient posture with his eyes concentrated between his eyebrows, he should perform maṭhana slowly. In six months, the state of maṭhana becomes natural like sleep in children. And it is not advisable to do maṭhana always. It should be done (once) only in every month. A yogin should not revolve his tongue in the path. After doing this for twelve years, siḍḍhi is surely obtained. Then he sees the whole universe in his body as not being different from Āṭmā. This path of the ūrḍhvakuṇdalinī (higher kuṇdalinī), O chief of kings, conquers the macrocosm. Thus ends the second chapter.

[1] Probably it here means some part below the skull.

[2] Certain motions of the fingers and hands in the pronunciation of manṭras.

CHAPTER III

Melanamanṭra.—ह्रीं (Hrīm), भं (bham), सं (sam), षं (sham), फं (pham), सं (sam), and क्षं (ksham).

The lotus-born (Brahmā) said:

O S'aṅkara, (among) new moon (the first day of the lunar fortnight) and full moon, which is spoken of as its (manṭra's) sign? In the first day of lunar fortnight and during new moon and full moon (days), it should be made firm and there is no other way (or time). A man longs for an object through passion and is infatuated with passion for objects. One should always leave these two and seek the Nirañjana (stainless). He should abandon everything else which he thinks is favourable to himself. Keeping the manas in the midst of s'akṭi, and s'akṭi in the midst of manas, one should look into manas by means of of manas. Then he leaves even the highest stage. Manas alone is the binḍu, the cause of creation and preservation. It is only through manas that binḍu is produced, like the curd from milk. The organs of manas is not that which is situated in the middle of banḍhana. Banḍhana is there where S'akti is between the sun and moon. Having known sushumnā and its bheḍa (piercing) and making the vāyu go in the middle, one should stand in the seat of binḍu, and close the nostrils. Having known vāyu, the above-mentioned bindu and the saṭṭva-prakṛṭi as well as the six chakras, one should enter the sukha-maṇdala (*viz.*, the sahasrāra or pineal gland, the sphere of happiness). There are six chakras. Mūlāḍhāra is in the anus; svāḍhishthāna is near the genital organ; maṇipūraka is in the navel; anāhaṭa is in the heart; vis'uḍḍhi is at the root of the neck and ājñā is in the head (between the two eyebrows). Having known these six maṇdalas (spheres), one should enter the sukha-maṇdala (pineal gland), drawing up the vāyu and should send it (vāyu) upwards. He who practises thus (the control of) vāyu becomes one with brahmāṇda (the macrocosm). He should practise (or master) vāyu, binḍu, chiṭṭa, and chakra.

Yogins attain the nectar of equality through samāḍhi alone. Just as the fire latent in (sacrificial) wood does not appear without churning, so the lamp of wisdom does not arise without the abhyāsa yoga (or practice of yoga). The fire placed in a vessel does not give light outside. When the vessel is broken, its light appears without. One's body is spoken of as the vessel, and the seat of "That" is the fire (or light) within; and when it (the body) is broken through the words of a guru, the light of brahmajñāna becomes resplendent. With the guru as the helmsman, one crosses the subtle body and the ocean of samsāra through the affinities of practice. That vāk [1] (power of speech) which sprouts in parā, gives forth two leaves in pas'yanṭī, buds forth in maḍhyamā and blossoms in vaikharī—that vāk which has before been described, reaches the stage of the absorption of sound, reversing the above order (*viz.*, beginning with vaikharī, etc). Whoever thinks that He who is the great lord of that vāk, who is the undifferentiated and who is the illuminator of that vāk is Self; whoever thinks over thus, is never affected by words, high or low (or good or bad). The three (aspects [2] of consciousness), vis'va, ṭaijasa, and prājña (in man), the three Virāṭ, Hiraṇyagarbha, and Īs'vara in the universe, the egg of the universe, the egg of man [3] and the seven worlds—all these in turn are absorbed in Praṭyagāṭma through the absorption of their respective upāḍhis (vehicles). The egg being heated by the fire of jñāna is absorbed with its kāraṇa (cause) into Paramāṭmā (Universal Self). Then it becomes one with Parabrahman. It is then neither steadiness nor depth, neither light nor darkness, neither describable nor distinguishable. Saṭ (Be-ness) alone remains. One should think of Āṭmā as being within the body like a light in a vessel. Āṭmā is of the dimensions of a thumb, is a light without smoke and without form, is shining within (the body) and is undifferentiated and immutable.

[1] Vāk is of four kinds (as said here) parā, pasyanṭī, maḍhyamā, and vaikharī. Vaikharī being the lowest and the grossest of sounds, and parā being the highest. In evolution vāk begins from the highest to the lowest and in involution it takes a reverse order, to merge into the highest subtle sound (Parā).

[1] The first three aspects of consciousness refer to the gross, subtle, and kāraṇa bodies of men, while the second three aspects refer to the three bodies of the universe. This is from the standpoint of the three bodies.

[3] The egg of man—this shows that man in his formation is and appears as an egg, just as the universe is, and appears as an egg.

The Vijñāna Āṭmā that dwells in this body is deluded by māyā during the states of waking, dreaming, and dreamless sleep; but after many births, owing to the effect of good karma, it wishes to attain its own state. Who am I? How has this stain of mundane existence accrued to me? What becomes in the dreamless sleep of me who am engaged in business in the waking and dreaming states? Just as a bale of cotton is burnt by fire, so the Chiḍābhāsa [1] which is the result of non-wisdom, is burnt by the (wise) thoughts like the above and by its own supreme illumination. The outer burning (of body as done in the world) is no burning at all. When the wordly wisdom is destroyed, Praṭyagāṭma that is in the ḍahara (ākās or ether of the heart) obtains vijñāna, diffusing itself everywhere and burns in an instant jñānamaya and manomaya (sheaths). After this, He himself shines always within, like a light within a vessel.

That muni who contemplates thus till sleep and till death is to be known as a jīvanmukṭa. Having done what ought to be done, he is a fortunate person. And having given up (even) the state of a jīvanmukṭa, he attains viḍehamukṭi (emancipation in a disembodied state), after his body wears off. He attains the state, as if of moving in the air. Then That alone remains which is soundless, touchless, formless, and deathless, which is the rasa (essence), eternal, and odourless, which has neither beginning nor end, which is greater than the great, and which is permanent, stainless, and decayless.

Thus ends the Upanishaḍ.

---

[1] It is the consciousness that becomes distorted and is unable to cognise itself through the bodies.

INDEX OF PROPER NĀMES

A

PRINTED BY ANNIE BESANT AT THE VASANTĀ PRESS, ADYAR, MADRAS.

9781440071249

WS - #0024 - 301122 - C0 - 229/152/16 - PB - 9781440071249 - Gloss Lamination